# Essentials of
# Strategic Human Resource Management
## & Organizational Behaviour

Second Edition

Helen Lam

Athabasca University
FACULTY OF BUSINESS

# NELSON

# NELSON

ISBN-13: 978-0-17-667010-8
ISBN-10: 0-17-667010-6

*Consists of Original Works*

Faculty of Business, Graduate Programs
Athabasca University
201, 13220 St. Albert Trail NW
Edmonton, Alberta, Canada T5L 4W1
Tel: 1-800-561-4650
Email: CAQ@fb.athabascau.ca

Website: http://business.athabascau.ca/

Editor, cover designer, indexer: Janet Thompson

# CONTENTS

# Contents

Contents

## CHAPTER 8

## REWARDS MANAGEMENT

## CHAPTER 9

## PERFORMANCE APPRAISAL AND PERFORMANCE MANAGEMENT

## CHAPTER 10

## DIVERSITY MANAGEMENT AND INCLUSIVENESS

## CHAPTER 11

## UNION-MANAGEMENT RELATIONSHIP

## CHAPTER 12

## THE FUTURE OF THE HUMAN RESOURCES ROLE

# ACKNOWLEDGEMENTS

A number of individuals have contributed in various ways to the successful completion of this book. First, the genesis of this book actually came from the MBA students of Athabasca University, who suggested that a custom-made textbook integrating human resource management with other relevant disciplinary areas would be most effective in delivering the Strategic Human Resource Management (HRMT) course. Second, this book would not have been possible without the encouragement and support of the then entire HRMT academic coaching team (Dr. Greg Berry, Mr. Glenn Coltman, Dr. Rob Dainow, Dr. Rocky Dwyer, and Dr. Gordon Hollis). I am very much indebted to them for taking time out of their very busy schedules to provide invaluable suggestions and feedback on the manuscript. Third, I have to thank the author of the previous HRMT Study Guide, Dr. Ron Edmonds, whose work has given me much inspiration. Fourth, the constructive comments from the external reviewer, Dr. Steven Havlovic, have certainly helped strengthen a number of areas of the book and provided me with added confidence that this book is a meaningful and worthwhile endeavour. Last but not least, the resource support provided by the Centre for Innovative Management, Faculty of Business, Athabasca University, has been instrumental to this publication. Specifically, I am grateful to Dr. Lindsay Redpath, former Executive Director of the Centre, for her ongoing advice and for providing me the necessary time in my work plan to accomplish this major book project. And I cannot thank Ms. Janet Thompson enough for her superb editorial work and all the coordination and design efforts made behind the scenes that helped bring this book to print.

Helen Lam

# What's New in the Second Edition?

Thanks to the feedback of the MBA students at Athabasca University who used the first edition of the textbook, the author knows that the concise style of the book has been appreciated. Hence, in preparing the second edition, the focus was on adding new content only where it would add value by enhancing readers' understanding and interest in HR and on making revisions that reflect the latest developments. Below are some areas of changes in this edition.

- A section named HRM in Action is added to provide real organization examples for each of the chapters from Chapter 1 to Chapter 11. This helps to show how the theories and concepts discussed in the chapter are actually reflected in organizational practices.

- More illustrations in tables and figures are included for better visual presentation that also can make it easier for readers to capture the main points.

- The chapter on Human Resource Flow is divided into two chapters, with Orientation, Training, and Development now being in a new chapter with broader coverage. Expanding on these topic areas is important as talent management and enhancing human capital have been considered a main challenge for organizations in the years to come.

- Statistics, trends, literature, and case laws have been updated. Examples of these changes include demographic/diversity statistics, union membership trends, mandatory retirement law changes, new developments in the Wallace factor in dismissals, social media implications on HR, and a new addition to Hofstede's national culture dimension.

 **Chapter 1**

# Strategic Human Resource Management

## Introduction

Strategic human resource management is increasingly important for organizations trying to gain a competitive advantage over others. The traditional approach to managing people, generally called personnel management, tends to focus narrowly on administrative and functional matters. Many in the human resource field no longer see this as a sufficient response to an ever changing business environment or as a way to bring out the best in people. The strategic human resource management (HRM) approach emerged around the 1980s. Its view is people are an asset, the contributor to the organizational strategies, and the driver of business success. Its emphasis is on effectiveness, rather than simply efficiency. Alignment of HRM strategies with the organization's strategy and congruence among HRM policies and practices as well as across policy areas are some of its key characteristics (Beer, Spector, Lawrence, Quinn Mills, & Walton, 1985; Schuler & Jackson, 1999; Wright & Snell, 1991).

Effective strategic HRM inevitably intertwines with many other disciplinary areas. Unfortunately, many strategic HRM books continue to focus on the traditional human resource (HR) area without integrating it with related disciplines. For example, the topics of motivation, organizational culture, leadership, and work groups or teams are all essential for promoting employee performance and organizational commitment. Yet they are often left to be separately covered in organizational behaviour books. Similarly, discussions on organizational contexts, structures, and design that have a significant impact on work content and conditions are generally considered as falling under the scope of organizational theory texts. The examination of union and management relationships that is critical for understanding workplace relationships and power balance is commonly regarded as within the territory of industrial relations publications. How can strategic

HRM be addressed and explored without a basic understanding of all these other important and relevant disciplinary areas? Reading four separate books to try to figure out the important strategic HRM concepts, as well as their linkages and integration, could be difficult for people interested in strategic HRM, whether they are students, HR practitioners, or line managers. This book, therefore, is written with the readers' interests in mind. A broad range of theories and concepts across disciplinary areas is introduced in a concise and integrated manner to help in the understanding and application of strategic HRM. The purpose of the book is not to train readers to be HR specialists. It is meant for managers in all areas, whether they work in private, non-profit, or public organizations, to gain an appreciation of HR from the strategic and macro perspective, taking an overall organizational view of people management.

This book starts with an introduction to strategic HRM in Chapter 1. In Chapter 2 topics on management philosophy and organizational culture are explored. Chapters 3 to 5 are devoted to organizational behaviour and organizational theory topics that have a large influence on the management of people, namely, work design, motivation, leadership, and teams. These concepts provide the essential foundation for the discussion on the design and implementation of HRM systems in Chapters 6 to 10, which cover human resource flow, training and development, rewards management, performance management, and diversity management respectively. While union-management issues are covered throughout the book in relation to the topic under discussion, Chapter 11 provides specific coverage on the laws, policies, and processes related to labour relations. Finally, Chapter 12 takes a look at the future of the role of HR and, hopefully, helps organizations further understand the importance of strategic HRM.

In this first chapter, a brief overview of the development of HRM is given and then a strategic HRM model is introduced. In discussing the various components of the model and their relationships with each other, many basic HRM concepts are introduced. Most of these concepts are revisited in later chapters throughout the book.

## HRM VERSUS PERSONNEL MANAGEMENT

Traditional management theory emphasizes control, predictability, and compliance by focusing on structures, rules, and procedures. Personnel management generally follows this line of thought. It worked well in North America for decades in the mid-twentieth century, when the organizational environment was generally stable and favourable, with little global competition, continuous market expansion, good labour supply, rapid technological advancement, and relatively minimal government intervention. Personnel management's role is basically one of administration, ensuring that employees are hired and paid and that company rules, government regulations, and collective agreement provisions (in an union setting) are enforced. Personnel decisions are rather straightforward, based on rigid and narrow job descriptions and preset rules, such as seniority provisions. The personnel department is seen as a service provider, a support department that plays a reactive role "peripheral to the organisation's purposes" (Handy, Barham, Panter, & Winhard, 1989, p. 14). Employees are regarded as passive agents (or just a factor of production) to be organized and controlled in order to optimize their use (Chiavenato, 2001; Walton, 1985).

While HR today is still responsible for the administrative and support functions mentioned above, its role has evolved over time. Starting from the 1970s, significant changes occurred in the organizational environment. With keen competition from abroad, especially from Japan, the North American way of doing business was greatly challenged. Customers could no longer be taken for granted. Well-priced, good quality products and services as well as flexibility and innovation became the keys to survival and success. The traditional way of managing people through control and compliance, though good for the production and provision of fairly standardized products and services, was no longer appropriate in all cases under the new environment. The workforce became more ethnically diverse. Women's participation in the workforce drastically increased. The baby boomers, much better educated than the previous generation, matured and entered the workforce. People in the management field soon realized that, among all the factors of production, workers were the only source that had excellent untapped potential to address the environmental challenges. Instead of using the top-down management approach, managers started to value the contributions from the bottom up. This is still an evolving process.

In the 1980s, largely due to the Japanese influence as well as the need to contain costs and enhance performance, initiatives like quality circles, quality of work-life programs, and semi-autonomous workgroups began to flourish. Basically, these initiatives are premised on the assumption that because workers are the ones doing the actual work, they should know best how to go about it and that their contributions could lead to continuous improvements. Workers should be motivated to do their best and provide useful input. If they have a voice in the work and feel a sense of ownership in the product or service, they will be much more willing to put forth good ideas for improvements. If employees can see where the organization would like to go, they will be able to help to make it happen. Hence, the management paradigm began to shift from command, control, and compliance to employee empowerment, alignment of individual and organizational goals, and

3

valuing of trust, flexibility, and creativity. This change can be seen to be basically in line with the philosophy underlying the strategic HRM approach.

Table 1-1 summarizes some basic differences between personnel management (PM) and strategic HRM.

**Table 1-1  Personnel Management versus Strategic HRM**

| | Personnel Management | Strategic Human Resource Management |
|---|---|---|
| **Relation to organizational strategies** | Reactive, responding to organizational goals and objectives set at the top | Proactive, HR as business partners contributing to the setting of (not just responding to) organizational goals and objectives |
| **Time line** | Short-term functional focus | Long-term strategic focus |
| **Emphasis on control** | Emphasizes external control, predictability and compliance (with laws as well as internal policies and procedures) | Emphasizes internal (self) control, trust, commitment, empowerment, and goal alignment (between individuals and the organization) |
| **Structures and systems** | Rigid rules and procedures; hierarchical structures; standardized roles | Flexible programs, systems and roles; organic structure |
| **Use of HR information** | To support HR administration | To help in HR planning and evaluation of HR effectiveness in addition to necessary HR administration |
| **HR Evaluation** | Efficiency and cost reduction | Effectiveness and value-added |

In practice, PM and strategic HRM exist on a continuum and an organization does not move from PM to strategic HRM overnight. Many organizations probably still fall closer to the PM end of the spectrum or are somewhere in the middle.

## A Strategic HRM Model

In short, strategic HRM can be defined as "a set of distinct but interrelated practices, policies, and philosophies whose goal is to enable the achievement of the organizational strategy" (Belcourt & McBey, 2000, p. 14). Organizational strategies are basically action plans to achieve organizational goals, which are in line with an organization's vision and are given in its mission statement. For an overall view of the various components involved in a strategic HRM model, please refer to Figure 1-1. The individual components of the model are discussed in the following pages.

**Figure 1-1 A Strategic HRM Model**

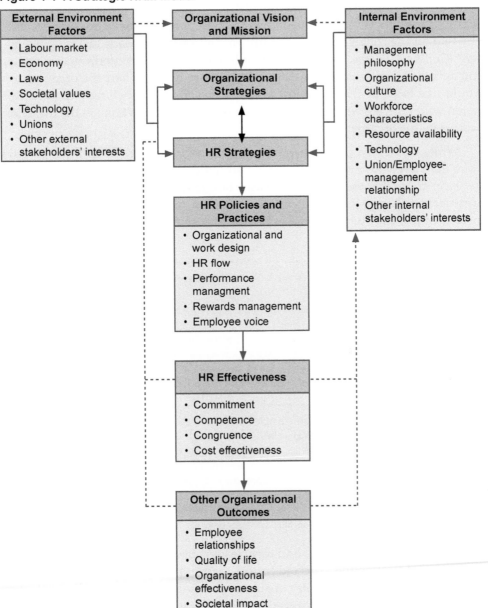

**Source:** The above is an extension of the model presented in Beer, M., Spector, B., Lawrence, P. R., Quinn Mills, D., and Walton, R. (1985). *Human resource management: A general manager's perspective* (p. 17). New York: Free Press, with an emphasis on the two-way influence between organizational strategies and HR strategies.

## Organizational Vision and Mission

An organization's *vision* is an overarching concept involving "a guiding philosophy that, in the context of expected future environments, leads to a tangible image" (Collins & Porras, 1991, pp. 32-33). It is about an organization's shared values and beliefs and its purpose for existence. It shows people where the organization would like to be in the long term (e.g., 5-10 years). A compelling and attractive vision will motivate employees and guide behaviour and actions in the direction desired by the organization.

While vision is a rather abstract concept and in practice often involves little more than a few nice-sounding words with little relation to operations, a *mission statement* translates the vision into clear, tangible, and achievable goals for the organization. A mission statement also provides the "how" and even the "why" instead of just the "what." Some examples of vision and mission statements are provided below:

---

**Motorola Canada** (a wireless and broadband communications provider):

*Vision:* "Seamless Mobility"

*Mission:* "Motorola Canada is dedicated to achieving market leadership in Canada and contributing to worldwide new product development. We will accomplish this by placing the customers first, by providing opportunities to our employees to contribute and grow, and by developing new and innovative partnerships."

---

**Source:** Retrieved May 1, 2008 from http://www.motorolacareers.com

---

**Alzheimer Society of Canada** (a non-profit organization):

*Vision:* "A World Without Alzheimer's and Related Diseases"

*Mission:* "The Alzheimer Society of Canada identifies, develops and facilitates national priorities that enable its members to effectively alleviate the personal and social consequences of Alzheimer's and related diseases, promotes research and leads the search for a cure."

---

**Source:** Retrieved May 1, 2008 from http://www.alzheimer.ca

The organization's founder and early leaders usually establish the vision, taking into consideration the expected future environment. Because vision and mission involve long-term goals, they are usually not influenced by temporary fluctuations in the environment. However, new organizational leaders may sometimes find it necessary to revisit the vision and mission to reinforce or redefine them.

## Organizational Strategies and HR Strategies

*Organizational goals* reflect the organization's ideal destiny. *Organizational strategies* are the plans to achieve these goals, taking into consideration the competitive environment and the constraints of the internal operating capabilities. Strategies show the business direction of the organization. Porter's (1980) widely adopted framework for generic organizational strategies involves low cost leadership, differentiation, and focus strategies. Such strategies undoubtedly have a degree of impact on HR strategies and policies. For example, if an organization adopts the low cost leadership strategy, quality probably is not paramount and thus a highly skilled workforce that requires a wage premium may not be necessary. If an organization goes for differentiation, then employee creativity may be highly valued and HR strategies are likely aimed at attracting, motivating, and retaining talented and creative employees. If the focus strategy is adopted, the organization targets certain customer groups, and HR strategies that emphasize flexibility and employee empowerment may be appropriate in order for employees to promptly and effectively serve customers.

Although HR strategies are often seen as operational strategies that relate to one functional area, their impact should not be underestimated. As Walker (1992) notes, "the capacity to implement changes called for in business strategies is dependent on people. People, not companies, innovate, make decisions, develop and produce new products, penetrate new markets, and serve customers more effectively. Typically, human resource issues are central to strategy implementation" (pp. 8-9). Strategic HRM has always called for HR strategies and policies to be aligned with organizational goals and strategies. At times, HRM books focus too much on the implementation aspect and interpret alignment as following in line. Such perspectives lack an emphasis on the role HR can play in shaping the organizational strategies.

An HR leader should not sit back and wait for the organizational strategies to be established and then just implement policies to help achieve them. HR strategies should be established alongside the organizational strategies with reciprocal influence, as both types of strategies are intertwined and should be well integrated. HR can contribute greatly to the development of organizational strategies as the human capital available in the organization—the number of staff, the competencies of the employees and their flexibility in work assignments (e.g., ability to handle multiple tasks)—can and should, to varying extent, determine the business direction and strategies. For example, if an organization has a pool of creative and talented employees who have become redundant due to technological changes, rather than laying off these employees, the organization could consider diversification into other product areas that may utilize such talents. In other words, HR should be a partner in the strategic business decision-making process, not a bystander waiting only to implement policies. Hence, the relationship between organizational strategies and HR strategies is clearly indicated by a two-way arrow in the Strategic HRM Model in Figure 1. Awareness at the very top levels of executive leadership of the importance of HR being a full partner in strategic planning is obviously required.

## External Environment

There are many factors in an organization's external environment. Although a large organization's actions can sometimes affect the environment, the model assumes the general situation where each organization has minimal impact on and thus very little control over the external factors.

The *labour market* condition has a direct effect on an organization's recruitment, compensation, and other staffing decisions. For example, in a tight market where labour supply is low, more innovative recruitment methods and flexible compensation policies may be needed to attract talent. Retention of employees is a high priority, and proper HR planning is essential. Consideration of just the overall supply and demand of labour is not enough. Because different types of labour (with varying skills, knowledge, and ability) are required by different organizations, the overall unemployment rate in the area is not always the best indicator of the availability of a specific type of labour. Also, the demographic trends in the broader market should be assessed to get a sense of the opportunities and constraints in future staffing. For example, with the aging of the baby boomers, labour shortage may be a concern for some occupations that require extensive experience. On the other hand, the trend of the young generation becoming more technically savvy provides the opportunity for organizations to take better advantage of technology and automation.

The *economy* determines to some extent the customer and financial market situations. Organizational strategies need to cope with supply and demand fluctuations and consider economic threats and opportunities. Is the industry booming? Are there economic barriers for market entries? Are the interest rates favourable? These are just some examples of the economic contexts. Moreover, international competition, which was relatively rare decades ago, is now a fact of life in most industries. With the cost of production or services in China and India far below those in North America (e.g., India's average wage is just 20% of the U.S. rate; Canada's average wage is 89% of the U.S. rate), competition from these countries is tremendous (Klie, 2006).

*Laws* and *societal values* affect organization decisions at both the strategic and policy levels. Illegal or unethical practices can bring a company to a grinding halt. With the implosion in the early 2000s of high profile companies like Enron, Arthur Andersen, and Worldcom in the United States and a series of organizational scandals in Canada, such as Nortel's accounting practices, Air Canada and Westjet's spying lawsuits, and the Liberal government's sponsorship (Canadian Broadcasting Corporation, 2002, 2006, 2007), ethical concerns have been brought to the forefront of the corporate world in North America. People are beginning to see that legality and ethics are often intertwined and that even if something seems legally right, it may not be so ethically. Legislation often tends to provide minimal protection for the vulnerable and to take a limited number of factors into consideration. For example, an employer can legally lay off an employee in the face of redundancy as long as certain legislative provisions are met. However, most people would think that laying off a long-time employee so that a relative of the owner can be hired is not morally acceptable. Throughout the subsequent chapters, legal issues and ethics will be incorporated as important considerations in various HRM initiatives.

*Technology* can impact greatly on the way an organization does its business as it affects the work design and the structure of the organization. For example, call centres can nowadays be set up half a world away to take advantage of the low cost of labour in some countries. Employees can have the flexibility of working at home as telecommuters. Virtual teams can be set up in organizations to bring together distantly located members to achieve a common task. These changes come with significant benefits but they can also have side effects and hidden costs, such as the adverse implications in the areas of an employer's corporate social responsibility to the community and employees' social needs. The latest developments in social media can also have significant implications for organizational strategies, policies, and practices, particularly in areas like customer relations, recruitment reach, and employee communications.

*Unions*, where properly certified in Canada, are exclusive bargaining agents for employees. That is, the terms and conditions of employment are determined by the employer and the union in a collective agreement, rather than by individual employees in employment contracts. A union's philosophy and power can greatly influence the union-management and management-employee relationships as well as the way work is done and people are rewarded. This is discussed further in later chapters, particularly in Chapter 11.

*Stakeholders* are people or parties who have an interest, or stake, in the organization. Such parties are not just shareholders, management, and employees.

Sometimes, external bodies such as professional associations, accreditation agencies, financial institutions, and interest groups have a direct or indirect effect on HRM strategic choices. For example, professional associations may require its members to abide by a certain code of ethics, while accreditation bodies may require certain professional and operational standards be met. Environmental groups or human rights activists may raise concerns or protest over an organization's emission level of pollutants or its way of treating its workers. Their influence can lead to stricter legislative enforcement or media disclosure affecting the organization's image. Unions from outside may try to organize members of the organization or raid an existing union, leading to possible turmoil in employment relationships. Banks and insurance companies can also have significant influence on an organization's strategic decision as they affect the resources available to and risks confronted by the organization.

Overall, there are many dimensions to the external environment, and it is important to realize that the environment is constantly in flux. Therefore, corresponding changes in organizational strategies and actions are often needed.

## Internal Environment

*Management philosophy* refers to the values, beliefs, and assumptions that management has about the nature of people and its employees in particular. It is the fundamental driver of all areas and levels of strategies, policies, and practices. For example, if management believes that employees are self-centred and must be controlled, it is unlikely that the organization supports participative management or employee empowerment. If management thinks employees are their best asset, they likely treat their workers with respect and trust. Beer, Spector, Lawrence, Quinn Mills, and Walton (1984) neatly summarize the role of management philosophy in strategic HRM as follows:

> No discussion of integrating an HRM system can be complete without considering [management's] values and how they are transmitted. The values of senior management, as expressed in words and deeds, either do or do not give employees a sense of confidence about the many different HRM practices. The degree to which management's respect for individual employees infuses HRM practices is especially crucial. Employees will not continue to be emotionally involved in the affairs of the business if their contributions are not respected by their managers. Similarly, employees cannot be expected to be actively committed to the organization if the organization does not show its commitment to them. The institutional commitment must be rooted in the sincerity and durability of the values of top management... The values managers hold are revealed in many ways besides direct ver-

bal expression. In fact, the old adage that actions speak louder than words applies incontrovertibly to the transmission of values ... (p. 190).

In Chapter 2 this concept of management philosophy is explored in greater detail, with various management philosophy frames provided to help in the understanding of management decisions.

*Organizational culture* is another internal environmental factor that heavily influences management decisions and choices. Organizational culture refers to the complex set of beliefs, assumptions, values, attitudes, expectations and norms held and shared by its members (management and employees) and exhibited in artifacts and behaviours. It can be reflected in something superficial and observable, like symbols and ceremonies, or something deeply rooted and subjective like people's collective value system (i.e., what they think is right, good, useful, normal, important, etc.). Organizational culture can shape the way work is done and how people act and interact. An understanding of the organizational culture is therefore particularly essential in the design of any work system and formation of HRM decisions. As such, this factor is covered in Chapter 2 before other HRM areas or concepts are explored.

An analysis of the *internal workforce characteristics* indicates the age profile, educational backgrounds, skill levels, and other attributes of the employees. Such data is useful in making decisions about organizational structure, work design, recruitment, training, and compensation. For example, a well-educated workforce with good skills is likely to require less supervision but higher compensation, commensurate with their qualifications, than a workforce that is not. A degree of diversity may be a favourable condition for the use of teams. Similarly, an analysis of the internal market is important to determine if there are staff shortages and where premium wages are necessary. Recognizing the demographic trends, such as the aging of the workforce and increasing ethnic diversity, helps in overall HR planning. The topics of diversity management and HR planning are further addressed in Chapters 6 and 10.

Besides human resources, organizations must have *financial resources* in the form of capital investment. The resources available constrain or enable certain types of strategies. Large scale automation to gain better productivity is not possible with limited capital outlay. Similarly, benefits from economies of scales are not available to a small company with little resources.

*Technology* is both an external and internal environmental factor. What is available outside of the company does not necessarily mean it can be available inside. Often, a company has to work within the limitations of its existing technology, at least in the short term future. In the long run, major changes can be made but, as discussed above, this relies heavily on the capital investment available. Whatever technology is adopted, it will have a huge effect on how people and work are organized. The amount of labour, worker training, and the types of supervision needed all depend to some degree on the technological applications.

The internal *union-management* or *employee-management relationship* is another situational factor that can affect managerial decisions. In a traditional adversarial setting, management decisions may tend towards a more authoritative approach as the parties are unlikely to work collectively. Hence, the organization may stay with the low-cost leadership strategy of tightly supervising employees and controlling costs because it is too difficult to adopt the differentiation strategy where creativity and employee motivation are the keys to success. In contrast, a cooperative setting where the parties seek common interests can lead to very different strategies and outcomes. A participative style of management may be pursued. For example, if the union or employee relationship with management is good, the company can look at adopting innovative approaches, quality initiatives, and flexible HR policies that promote employee commitment to support the differentiation or focus strategies.

Each organization has many *internal stakeholders*, each with a different set of interests in, expectations for, and influence over the organization. Shareholders are likely interested in the return on their investment and the long-term prosperity and profitability of the organization. Management, although likely to value prosperity and profitability, may not always be as concerned about the long-range future, especially if they have bonuses tied to short-term performances. As recognized in agency theory, the motives and interests of management (the agent) can be quite different from those of the owners (the principal). Unions, concerned about membership support, their representational rights, and relative bargaining power, may want better job security for their members, which can be a constraint in strategies that call for greater organizational flexibility. Employees are another group of stakeholders. Whether represented by a union or not, employees are not a homogenous group. Older members of an organization probably prefer more stability and fewer changes or uncertainties. They are also more likely to be interested in pension and health benefits than their younger counterparts. An effective organization must be able to consider and properly balance the interests and concerns of its various stakeholders.

In theory, the external and internal environments are separate. In practice, they are often intertwined and interdependent. For example, an organization can choose to operate in a different external environment by changing location or industry (even if it cannot change things in the external environment). The various external factors to which an organization is exposed can certainly influence the internal environment (e.g., organizations may seek to mimic other successful ones).

## HRM Policies and Practices

The HR system consists of various components, each involving a set of policies and practices intended to meet the organizational goals. The key components include organizational and work design; human resource flow; performance management and rewards management; and employee voice and involvement. All these areas are intertwined as discussed below. Therefore, rarely should one area be designed independently of another. Achievement of congruence among the different policy areas is fundamental to HR effectiveness.

### *Organizational and Work Design*

How should an organization be structured? Should it be along functional lines, product lines, or by geographical location? Should decisions always be made at the top? Is a tall hierarchical structure appropriate? Should standardized policies and procedures be adopted? These are just some of the questions related to organizational design.

Daft (1998, pp. 17-18) provides a number of structural dimensions in an organizational design. They are described in Table 1-2:

**Table 1-2  Dimensions in Organizational Design**

| Dimension | Relates to |
|---|---|
| Formalization | Amount of written documentation |
| Specialization | Division of labour – how fine the job is divided |
| Standardization | Uniformity in the way work is done |
| Hierarchy of authority | The reporting relationship – who is the "boss" |
| Complexity | The number of activities, organizational layers, departments/units, locations, etc., and how they intertwine |
| Centralization | Whether decisions are made at the top level |
| Professionalism | Level of education and training of employees |
| Personnel ratios | Number of employees assigned to a function/unit divided by the total employee number |

Although *organizational design* is not always totally within the bounds of HRM and involves every functional area, the structural design of the organization really cannot be made without thorough consideration of the area of HR. For example, an organization with creative employees that values such employee talents is unlikely to be designed with a high degree of formalization, standardization, and centralization or with a tall hierarchical structure. Proper organizational design will help an organization realize its goals and potential.

Work design and organizational design are closely related. Organizational design relates more to the structural aspect of the organization whereas work design has more to do with the design of employees' work, which to a large extent is affected by the type of organizational design. Organizations with a high level of formalization, specialization, and standardization probably leave little room for employees to have autonomy over how their work is done.

*Work design* involves the organizing of workers and their activities, taking into consideration the utilization of technology and information. It affects all other areas of HRM. An assembly line type of operation likely selects workers who care about money more than work autonomy, provides limited training, has tight monitoring of performance, and bases compensation on hourly rate or piece rate. Work design is discussed in Chapter 3 in conjunction with motivation theories, after the concepts of management philosophy and organizational culture are covered.

## Human Resource Flow

*Human resource flow* (HRF) is a term used to describe how people move into, within, and out of the organization. It includes the area of recruitment and selection, promotions, transfers, layoffs, and terminations. Orientation, training, and development can also be considered as part of HRF, as they are very closely associated—although in this book, these topics will be covered in a separate chapter. Strategic HR planning is essential in the HRF area to provide the organization with the right people at the right time to ensure the needs of the organization, both in the long- and short-term, are met.

HRF affects various HR policy components. For example, the availability of skilful and experienced workers may mean that greater work autonomy can be built into the work design. Pay levels need to be commensurate with the qualifications of the people recruited. Performance management is very different if the employees hired are new school graduates rather than experienced workers. Indeed, training and development is as much an area under HRF as it is under performance management, and many areas are really interdependent on each other.

## Performance Management and Rewards Management

*Rewards management* and *performance management* are two different, but very much interrelated, concepts. Often, one of the purposes of a reward system is to provide the incentives for better employee performance, and performance measurement systems are devised to serve as the basis for compensating employees according to their level of performance. A few concepts should, however, be clarified at this stage. First, rewards do not necessarily mean money. A simple "thank you" or a pat on the shoulder can sometimes do wonders. Second, rewards do not necessarily have to always relate to performance (e.g., a seniority-based pay system). Third, where the two concepts are tightly tied together, organizations must be cognizant not to allow budget incentives to drive performance measurements. An employee's performance should always be reviewed based on valid criteria. In a situation where an employee performs well but cannot be granted an increase due to financial constraints, it is important that the company does the right thing by giving the employee the proper performance assessment, rather than downgrading the performance rating purely for the sake of justifying the salary freeze. Fourth, performance management is much broader than performance measurement or performance appraisal. It has a heavy emphasis on reviewing performance with a view to furthering performance improvements and employee development. Hence, while it does look at past performance for wage, promotion, or other administrative considerations, it has a strong future orientation to ensure that the organization has the desired staff for future needs.

Performance management provides information on the strengths and weaknesses of employees that can help determine promotions, transfers, or outplacements. It also influences the work design. An employee or group who has demonstrated a high degree of motivation and self-control in performing work will be well suited to an autonomous work design. An organization with very competent employees good at multi-tasking may also favour a flatter organizational structure with good opportunities for lateral movements.

Rewards management sends important signals to employees about what the organization values most. Does the organization emphasize employee input in the work design process? Does the pay system emphasize group work or individual work? To what extent are employees rewarded for multi-skilling and multi-tasking? Are employees basically managing their own performances or are they closely supervised? Will they be rewarded with promotions for excellent performance? Are the criteria for rewards congruent with what are evaluated in performance management? Are the current rewards driving the desired performance? These questions clearly show how closely linked rewards management is with the other HR components.

### Employee Voice and Involvement

Researchers have long noticed that employees prefer to have more influence in organizational decisions that significantly affect their work lives (e.g., Freeman &

Rogers 1993, 2006; Singh, 2001; Taras & Kaufman, 2006). Hirschman (1970) claims that if employees have concerns over their work or work environment, they can either express so through voice or through exit. Exit simply means quitting the organization while voice refers to "any attempt at all to change, rather than to escape from, an objectionable state of affairs, whether through individual or collective petition to the management, through appeals to a higher authority ..., or through various types of actions and protests" (Hirschman, p. 30). Voice can take either individual or collective form. The former involves employees bringing their issues to the attention of management to hopefully work out a solution in their favour. The latter involves the expression of collective voice through such avenues as joint labour-management committees and unions representing the employee members. The obvious advantages of collective voice over individual voice for employees are its likelihood of getting more attention and the reduction in the possibility of employer retaliation on individuals. Employees are important stakeholders in the organization and how much authority and power they have has a huge impact on how work is done and what gets done. Paying attention to employee voice is a good retention strategy.

The way HR policies are designed can determine the level of employee involvement. Employee can have their voice heard through various channels, such as through their supervisors, company suggestion programs, formal or informal work group recommendations, formal committees (e.g., health and safety), and union representation (e.g., collective bargaining and the grievance process). Although employee involvement has many potential benefits and there is a rising trend to such, it is not uncommon to hear of organizations paying only lip service to it. Hearing is not the same as listening and involvement is not necessarily the same as empowerment. Therefore, even when two organizations indicate that they both have employee involvement programs, the real level of involvement can be drastically different.

Many managers are skeptical of employee involvement because involving subordinates in decisions appears to diminish their authority and power. What they do not consider is the *paradox of control* (Nutt, 1999). Managers who want to control their employees are focusing on the organizational type of control, through rules and hierarchies as well as rewards and punishment. What they miss are the other aspects of control, namely self control (people like to do what they want to do, something that is meaningful to them) and social control (people want to do work that conforms to the social or group norms). If employees have to choose between compliance with the group norm and with management's expectations, the former tends to win over (as indicated in some of the human relations studies such as the Hawthorne studies done around 1930). Allowing employees to have more autonomy over their work often motivates them and increases their commitment towards the organizational goals, especially if the goals are jointly set. On the contrary, tight organizational control results in employees trying to shirk work, "beat the system", or doing just enough not to get fired. The greater the control force, the greater the repulsion. Of course, that is not to say that all will be fine by giving the employees all the control. Various HR components have to be in congruence to make things work to promote self control and social control and to align individual and group goals and interests with those of the organization.

Employee involvement is certainly closely related with all other areas of HR policies. How the work is organized depends largely on the level of delegation of authority to the employees. Usually, organizations emphasizing employee involvement tend to be flatter (rather than having a tall hierarchical structure) with less formalized rules. Their performance management and rewards systems focus on achievement of goals related to the contribution to process improvements. Employees are encouraged to provide constructive criticism and are offered training on effective communication and critical thinking, in addition to training that broadens job knowledge and skills.

## HR Effectiveness

There are different ways to measure HR effectiveness. For example, Beer et al. (1985) use the four Cs to evaluate the overall impact of HRM policies and practices. Descriptions of the four Cs is provided are provided in Table 1-3.

**Table 1-3 The Four Cs in Measuring Overall HR Effectiveness**

| Dimension | Description<br>How well do the HR policies and practices help in these areas? |
|---|---|
| Commitment | Employee commitment to the organization, for example, in terms of loyalty to the organization, identification with the organization, psychological engagement in their work, and citizenship behaviour (employees' willingness to do things for the organization beyond their job requirement) |
| Competence | Development of employee competence (e.g., skills, knowledge, and ability critical to the organization) and the organization's ability in attracting and retaining competent employees |
| Cost Effectiveness | The costs and efforts are worthwhile and lead to the desired outcomes. Note that some costs are not always easily measurable, such as lost productivity due to stress, turnover, and absenteeism |
| Congruence | Alignment of goals and interests of various stakeholder groups in the organization, such as those between management and employees and among employee groups |

Most traditional organizations tend to focus mainly on cost effectiveness rather than other measures because the financial numbers are of overarching concern. However, such a focus can have repercussions on the overall organizational effectiveness if organizations take a short-run approach and allow the achievement of this C at the expense of the other Cs. For example, placing a hiring freeze and removing the training department can lead to an immediate increase in cost effectiveness but give rise to a long-term problem of not having competent employees to do the job in the future. Similarly, downsizing and outsourcing can lower cost in the short run but may adversely affect commitment. On the other hand, organizations that focus on the other Cs have more competent or committed employees, or employees who see the HR programs and policies as being in line with what they personally prefer, which likely leads to greater HR cost effectiveness in the long run. Using all the four Cs can be viewed as providing a holistic approach that involves a more comprehensive assessment of HR programs and policies than using just a subset of these dimensions.

At the individual HR program level, there are further areas of measurement that can be considered. For years, the *return on investments* (ROI) methodology as an assessment tool has been widely advocated because senior executives often want to see supporting data to justify their HR cost and investments. The HR department also likes having some means of demonstrating their accountability and influence. But as mentioned above, an overemphasis on the cost or quantitative aspects may have its drawbacks. Nevertheless, ROI is a valuable tool that can be integrated with other measurement methods. Phillips (2003) suggests five levels of measurement focus for HR programs, plus the consideration of the intangibles, as described in Table 1-4. Intangibles are measures purposely not expressed in monetary terms, either because it is inappropriate to assign a dollar value to them (such as for trust and recognition) or because too many assumptions need to be made that would cast doubt on the validity of the measures if they were to be converted to monetary terms:

**Table 1-4  Measurement Focus for Individual HR Programs**

| Measurement Focus | Description |
|---|---|
| Reaction and Planned Action | Whether planned actions for the program occurred, how satisfied participants are with the program, and what they plan to do with their learning |
| Learning | What has been learned from the program – increase in knowledge or improvements in skills and attitudes |
| Application | The extent to which the learning from the program is applied to the job |
| Business Impact | The extent the application results in improved performance such as improved productivity |
| ROI | The ratio of benefits to cost to determine if benefits outweigh cost for the program |

Tsui and Gomez-Mejia (1988) also suggest assessing HR effectiveness along some of the aforementioned dimensions and according to the level of analysis:

- *Strategic level* – HR policies and programs should be measured against their consistency with the organizational strategy.

- *Management level* – Cost effectiveness is often the common criteria as the emphasis is on control.

- *Operational level* – Effectiveness may need to be measured from the perspective of the various constituents, that is, how they view the quality of the HR services.

Enhancing and monitoring HR effectiveness often relies on the availability of good HR information. Such information is useful for records, reports, and administration as well as for analysis, planning, and decision-making. A formal system—called an HR Information System (HRIS)—to capture such information may be very beneficial, especially for large organizations. An HRIS usually involves the use of computer applications and databases that not only allow the input, organization, and storage of HR data but also provide the tools for managing and reporting the data as needed. Retrieval and updating of information needs to be simple, particularly if employees are expected to be directly involved in this process in relation to their own personal records. HRIS can be useful in most areas of HR, such as salary and benefits administration; HR planning, training, and development; recruitment; and redeployment. In the early days of HRIS, its function was mainly for administration but now it is increasingly used to provide the support for strategic HR management and organizational decision-making needed to help organizations gain a competitive advantage (Broderick & Boudreau, 1992; Ngai & Wat, 2006). HRIS is said to be making "vital contributions to knowledge management by advancing organizational learning" and fostering "systems thinking" in an organization (Mayfield, Mayfield, & Lunce, 2003, p. 143).

## Organizational Outcomes and Effectiveness

Evaluating HR effectiveness is important because it has an impact on not just the overall organizational effectiveness, but also on the individuals involved and, possibly, society. At the individual level, low congruence can lead to stress, low competence can affect one's future job opportunities, and low commitment can be associated with disinterest and disengagement from work. These areas can affect an individual's health, quality of life, career path, and motivations as well as the employment relationship. At the societal level, changes in government policies and legislation can be prompted by disgruntled or mistreated employees protesting over some undesirable, or even unacceptable, employment conditions. Poor labour relations policies in an organization can also lead to strikes or lockouts that affect the general public, who are the consumers of the product or services. The relation between HR effectiveness and organizational effectiveness involves some in-depth discussion and is addressed in the following paragraphs.

How would we know if an organization is successful? Other than having good current financial performance, organizations must be able to survive in the long run as well. Often, organizations that flourish at one point in time may not do so well at other times. What distinguishes effective organizations from others is their ability to gain a competitive advantage.

For something to provide a competitive advantage, it must have the following three main characteristics:

1. It must be something unique that is distinguishable from what competitors have.

2. It must provide added value or economic benefits to the organization.

3. It must not be easily copied by other organizations (i.e., the competitive advantage must be "sustainable").

An organization's purchase of expensive software to automate its processes is unlikely to give rise to a competitive advantage unless the cost is so high as to be a barrier for others to adopt similar technology. On the other hand, resources that reside in the collective employee group (that is, their tacit knowledge) and the organizational culture are very difficult to directly transfer to another organization. Even if the same group of employees leaves the organization to join another one, their effectiveness may not necessarily carry over due to various organizational differences such as management philosophy, leadership, culture, and other contextual factors. Southwest Airlines' well-known success is due to its low-cost, no-frill, quick-turnaround short haul flights and unique HR philosophy, leadership, and culture that generate a very positive and highly committed workforce. Some other U.S. airlines, such as United and Continental, have tried to imitate the Southwest model by introducing similar discount carriers without success. While these airlines are able to copy some of the operational aspects, such as routes, pricing, and no-frill services, they never achieve the "Southwest spirit", the people aspect. Westjet in Canada is one of the more successful low-cost carriers that has been able to build a system (rather than just parts of it), both culturally and operationally, that is similar to the Southwest model.

As the environment changes, organizations need to reinvent themselves in order to sustain their existing areas of competitive advantage and to create new ones.

Traditionally, organizations tend to measure performance simply based on the financial aspect. This view has changed somewhat since Kaplan and Norton (1992) proposed the balanced scorecard that links performance measures to four specific perspectives:

- financial
- customer
- internal business process
- innovation and learning (called learning and growth in subsequent balanced scorecard models)

The financial perspective caters most to the shareholders. The customer perspective focuses on the aspect of service to customers. The internal business perspective looks at the operations side to see how processes can be improved to meet customer needs, while learning and growth is a forward-looking perspective addressing how well the company prepares itself for value creation in the future.

Where does HR fit in this model? The most direct area is the learning perspective. Employee training and development is the key to improving the knowledge and skills of the workforce for future changes. Employees are the ones who can come up with innovative ideas for products and services that can better meet customer needs and enhance the current operational efficiency. This, in turn, has a positive impact on the financials. Therefore, it is of no surprise that in some of the sample models shown in Kaplan and Norton's (2007) balance scorecard article, employee satisfaction and staff development were considered main drivers of performance in other areas.

In sum, HR management is integral to an organization's success. Organizations that view HR as simply a support function and a cost centre with no revenues or contribution to the bottom line are missing the big picture.

## CONCLUSION

In this chapter, an overview was given of a strategic HRM model involving various components: the external and internal environments, organizational vision and mission, organizational strategies, HR strategies, HR policies and practices, HR effectiveness and other organizational outcomes. The organizational and HR strategies, which are influenced by the environments and the organization's vision and mission, should be well aligned. The strategies should determine the HR policies and practices, which in turn, should drive performance and outcomes. The models for evaluating HR effectiveness, such as the four Cs, are particularly helpful as an analysis tool for various HR systems that are discussed in later chapters.

# HRM in Action
## Strategic HRM at Harley-Davidson

Harley-Davidson was founded in Milwaukee over 100 years ago. It is a well-known manufacturer of high-end motorcycles. It has a loyal customer base as well as a satisfied workforce. In the early 2000s, despite rapid growth and continuing success, the organization was aware that to sustain its growth and to further excel in the market, its workers could not be complacent and simply rely on past successes. Its VP of HR was concerned that HR had not yet been a strategic partner in the company's strategic decision-making. Also, due to the increased demand for labour in the previous decade, the HR function had overly focused on recruitment, to some extent at the expense of other HR areas. With over half of the workforce having five or fewer years of service, employee development and engagement were critical. The company needed to have a strategic plan to invest in its people and the HR processes. Realizing this, the company embarked on a strategic HR transformation journey. With the help of a management consultant firm, the company adopted a framework to assess its human capital capabilities and processes, the alignment of HR practices with the organization's mission and strategies, as well as the linkages between the HR assets and the business performance. Qualitative data from interviews and surveys and quantitative data from HR and Finance were analyzed to assess four dimensions: business results, key performance drivers, human capital capabilities, and human capital processes (that help produce the human capital capabilities). Results available in early 2004 indicated that while the company was doing well in a number of HR processes, the company would benefit most from improvements in the following areas:

- Career development
- Employee relations
- Human capital strategy
- Human capital infrastructure (e.g., HR information system [HRIS], payroll, and benefits administrative processes).

The HR executives chose to focus first on human capital infrastructure (as it would help consolidate systems and share knowledge, thereby improving the overall HR function and increasing its credibility for strategic involvement) and the human capital strategy processes (e.g., by further collecting data on the effectiveness of HR programs and prioritize them according to business benefits). The organization also established a three-year master plan in which senior management would actively help set human capital management priorities, while HR executives would ensure HR processes are aligned with organizational goals and strategies. The changes led to a much more strategic HR function. In 2007, the strategic HR initiatives in employee development earned the company one of the few finalists' spots for the Strategic HR Leadership Award by the Society of Human Resource Management.

Sources:
Scott, H., Cheese, P., & Cantrell, S. (2006). Focusing HR on growth at Harley-Davison: Sustaining widespread success by prioritizing employee development. *Strategic HR Review, 5*(2), 28-31
Accenture. (2005). *Harley-Davidson Motor Company: Strategic HR function.* Retrieved January 28, 2012 from http://www.accenture.com
SHRM. (n.d.) 2007 Human Capital Leadership Awards winners and finalists. Retrieved January 28, 2012 from http://apps2.shrm.org/www/leadershipawards/07winners.asp

## References

Beer, M., Spector, B., Lawrence, P., Quinn Mills, D., & Walton, R. (1984). *Managing human assets*. New York: The Free Press.

Beer, M., Spector, B., Lawrence, P., Quinn Mills, D., & Walton, R. (1985). *Human resource management: A general manager's perspective*. New York: The Free Press.

Belcourt, M., & McBey, K. (2000). *Strategic human resources planning* (2nd ed.). Toronto, ON: Nelson Thomson.

Broderick, R., & Boudreau, J. W. (1992). Human resource management, information technology, and competitive edge. *Academy of Management Executive, 6*(2), 7-17.

Canadian Broadcasting Corporation. (2002, May 8). Sponsorship scandal: Breaking all the rules. *CBC News: The National* [Television broadcast]. Retrieved May 8, 2008, from the CBC Digital Archives website: http://archives.cbc.ca/politics/federal_politics/clips/1700-11687/

Canadian Broadcasting Corporation. (2006, May 30). Air Canada, WestJet settle spying lawsuit. *CBCNews.ca*. Retrieved May 8, 2008, from http://www.cbc.ca/money/story/2006/05/29/westjet-aircansettle.html

Canadian Broadcasting Corporation. (2007, February 27). Nortel: Canada's closely-watched tech [In Depth feature]. *CBCNews.ca*. Retrieved May 8, 2008, from http://www.cbc.ca/news/background/nortel/

Chiavenato, I. (2001). Advances and challenges in human resource management in the new millennium. *Public Personnel Management, 30*(1), 17-26.

Collins, J. C., & Porras, J. I. (1991). Organizational vision and visionary organizations. *California Management Review, 34*(1), 30-52.

Daft, R. (1998). *Organization theory and design* (6th ed). Cincinnati, OH: South Western College Publishing.

Freeman, R. B., & Rogers, J. (1993). Who speaks for us? Employee representation in a nonunion labor market. In B. E. Kaufman & M. M. Kleiner (Eds.), *Employee representation: Alternatives and future directions—Industrial Relations Research Association* (pp. 13-81). Madison, WI: Industrial Relations Research Association.

Freeman, R. B., & Rogers, J. (2006). *What workers want* (Updated ed.). Ithaca, NY: ILR Press.

Handy, L., Barham, K., Panter, S., & Winhard, A. (1989). Beyond the personnel function: The strategic management of human resources. *Journal of European Industrial Training, 13*(1), 13-18.

Hirschman, A. O. (1970). *Exit, voice, and loyalty: Responses to decline in firms, organizations, and states*. Cambridge, MA: Harvard University Press

Kaplan, R. S., & Norton, D. P. (1992). The balanced scorecard – Measures that drive performance. *Harvard Business Review, 70*(1), 71-79.

Kaplan, R. S., & Norton, D. P. (2007). Using the balanced scorecard as a strategic management system. *Harvard Business Review, 85*(7/8), 150-161.

Klie, S. (2006, November 6). HR around the world. *Canadian HR Reporter, 19*(19), 7.

Mayfield, M., Mayfield, J., & Lunce, S. (2003). Human resource information systems: A review and model development. *Advances in Competitiveness Research, 11*(1), 139-151.

Ngai, E. W. T., & Wat, F. K. T. (2006). Human resource information systems: A review and empirical analysis. *Personnel Review, 35*(3), 297-314.

Nutt, P. C. (1999). Surprising but true: Half the decisions in organizations fail. *Academy of Management Executive, 13*(4), 75-90.

Phillips, J. J. (2003). ROI best practices. *Chief Learning Officer, 2*(6), 50-52.

Porter, M. E. (1980). *Competitive strategy: Techniques for analyzing industries and competitors.* New York: Free Press.

Schuler, R. S., & Jackson, S. E. (Eds.). (1999). *Strategic human resource management.* Oxford, UK: Blackwell.

Singh, G. (2001). Supplements and complements to the current employee representation system in the United States. *Employee Responsibilities and Rights Journal, 13*(2), 107-124.

Taras, D. G., & Kaufman, B. E. (2006). Non-union employee representation in North America: diversity, controversy and uncertain future. *Industrial Relations Journal, 37*(5), 513-542.

Tsui, A. S., & Gomez-Mejia, L. R. (1988). Evaluating human resource effectiveness. In L. Dyer (Ed.), *Human resource management — Evolving roles and responsibilities* (pp. 187-225). Washington, DC: Bureau of National Affairs.

Walker, J. W. (1992). *Human resource strategy.* New York: McGraw-Hill.

Walton, R. E. (1985). From control to commitment in the workplace. *Harvard Business Review, 63*(2), 77-84.

Wright, P. M., & Snell, S. A. (1991). Toward an integrative view of strategic human resource management. *Human Resource Management Review, 1*(3), 203-225.

*Chapter 1*

# Management Philosophy and Organizational Culture

## Introduction

What does management believe in? Is labour just another factor of production like raw materials that can be just bought off the market? What does management really value: profits, fairness to people, contributing to the community? What are management's assumptions about the average workers: are they hard workers, can they be trusted, what do they like, and what will motivate them? The answers to these questions often determine the organizational and HR strategic and policy directions. In sum, *management philosophy* is the collective ideology, beliefs, values, and assumptions shared by management members of the organization. Of course, managers in an organization do not always have exactly the same philosophy, but generally people tend to be attracted to organizations and colleagues with whom they can identify. Organizations also tend to hire new people whose beliefs and values are congruent with those of the existing management team. As management philosophy is not usually stated expressly— even if it is, actions may speak louder than words—the simplest way to get a sense of an organization's management philosophy is to look at what is valued by the leaders, what gets rewarded, and how people are treated in the organization.

As stated in Chapter 1, *organizational culture* refers to the complex set of beliefs, assumptions, values, attitudes, expectations, and norms held and shared by its members (management and staff) and exhibited in artifacts and behaviours. Organizational culture can be greatly influenced by the management philosophy. Organization members tend to respond according to the management philosophy because either they share in management's beliefs and values or they want to behave as management expects for the sake of their own career or as a self-fulfilling prophecy. This, in turn, shapes to varying extent the overall organizational cul-

Note: An earlier version of some sections of this chapter written by the author was included in the *Human Resource Management Study Guide* (2007), Centre for Innovative Management, Athabasca University.

ture. Therefore, in this chapter, management philosophy and organizational culture are addressed together.

This chapter starts by looking at some theories and framework related to management philosophy. A theory is basically a model of patterns of observed phenomena and relationships of factors of concern. It helps to explain general behaviours, but it may not necessarily be applicable to all cases and situations. Next, organizational culture, its symbolism mechanisms, and culture types are discussed. Finally, a very important organizational culture dimension is discussed: ethical HRM. Ethics is a fundamental consideration in all HRM decisions.

## THEORIES X AND Y

In 1960, McGregor introduced the renowned and influential theories on managing employee behaviour: *Theory X* and *Theory Y*. The characteristics of these theories are found in many organizational behaviour books and are summarized in Table 2-1.

**Table 2-1  McGregor (1960) – Theory X and Theory Y**

| Theory X Assumptions | Theory Y Assumptions |
|---|---|
| 1. "The average human being has an inherent dislike of work and will avoid it if he can." | 1. "The expenditure of physical and mental effort in work is as natural as play or rest." |
| 2. "Because of this human characteristic of dislike of work, most people must be coerced, controlled, directed, or threatened with punishment to get them to put forth adequate effort toward the achievement of organizational objectives." | 2. "External control and the threat of punishment are not the only means for bringing about effort toward organizational objectives. Man will exercise self-direction and self-control in the service of objectives to which he is committed." |
| 3. "The average human being prefers to be directed, wishes to avoid responsibility, has little ambition, and wants security above all." (pp. 33- 35) | 3. "Commitment to objectives is a function of the rewards associated with their achievement." |
| | 4. "The average human being learns, under proper conditions, not only to accept but to seek responsibility." |
| | 5. "The capacity to exercise a relatively high degree of imagination, ingenuity, and creativity in the solution of organizational problems is widely, not narrowly, distributed in the population." |
| | 6. "Under the conditions of modern industrial life, the intellectual potentialities of the average human being are only partially utilized." (pp. 47-48) |

Note that these theories are about the assumptions made by managers, not that they necessarily describe the actual workers. The theories are also not intended as a categorization tool. Therefore, no attempt should be made to slot individual employees into different categories using these theories.

So what are the practical implications of these theories? How will the organization's HR policy and practices differ under these two philosophies?

Managers with the Theory X philosophy are likely comfortable with a tall hierarchical structure and centralized control, standardized work, and high degree of division of labour. Employees are closely monitored to ensure compliance. Job shirking is punished through monetary losses or disciplinary actions.

Managers with the Theory Y philosophy are the opposite. They likely favour work autonomy, employee empowerment, and broad job descriptions. The emphasis is on employee commitment rather than compliance. Intrinsic rewards, such as meaningful work, are used to motivate employees.

## SCHEIN'S FOUR MODELS

Schein (1980) provides a more expanded discussion of management philosophy, involving four models, namely *rational economic man, social man, self-actualization man,* and *complex man.* In the following discussion, the term "person" is used instead as the models apply to both genders.

### Rational Economic Person

The rational economic person model is similar in many ways to McGregor's Theory X. For example, both assume that employees are generally lazy and self-centred. They care little about the organization and so must be tightly controlled. Since they are not self-motivated, external incentives are needed. The rational economic person model proposes that employees are interested in monetary incentives and they make rational decisions that are calculated, involving the choice that will bring the most monetary return. Under this model, if a person is not maximizing his or her economic benefits, then the person is not rational.

In this model and the Theory X model, management believes in the availability of a small set of individuals who are different (more mature, committed, and capable) and who will lead the organization. These individuals are able to plan, organize, and coordinate the organization's activities. On the other hand, the average workers are there just to implement the management decisions. Hence, the rational economic person model and Theory X both emphasize narrow job classifications for the average workers—who need external drivers (e.g., money) to get the work done—and separation of planning and execution.

## Social Person

This model probably arose out of the findings of a series of studies done by researchers in the human relations school in the 1930s (see Mayo, 1960). In this model, management views satisfying social needs as employees' primary motivation in work. Informal work groups are important for the workers' identification and sense of belonging whereas economic incentives or the meaning of work itself are not as significant. Thus management with this view emphasize organizing work groups in such a way that meets workers' social and relationship needs and benefits the organization. Rewards are likely group-based or organization-based. Teams are formed to perform tasks. Managers and supervisors tend to use friendship and group norms as the tools to get employees to work rather than their position power. Employee selection focuses on the ability to fit in.

## Self-Actualization Person

The above two models view workers' behaviours as mainly driven by external factors. This model, the self-actualization person, sees people in a more positive light: basically their behaviour is internally driven. The model can be regarded as stemming from the theories of researchers like Maslow (see Chapter 3) and McGregor (see Theory Y above). It proposes that self-actualization is a very important need for individuals. Where possible, people want work autonomy and personal growth. They are self-motivated to do a good job to achieve their goals, which in desired situations are quite congruent with the organizational goals.

This management philosophy reflects the basic tenets for strategic HRM. According to this philosophy, employees should be given interesting and challenging work with little supervision. Adequate resources and authority are given to allow employees to do their work the way they see fit. Training and development is heavily emphasized to help the employees grow. Employee involvement and empowerment should be common practices throughout the organization. Fair external rewards, while necessary, are not the main driver of good performance. Employees work to the best of their ability because they want to do so themselves, not because they are driven by outside forces.

## Complex Person

The above three models are all premised on some basic assumptions about human beings that later research found too simplistic. In the real world, people are often more complex and their responses are dependent on the circumstances. This is called the contingency school of thought. According to the complex person model, people can behave differently across situations and time, and their behaviour can change with new experiences. They have a variety of needs, and not all of them require satisfaction through work.

Simply put, workers are not a homogenous group with identical responses to similar stimuli. As such, management who hold this philosophy are dealing with individual employees in individual situations: what works for A may not work for B and what works for C in situation X may not work for C in situation Y. For small organizations, such a form of micro-level management is possible, but implementing different policies for different employees in a large organization is not only a daunting, or near impossible, task, it can also easily give rise to accusations of favouritism and discrimination, which in turn could demoralize the workplace and lead to legal concerns. At best, an organization with this philosophy sets up different policies for different groups of employees, according to what management believes the group needs are.

When it comes to adopting a philosophy to establish policies and practices, management usually goes with one of the first three models due to the impracticability of the fourth. It does not mean that all managers in the organization must embrace exactly the same model, nor does it mean that all workers will share the traits that management believes they have in common. It basically reflects the organization's overall way of treating its employees, especially in terms of the amount of trust management has of them. Obviously, the rational economic person model assumes employees cannot be trusted, while the self-actualization person model assumes the contrary.

## CONTROL VERSUS COMMITMENT

Theory X and the rational economic person model reflect a strategy of command and control in the management of the workforce. Managers with such philosophies think they have the power to get the most out of their employees. They exercise their control through close supervision, tall hierarchies, sets of rules and regulations, use of monetary rewards as incentive, and punishment to force compliance. And they may get compliance, but it is unlikely that employees go beyond their call of duty. The psychological contract an employee has with such an organization (i.e., the unstated contract involving sets of expectations between the employee and the organization) is basically transactional in nature. Most employees dislike being constantly monitored and may choose to avoid work when the opportunity arises, partly due to a self-fulfilling prophecy. That is, why would employees want to work hard when management assumes they are shirking anyway? What management in this situation overlooks is the power within individuals and the influence of social groups. Why do people work as volunteers for non-profit organizations when there is no monetary return? Why do employees willingly help or mentor their colleagues when it is not specifically written into the job description? Management that fails to recognize the importance of these forces is most unlikely to obtain a high level of HR effectiveness.

On the other hand, management that chooses the commitment strategy may actually get more productive employees and gain greater HR effectiveness although, on the surface, they may be relinquishing control to the employees (i.e., by empowering them). Given the right support and empowerment, employees have the intrinsic incentive to perform well. By engaging in strategic HRM, organizations are able to attract, retain, and motivate employees whose interests align with those of the organization.

## ORGANIZATIONAL CULTURE

When newcomers to an organization say they have a problem of fitting in, often they are referring to a lack of understanding or appreciation of the organizational culture. Organizational culture is something that is generally taken for granted by management and employees. Yet it is critical for new members to be socialized properly and to learn the ropes; that is, to have a good idea how things are generally done in the organization and what to expect in terms of the behaviours and attitudes. Culture can be seen as the social glue that binds the organization's people together, shaping their attitude and guiding their behaviour. It is also something that distinguishes one organization from another.

Culture can be communicated in formal or informal ways. For example, it can be explicitly written in the vision and the mission statement and reinforced by various HR policies (e.g., in the structuring of work, setting of performance goals and measurement standards, use of rewards). Culture can also be communicated implicitly by leadership action and symbolism. Schein (1983) identifies 10 symbolic mechanisms used to establish culture (generally listed in descending order of explicitness):

1. Formal statements of organizational philosophy, charters, creeds, materials used for recruitment and selection, and socialization.
2. Design of physical spaces, facades, buildings.
3. Deliberate role modeling, teaching, and coaching by leaders.
4. Explicit reward and status system, promotion criteria.
5. Stories, legends, myths, and parables about key people and events.
6. What leaders pay attention to, measure, and control.

7. Leader reactions to critical incidents and organizational crises (times when organizational survival is threatened, norms are unclear or are challenged, insubordination occurs, threatening or meaningless events occur, and so forth).

8. How the organization is designed and structured. (The design of work, who reports to whom, degree of decentralization, functional or other criteria for differentiation, and mechanisms used for integration carry implicit messages of what leaders assume and value.)

9. Organizational systems and procedures. (The types of information, control, and decision support systems in terms of categories of information, time cycles, who gets what information, and when and how performance appraisal and other review processes are conducted carry implicit messages of what leaders assume and value.)

10. Criteria used for recruitment, selection, promotion, levelling off, retirement, and "excommunication" of people (the implicit and possibly unconscious criteria that leaders use to determine who "fits" and who doesn't "fit" membership roles and key slots in the organization). (p. 22)

It is not unusual that conflicting messages are sometimes sent by different leaders in the organization or even from the same leader. It is also not uncommon that the implicit messages do not always match the explicit ones, in which case it is necessary to see if the leader really "walks the talk". So often leaders may say employees are their most important asset, yet remove all training and development programs or even lay off a large number of employees at the slightest sign of an economic downturn. In this case, it is not difficult for members to see through the veil. Similarly, an organization may say that they value employee input and hence have an open door policy. Yet inputs are never seriously considered. The door is open, but management's ears are shut. It does not take long for employees to realize that management is simply paying lip service to the high-sounding idea.

Among the 10 mechanisms, Schein suggests that item 3 on role modeling, item 6 on what leaders pay attention to, and item 7 on leader reaction to critical events are most important in sending potent messages about the organizational culture. Knowing the relative importance of these mechanisms is helpful in deciphering conflicting messages.

People often say things about organizations and, surprisingly, sometimes even a very simple statement speaks volumes about the organization's culture. Edmonds (2000) provides a number of such examples:

1. Win at all costs.

2. People get ahead by being patient and paying their dues.

3. Decisions are made by consensus.

4. Desks and work areas are neat and tidy at all time. Look organized.

5. Be careful what you say to your boss (or anybody's boss for that matter).

6. Teach people the ropes. Help them get ahead. A boss is a mentor.

7. You have to be tough to survive in this business.

8. No surprises.

9. Work should be exciting. Take risks. Try it!

10. Commitment and loyalty to the organization are important. If you are not committed, you don't belong here.

11. You get and keep business by paying attention to customers. Listen to them!

12. Get results, but do so ethically.

13. Talk to others. Listen. Ideas should be expressed. Good ideas know no hierarchy or job description.

14. It's not your job to think. We have people who are hired to think.

15. Innovate! We stay in business by being state-of-the-art.

16. Avoid direct conflict if at all possible.

17. Loyalty to your group is more important than loyalty to your boss.

18. Keep things on a small scale. Decentralize.

19. Keep things simple. Question paperwork.

20. Survival of the fittest.

21. If you do your job, you'll be here for a long time.

22. When in doubt, go by the book. (Section 4-3 Leadership and Organizational Culture)

When a newcomer hears statements like any of the above, inevitably he or she will become aware of how to behave in a way acceptable to the organization. Outsiders hearing this will also form an image of what the organization and its members are like.

## CULTURE TYPES

Handy (1993, pp. 181-191) describes four organizational culture types that are summarized here.

### The Power Culture

Often found in small entrepreneurial-type organizations, the power culture relies on a *central power source*. This central figure (power source) exerts rays of power and influence outwards. Trust and empathy are characteristics on which the organization depends for its effectiveness. For communication, the reliance is on personal conversation and, in effect, telepathy. Rules, procedures, and bureaucracy are sparse in this form of organization. Control is exerted by the central power source through key individuals. Hence, careful selection and succession planning for such individuals are crucial. Decisions are often political in nature and not necessarily based on rules or logic. Organizations with a power culture have the ability to move quickly in response to changes. However, growth of an organization with this culture may pose a problem if the linkage to the central figure weakens.

### The Role Culture

The role culture is analogous to a *Greek temple*, with its pillars representing the organization's functions. These functions (the pillars) are controlled by rules and procedures that are coordinated at the top of the temple by a group of senior executives. The role organization can work well in a stable environment. However, it does not react quickly to change even when faced by the need to do so. Role culture provides a secure and predictable organizational environment for workers, but holds no appeal to individuals who are power-oriented or who want more autonomy and flexibility over their work. The role culture is predominant in organizations "where economies of scale are more important than flexibility or where technical expertise and depth of specialization are more important than product innovation or product cost" (Handy, 1993, p. 186).

### The Task Culture

The task culture suits an organization that has a job or project focus. Its structure resembles a *net* or *matrix* with most of the power and influence occurring at the knots. The essence of this culture is to get the work done, often by bringing together necessary resources, such as people. The task culture frequently adopts the team approach, enhancing organizational performance through integration of the efforts and powers within the group and the alignment of these with the organizational goals. The task culture is incredibly adaptable, enabling groups, project teams, or task forces to be created, changed, or discontinued as appropriate. Such a group orientation also allows work to be done quickly and efficiently since group members, desirably, have the necessary decision-making powers. Individuals exercise considerable control over their work and people are judged by results (i.e., what they do rather than who they are). This culture is suited to markets or environments where flexibility and the speed of response are important but not when economies of scale or a high degree of specialization is preferred. This culture mirrors the current business thoughts being championed for change and adaptation and for employee autonomy and empowerment, but it may encounter problems when resources are scarce and teams begin to compete against each other.

### The Person Culture

This culture is uncommon in that the individual is the centre of attention. An organization with such a culture exists only for the individuals within it, and there is no singular, overarching control. Examples are architects' partnerships, small consultancy firms, social groups, and families. Organizational structure under this culture is minimal and the best description for this culture would be a *cluster*.

There are other culture typologies that can be considered. For example, Cameron and Quinn (1999) used a competing value framework to distinguish four culture types along two dimensions, as shown in Table 2-2.

**Table 2-2  The Clan, Adhocracy, Market, and Hierarchy Cultures**

| Flexibility/Discretion | Clan Culture | Adhocracy Culture |
|---|---|---|
| | Family-like friendly organization | Highly adaptive organization striving for innovation |
| Stability/Control | Hierarchy Culture | Market Culture |
| | Highly structured workplace relying on rules, policies, and procedures for effective functioning | A competitive workplace emphasizing productivity and results |
| | *Internal Focussed* | *External Focussed* |

Readers may want to go through Edmond's (2000) examples of statements about organizations again and see if some may be matched with the above organizational culture types. For example, what do "go by the book", "get results", "talk to others and listen", and "be careful what you say to your boss" statements suggest about the organizational culture?

## Culture and the Psychological Contract

Different cultures call for differing psychological contracts (the implicit under-standing of the expectations between employer and employee). An example of such contracts is an employee expects to have stable employment, good pay, and promotion opportunities in return for hard work and loyalty to the organization. Psychological contracts are very important in an employment relationship. Seri-ous consequences may result from a breach of such contract. For example, when an employee expects the organization to value employees and support job security but sees long-term employees being laid off in an economic downturn, trust can be lost and morale can suffer. The employee then becomes skeptical of what the employer tells him or her, performs less effectively, and has lower commitment to the organization.

Certain types of people will be happy and successful in one culture but not in another. It is therefore important to ensure a match among the organization's environment, its culture, its people, and their psychological contracts.

## Ethical HRM

The issue of business ethics has been brought to the limelight ever since the col-lapse of some big corporations (e.g., Enron, Worldcom, Arthur Andersen) and the outbreak of major corporate scandals (e.g., the Canadian Liberal government's sponsorship scandal and the Canadian airlines' spying lawsuits) due to ethically questionable behaviours. Organizations are often concerned about the morale of employees because it affects employee productivity and commitment. It is bad enough for an organization to have poor morale, but an organization is in much greater trouble if it has a *moral* problem (in that management and/or employees do not know what is ethical). Moral problems can and will severely and adversely affect morale because unethical processes and decisions breed employee dissat-isfaction. HR can be seen as the "keeper and voice" of ethics in an organization and thus has a major role to play in helping the organization build an ethical culture (Mathis, Jackson, & Zinni, 2008, p. 25). HR is the holder of confidential personal employee information and is involved in many decisions that have a major bearing on employees' livelihood. Ethics is inherently an important com-ponent in almost all aspects of HRM policies and activities. Unethical behaviours within HRM can occur in various ways: favouritism in recruitment and selection, promotion and deployment, layoffs and termination as well as intentional bias in performance assessment and rewards. Similarly, in disciplinary actions, con-doning certain misbehaviours for some employees but not others is unethical. Ignoring unsafe work conditions or workplace harassments can result in outcomes that are both unethical and unlawful. Providing misrepresented information to employees or potential hires and allowing or encouraging employees to provide misleading information in order to achieve better bottom-line profits are also unethical behaviours.

Ethical behaviour is largely dependent on the organizational culture, which in turn, is mainly attributed to the signals or symbols given by organizational leaders relating to the values embraced by the organization and what are acceptable and unacceptable behaviours. To help build an ethical culture, Blanchard and Peale (1988) offer the following suggestions.

- Organizations should have a clear mission that is based on integrity, with employees understanding and appreciating that they play an important role in achieving that mission.

- Employees are likely to engage in ethical behaviours if they feel good about themselves, and they like what they are doing.

- Organizations need a genuinely open policy, to be concerned about the fairness of both the means and the ends in achieving organizational goals, and to establish reliable organizational systems premised on integrity and consistency.

- Review of organizational values and reinforcement of them on an ongoing basis with employees also helps in maintaining an ethical culture.

How would one know if a decision is ethical? A couple of frameworks or guiding questions have been developed that may help. These are provided in Table 2-3.

Ethical decisions in both processes and outcomes are crucial to organizations. If something is not right because it should not be done in the first place, then there is no right or ethical process for doing it. Even if something is the right thing to do, it can still be unethical if the process in achieving it is not fair.

**Table 2-3 Guidelines for Ethical Decision-Making**

| Blanchard and Peale (1988) | |
|---|---|
| Is it legal? | If something is illegal, chances are it is also not ethical. However, something that is legal still does not always guarantee that it is ethical, as the law sometimes sets only minimal standards. |
| Is it balanced? | Is the decision fair to all of the stakeholders? Will one group of stakeholders gain disproportionately at the expense of another? Will it lead to a win-win situation for the various parties such that a favourable and sustainable relationship can be maintained? |
| How do you feel as the decision-maker? | Will you feel good and proud about it? |
| **Wheeler (2004)** | |
| Reciprocity | Do you want others to treat you the same way? |
| Publicity | Are you comfortable letting the public know of your decision? |
| Trusted friend | Are you comfortable telling close friends what you are doing? |
| Universality | Will you advise others to act this way? |
| Legacy | Does your action reflect how you want to be known down the road? |

## CONCLUSION

Management philosophy has a major influence on organizational culture as well as the organization's policies and practices. While management philosophy may change with new leadership, organizational culture that is well ingrained within all parts of the organization may take a long time to change, probably even longer than changing the organizational structure. In an age of constant environmental changes, the role culture may become less appropriate for sustaining organization effectiveness. On the other hand, the task culture may gain in popularity especially with the trend towards computer-mediated communications and the use of virtual teams. (Teams will be discussed further in Chapter 5.) A main role of management is to foster a culture that will allow both the organization and its members to grow and prosper, and ensure that decisions made are ethical and lawful.

# HRM in Action
## Organizational Culture at Google

Google's rather unique organizational culture has been well known in the business setting. Despite the fact that it is now a multi-billion dollar global enterprise and leader in information technology with more than 20,000 employees worldwide, it still maintains a culture somewhat similar to its start-up stage. Google's mission is to "organize the world's information and make it universally accessible and useful." It recognizes its employee resource as critical to the accomplishment of its mission and sustainable success. Hence, it offers employees a great degree of latitude in managing their work, stretch their imagination, share ideas, and innovate. Most employees' work is project-based, with collaboration a key element. Their workplace is atypical in its setting with few offices and many amenities, while its work hours are flexible. Fun is an important part of its culture to keep employees happy, energized, and motivated. The main office was even given a nickname, Googleplex , to reflect the many fun things one can do in it.

In terms of staffing, particular attention is given to finding employees with the right fit (in addition to the ability, knowledge, and skills requirements) – those who are highly flexible, adaptable, team-oriented, and eager to get work done without much concern for rank and status. Employees' professional growth and development are emphasized to develop and retain top-notch talents. Employees are also provided with generous perks, including free healthy food throughout the day. The organization also recognizes the need for work-life balance and has various programs to support it.

With rapid expansion that could diffuse or jeopardize its cultural advantages, Google took a rare initiative of hiring a chief culture officer in 2003, whose role was dedicated to maintaining the unique culture and to make employees happy. The incumbent also assumed the role of director of human resources.

Below are some more tidbits about Google's organizational culture:

- Weekly meeting where employees can directly ask questions of the top leaders
- Employees have lots of opportunities to share time together socially, e.g., happy hours, parties, and other celebrative occasions
- Break rooms with snacks and drinks are available for employees' rest and enjoyment
- Ball courts, video games, pianos, gym equipment, pool tables, ping pong tables, massage chairs, and other amenities are available on site for health and entertainment
- Interest groups of all sorts formed by employees are welcome, e.g., dancing, wine tasting, exercise classes
- Bicycles, scooters, and even dogs can be brought to the office as employees prefer.

Sources:
Google. (n. d.). *Our culture*. Retrieved January 30, 2012 from http://www.google.com/about/corporate/company/culture.html
Mills, E. (2007, April 27). *Newsmaker: Meet Google's culture czar.* Retrieved January 30, 2012 from http://news.cnet.com/2008-1023_3-6179897.html

# HRM in Action

## A Cultural Revolution at General Electric (GE)

When Jeffrey Immelt took over the position of Chairman and CEO at GE from Jack Welch in 2001, GE had been well known for its continuous operational improvements and success at "cost-cutting, efficiency, and dealmaking." Promotion-from-within was the norm, but employees would have to be prepared for frequent transfers to climb the career ladder. Management kept a tight control over performance evaluations and the bottom 10% performers would not be retained. While the company was doing well at that time, Immelt knew that to excel in the new era, with keener global competition and slower domestic market growth, fundamental changes would be needed in the way things were done. Basically, he initiated a cultural revolution to "transform the hard-driving, process-oriented company into one steeped in creativity and wired for growth," with an emphasis on "risk-taking, sophisticated marketing, and above all, innovation".

To embark on this cultural transformation, a number of initiatives were implemented, some of which include:

- Diversifying the top ranks by hiring outsiders: new executives could act as a change agent to bring new expertise and vision
- Establishing a high-profile Commercial Council: the council, comprised of top sales and marketing executives, met monthly to discuss marketing growth strategies and innovative ideas
- "Imagination Breakthrough" proposals: business leaders were expected to submit three breakthrough proposals each year, involving a new line of product or a new market, with each proposal having a potential to increase revenue by $100 million
- Executive compensation was tied with creativity and growth: purely meeting the bottom line was no longer good enough. Rather, ability to envision and meet customer needs and to generate growth would be rewarded. Risk-taking was encouraged, and there seemed to be more flexibility in determining and removing the bottom performers
- Investment in R&D in high-growth business areas: low-margin and slower-growth business areas (like appliances) were trimmed in favour of high-potential areas like bioscience, wind power, and film entertainment. Globalizing research would help to tap into worldwide talent
- Training and development focused on marketing and creativity: the top marketers were even offered a commercial leadership program that involved two years of intensive development
- Programs and rewards for new ideas: examples are "virtual idea box" (brainstorming using the Web) and "Excellerator awards" at GE Energy.

Source:
The Immelt revolution. (2005, March 27). *Businessweek*. Retrieved January 30, 2012 from http://www.businessweek.com/stories/2005-03-27/the-immelt-revolution

## References

Blanchard, K. H., & Peale, N. V. (1988). *The power of ethical management.* New York: Ballantine.

Cameron, K. & Quinn, R. (1999). *Diagnosing and changing organizational culture.* Reading, MA: Addison-Wesley.

Handy, C. (1993). *Understanding organizations* (4th ed.). London: Penguin Books.

Edmonds, R. (2000). *Human resource management (HRMT-502) Study Guide—Lesson 4: Leadership* [Unpublished course materials]. St. Albert, AB: Centre for Innovative Management, Athabasca University.

Mathis, R. L., Jackson, J. H., & Zinni, D. M. (2008). *Human resource management* (Canadian ed.). Toronto, ON: Nelson Thomson.

Mayo, E. (1960). *Human problems of an industrial civilization.* New York: Viking Press.

McGregor, D. (1960). *The human side of enterprise.* New York: McGraw-Hill.

Schein, E. H. (1980). *Organizational psychology* (3rd ed.). Englewood Cliffs, CA: Prentice Hall.

Schein, E. H. (1983). The role of the founder in creating organizational culture. *Organizational Dynamics, 12*(1), 13-28.

Wheeler, M. (March, 2004). Fair enough? An ethical fitness quiz for negotiators. *Negotiation* [Harvard Business School newsletter], *7*(3), 3-5.

# Work Design and Motivation

## Introduction

Work of the same nature need not be created equally. For example, manufacturing of a product can be done by a team or on an assembly line. An accountant can be given purely repetitive clerical responsibilities or be given full budget accountabilities. How work is designed has a significant impact on how work is actually done, how it is coordinated amongst employees, and, most importantly, how much it makes the job appeal to individuals and motivates their performance. While it is generally recognized that work design and rewards are both closely related to employee motivation, intrinsic rewards related to the work content (such as growth and actualization) are often more important than extrinsic factors (such as pay and working conditions) in driving high employee performance. Hence, in this chapter, work design and motivation are discussed together. The chapter starts with an introduction to work design and its components. This is followed by an examination of the popular management schools of thoughts, each of which relates to a different set of recommendations for work design. The second part of this chapter is devoted to a discussion of motivation. Various motivation theories are introduced and their implications on work design addressed. An integrated model of motivation is also provided for practical reference. The concept of the self and its role in motivation as well as some recent developments of motivation in the global context are covered before the close of the chapter.

## Work Design

In designing or redesigning work for motivation, it is often useful to start by looking at the various job dimensions. Two of the most common job characteristics models are described here.

Note: An earlier version of some sections of this chapter written by the author was included in the *Human Resource Management Study Guide* (2007), Centre for Innovative Management, Athabasca University.

Hackman and Oldham (1980) identified five core dimensions of job characteristics that would affect employee behaviour, as shown in Table 3-1.

**Table 3-1  Hackman and Oldham (1960) – Dimensions of Job Characteristics**

| | |
|---|---|
| **Task/skill variety** | The extent of the variety in the tasks of the job and the variety of skills or talents required. |
| **Task identity** | The extent to which the job leads to an identifiable piece of work produced that can be viewed more as a "visible whole" than as a "not-so-visible part." |
| **Task significance** | The extent of importance of the task to the final product, the organization, and/or the society. |
| **Autonomy** | The amount of discretion or control the job allows the employee to have, such as in scheduling the work and determining how the work should be done. |
| **Task feedback** | The amount of feedback the job provides the employees about how well the job has been done. |

Similarly, Dawson (1996, p. 19) listed fourteen basic elements of job design, as described in Table 3-2:

**Table 3-2  Dawson (1996) – Elements of Job Design**

| | |
|---|---|
| **Task** | Objective(s) of activity(ies) |
| **Method** | How job is done (nature of activities) |
| **Technology** | Plant, equipment, machinery involved |
| **Variety** | How many activities included |
| **Sequencing** | Order in which activities are undertaken |
| **Timing** | Time for completion of sequence(s) of activities |
| **Pace** | Pace of work |
| **Quality** | Standards required |
| **Specialization** | Degree of specialization in division of labour |
| **Independence** | Relation of activities to those undertaken by others |
| **Partialness** | Relation of activities to completion of overall product |
| **Performance** | How is performance measured |
| **Monitoring** | Who decides action in light of performance information? |
| **Accountability** | What happens if performance information shows good/bad performance? |

Work design does not need to be a static concept since jobs can change over time, either by necessity or by intention. *Job enlargement* and *job enrichment* are two common initiatives that involve changes to work. Job enlargement is the merging of two or more specialized jobs that provide a worker with a wider range of tasks at a similar level of responsibility (horizontal loading). For example, an employee whose job has been photocopying documents for department A is asked to do so for department B as well. Job enlargement may add more work and a bit more variety, but it does not make the job more meaningful or help with employee growth and development. Job enrichment, on the other hand, provides employees with a higher level of responsibilities and discretion and at the same time offers more variety (vertical loading). It can make the job more challenging, and enhance learning opportunities for employees. *Job rotation* is a related initiative that does not actually involve changes in jobs: job incumbents move across jobs periodically. Job rotation allows workers to achieve greater variety of work and widens their exposure. It helps an organization achieve greater flexibility when it comes to future job assignments.

Constant and rapid technological changes inevitably have a significant impact on work design. Web conferencing and other virtual tools have greatly enhanced the effectiveness of meetings held with members at a distance. Tools that facilitate document sharing and updating give tremendous support to team collaboration and can allow for more efficient sequencing of work. Electronic monitoring devices and programs that are now more commonly available for employees' phone or computer activities can serve as a basis for performance review and better work design (although the desirability of such monitoring is often subject to debate). Social media advances also dramatically change the communications amongst organizational stakeholders (including potential clients and employees). This can provide an extra feedback channel for the organization and its employees on various initiatives and activities.

## SOME MANAGEMENT SCHOOLS OF THOUGHT

Of the management schools of thought developed in the twentieth century that have had a lasting effect on organization and job design, Frederick W. Taylor's scientific management has probably been one of the more influential, especially in the earlier decades. This and other major developments in management approaches, including the human relations school of thought, the socio-technological approach, and total quality management, are examined here.

### Taylorism

Taylor's (1911) book, *The Principles of Scientific Management*, has had profound impact on management and work organization. Taylor was well known for using scientific methods (time-motion studies) to examine individual job components to determine how the parts could be best performed and coordinated. Hence, an important feature of Taylorism is the high degree of division of labour and specialization. Work can be repetitive. The level of discretion workers have on the job is low. Training is therefore not necessary or is minimally required, just to ensure the workers can carry out the specific component of work assigned. Efficiency is the key. Because maximization of workers' physical capacity and productivity is emphasized, worker selection tends to focus on physical fitness. Workers are also considered lazy; "soldiering" must therefore be managed by close supervision and control. Separation of planning and execution of work is also a main characteristic of Taylorism, with the former task to be performed by management staff and the latter by the workers. Workers are believed to be motivated by economic incentives and thus hourly rate or piece-rate is common under this type of management approach. The assembly line concept is a good example of the Tayloristic approach towards work design. Products are standardized and each worker on the line is responsible for a very tiny part of the process. Skill workers are not required and the pace of work is tightly controlled.

The Tayloristic approach flourished for a number of decades after its introduction, and it is still in place to various extents in manufacturing organizations. It is particularly appropriate for use at a time when the organizational environment is relatively stable and customer demand for standardized products through mass production is high. However, it likely is not flexible enough to meet a constantly changing environment where employees need to have creative ideas and to work together for synergies in efforts. Nor can it meet the new expectations of customers for better service and higher level of customization of products. The assumption that workers are motivated by money is also subject to challenge. As discussed later in the chapter, many motivation theories indicate the real motivators are more likely to be intrinsic in nature (Herzberg, 1968). The individualistic nature of this approach also fails to meet workers' social needs (Maslow, 1954). The latter area is addressed by the human relations school.

## Human Relations School

Interestingly, the human relations school started more by accident than by intention. Studies were initially conducted to determine the effect of illumination on workers' output (see Mayo, 1960). In 1927, Elton Mayo studied six female telephone equipment assembly operators who were isolated in a special room. Their production increased over time regardless of the changes made to the work setting— even when the working conditions were worsened. The result was mainly attributed to the positive group relations with each other and the supervisor and the feeling of being special or important (they were selected by management). Further studies with a bank-wiring group of men discovered that the group felt its own identity and established its norms (meaning that no one should be producing too fast or too slow). While Taylorism focuses on the physical and economic aspects, this school of studies shows that the human element and social relations have a major and direct effect on worker performance and organizational effectiveness. It offers a different view from Taylor on the understanding of satisfaction and motivation and of work groups.

## Socio-Technological Approach

Emphasis on the technical environment as well as social relations is increasing with rapid technological advancement over the past decades. The human relations school tends to see technology as a given (or a constant factor) while the socio-technological approach takes the view that technology can and should be chosen or developed integrative with the development of the social environment. Focusing on only the technical aspects may have undesirable social costs and focusing on only the social aspects may result in poor performance by overlooking the technical issues. To avoid sub-optimization, both the social and technical factors should be considered as a whole. The socio-technological approach is more commonly adopted in organizations that use technology extensively, such as those in the chemical processing industry.

## Total Quality Management (TQM)

Back in the 1950s, TQM's pioneer, Dr. Edward Deming, tried with little success to advocate total quality management (TQM) principles to North American organizations. TQM was, however, embraced in Japan, leading to some best business practices that other nations strive to follow or surpass decades later. The general principles of TQM, as outlined by Greer (2001) are:

- articulation of a strategic vision
- objective and accurate measurements
- benchmarking
- widespread employee empowerment and team building
- striving for continuous improvement
- emphasis on a systems view of quality that conceptualizes quality-related activities as being highly interdependent
- leadership committed to quality
- great emphasis on customer satisfaction (p. 52)

TQM is not just a set of principles specifically for work design. It is a management philosophy, and involves a paradigm shift. Under the Tayloristic environment, work is fragmented, training is minimal, and empowerment is non-existent.

47

Workers are tightly controlled and inspection is the proper method for ensuring that the products are acceptable. In contrast, TQM maintains that workers know best what they do and that their input into the process or system is important for continuous improvement. Cross-functional teamwork is common in organizations adopting TQM. Recognizing that most poor quality output and work mistakes are due to the system rather than the individual workers and that reworking is costly, the emphasis is to do work right the first time. Work is designed so that any monitoring is built into the process instead of requiring an inspector at the end of the process. TQM impacts the organizational structure, work design, and various HRM systems. It involves the fundamental belief that everyone can contribute to the organization to continuously improve on the system and make the organization successful. It is customer-orientated and quality-focused. Statistical process control is frequently adopted for quality assurance and improvement.

TQM should be distinguished from *re-engineering*, although both are initiatives aimed at improving quality. TQM emphasizes gradual continuous improvements that build on the strengths of the existing system, while re-engineering involves "the fundamental rethinking and radical redesign of business processes to achieve dramatic improvements in critical contemporary measures of performance, such as cost, quality, service, and speed" (Hammer & Champy, 1993, p. 32). Re-engineering involves throwing out the old and reinventing the processes. Organizations are likely to undergo re-engineering in response to or in preparation of substantial environmental changes. Re-engineering can at most happen periodically. TQM, on the other hand, is an ongoing process best used between re-engineering times or in a relatively stable environment. While the impact of TQM can be very significant, it is not something that can happen overnight. There must be management commitment, employee buy-in, and a corresponding culture change for positive outcomes to be realized.

Closely related to TQM is the Six Sigma approach that many high-profile organizations, such as 3M, Honeywell, and GE, have adopted. Six Sigma was first developed by Motorola in 1987. The term "Six Sigma" basically refers to a statistical concept – the chances of having product variation beyond the six sigma range under normal distribution is only 3.4 in a million, and this is the level of close-to-zero defects to which Six Sigma organizations strive (Pyzdek, 1997). Similarly to TQM, Six Sigma aims at achieving high performance through improved work processes, a customer focus, top management commitment, and the fostering of a quality-oriented culture. While TQM tends to be more of an organization-wide concept generally involving all employees, Six Sigma seems more specifically targeted at certain strategic tasks and training is often more selective. It is not uncommon for full-time improvement specialists to be appointed and provided with intensive training so that they can devote their efforts totally to the quality initiative. Moreover, Six Sigma is very much results-oriented, while TQM emphasizes the process and expects results to follow naturally. Six Sigma also requires a more structured method than past quality initiatives in terms of data collection and analysis, as well as more specific and well-defined measurement metrics. As Schroeder, Linderman, Liedtke, and Choo (2007) describe, "much of what is being done is not entirely new with respect to prior quality tools or principles, but the deployment approach and emergent structure of Six Sigma are new" (p. 548). Organizations may find that the Six Sigma approach gives them a more concrete roadmap for achieving quality standards.

## THE CHOICE OF WORK DESIGN

Since there are so many job dimensions, jobs can be designed in numerous ways. Overall, there is no one right approach. Work design is largely affected by the management philosophy. For example, if management believes workers can be trusted and are an asset that can provide a competitive advantage for the organization because of their skills and knowledge, then work will be designed with much autonomy, flexibility, and task significance. Team work will be emphasized if management believes in the synergies of sharing and cooperating. Ongoing feedback will be provided if management values continuous improvement. On the other hand, if management subscribes to the Tayloristic approach, workers will have closely supervised jobs with limited task variety or significance. In deciding on the choice of work design, management must understand its implications for employee motivation. Some types of design may be able to generate an acceptable level of employee performance but may not be sufficient to drive excellent and sustainable performance. The logical step is to consider how motivation occurs. Various motivation theories are introduced next.

## MOTIVATION THEORIES

One of the main tasks of organizational leaders is to ensure staff members do their job well. An understanding of what drives behaviour is, therefore, essential. Why do employees want to do something and how much effort are they willing to put in? This is at the heart of the concept of motivation.

Motivation theories are developed to explain such human behaviours. As with any other theories, they are models of patterns of observed phenomena and relationships of factors of concern. A theory may be able to explain the general behaviour of many people but it does not explain the behaviour of everyone, nor does it explain behaviour in all circumstances. Nonetheless, a good understanding of what motivates employees goes a long way in enhancing organizational effectiveness.

Motivation theories can be classified into two main types: *needs (or content) theories* and *process theories*. Needs theories look at what the individuals' needs are that drive their behaviour. Examples of needs theories are Maslow's hierarchy of needs, McClelland's theory of needs, and Herzberg's two-factor theory. Process theories have a different focus: they are concerned about the process that motivates performance. Common process theories include equity theory, expectancy theory, and goal-setting theory.

## Needs Theories

## Maslow's Hierarchy of Needs

Maslow (1954, 1971, 1998) proposes a theory of motivation based on a hierarchy of needs, as illustrated in Figure 3-1:

**Figure 3-1  Maslow's Hierarchy of Needs**

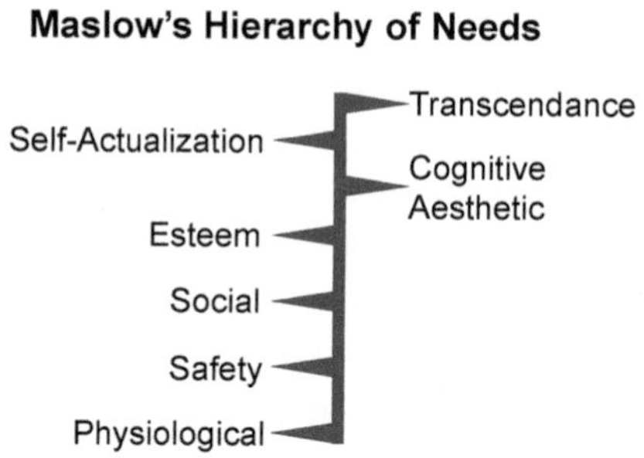

Maslow refined this hierarchy model over time. The five needs on the left are from the original model, which has been commonly used for decades. The lower four needs are basic needs, called *deficit needs* (D-needs). They are only motivating when unsatisfied. If satisfied, D-needs offer no continued motivation (e.g., if a person already has enough safety protection, providing further safety arrangements is not any more motivating). The higher level self-actualization need is different, it involves an ongoing desire to achieve one's potential to the fullest; thus such a need is called a *growth or being need* (B-needs) (Boeree, 2006).

The three needs on the right were added later to the original model. Cognitive needs involve knowing and understanding; aesthetic needs refer to the appreciation of beauty, order, form, and balance; while transcendence needs are about being "able to do more than one thought one could do" (Maslow 1971, p. 274).

Transcendence goes beyond the actualization of self to the actualization of others: to help others appreciate life, develop, grow, and achieve what they can possibly achieve. It "refers to the very highest and most inclusive holistic levels of human consciousness, behaving and relating, as ends rather than means, to oneself, to significant others, to human beings in general, to other species, to nature, and to the cosmos" (Maslow 1971, p. 279).

According to this model, it is important that the lower needs are satisfied first. Only then will the higher level needs become important. That is, people without food and shelter are concerned about meeting these needs before any higher level needs. Such an assumption, however, has not gone without challenge.

## Herzberg's Two-Factor Theory

Herzberg (1968) suggests that the "opposite of job satisfaction is not job dissatisfaction but, rather, *no* job satisfaction; and similarly, the opposite of job dissatisfaction is not job satisfaction, but no job dissatisfaction" (p. 56). Factors that lead to job satisfaction are called *motivating factors* or *motivators*. These differ from factors called *hygiene* or *maintenance factors* that, if present, are not motivating, but if lacking, lead to dissatisfaction. Hygiene factors are those associated with the work context, such as the working conditions, pay, job security, and supervision. For example, a very nice office is unlikely to motivate good performance but a poorly lit and ventilated workplace can make an employee unhappy. Job security is not a sufficient condition to motivate performance but a lack of job security can cause concern and dissatisfaction. Some managers think that extrinsic rewards and punishments are a good way to get people to work hard. These factors, however, can only make employees move, not motivated. In other words, they drive compliance, not commitment. Employees will not go above and beyond what is required of them. Motivators, on the other hand, are characteristics people find intrinsically rewarding. They are factors such as the work itself (being interesting, meaningful, or challenging); opportunities for personal growth and advancement; a sense of self-fulfillment and achievement; and a desired level of responsibility. Motivators provide ongoing incentive to perform better.

Given the intrinsic nature of the motivating factors, organizations can focus on job design to meet employees' growth and achievement needs. For example, applying the Hackman and Oldham (1980) model of work design presented at the start of this chapter, task or skill variety may make a job interesting, high task identity and significance may provide for a more meaningful job and a sense of achievement, autonomy can be associated with responsibilities and challenge, while feedback may offer the opportunity for growth and development.

In conclusion, motivators are important to an organization that wants high performance employees. But it cannot overlook the hygiene factors because, even though they may not raise performance, they can lower it or prompt dissatisfied employees to leave the organization.

## McClelland's Theory of Needs

McClelland (1961), building on the work of Murray (1938), offers a different view of motivation that focuses on satisfying *manifest needs*. These needs may vary with individuals and their environment. He theorizes that people specifically have a need for *affiliation*, a need for *achievement*, and a need for *power*. The need for affiliation is a desire to make friends and have a good relationship with others. The need for achievement refers to the drive to succeed, to do well in complex and high level tasks, and to meet or exceed high standards of expectations. The need for power is the desire to have control over others and to influence them.

Accordingly, employees with a high need for affiliation like a warm, harmonious work environment. They prefer work that provides opportunities for sharing, communication, and cooperation. They likely enjoy teamwork. Employees with a high need for achievement prefer jobs with challenging responsibilities, and good feedback for even better performance. Employees with a high need for power want to work in a job associated with position power or other forms of power such as resource power. They like to be in the limelight.

Although these three needs may motivate positive behaviour, a high need for power may result in authoritarianism; a high need for achievement may lead to overly individualistic behaviour; while a high need for affiliation may result in low task-orientation. Managers must also be cognizant about overemphasizing the extrinsic rewards for those with a high need for achievement. It could be seen as demeaning the job and cause motivation loss. Overall, different people have different degrees of the three needs. With good work design, organizations can meet these needs by placing employees in appropriate jobs where they can excel in their strong areas and make constructive contributions. Moreover, as McClelland posits, these needs "are acquired over time, as a result of life experiences" (Schermerhorn, Hunt, & Osborn, 1997, p. 90). Hence, it is plausible that the combination of these employee needs can be shaped to more closely resemble the needs profile of successful executives, if such a profile is identified.

## Process Theories

The process theories are generally based on the premise that individuals are rational and they are concerned about their self-interest. They also assume that individuals have all the necessary information, such as the various options available for action and their associated outcomes; are able to attach a value to each of the outcomes; and are free to choose the option that makes the best sense to them or, in other words, one that will most satisfy their self-interest.

## Expectancy Theory

Expectancy theory, advocated by Vroom (1964), has had encouraging support from researchers throughout the past decades. The theory is easily applied to situations of job choices and can predict to some extent the amount of effort a person will exert in an endeavour. Basically, it comes down to three main questions:

- Can I do the job satisfactorily?
- If I can do the job, will I get the reward?
- If I get the reward, what does it mean to me? How much do I value it?

Naturally, a person will not want to try doing the job if the person does not believe in the first place that it can be successfully done. If the job can be done but there is no incentive for doing so, it does not make sense for the person to do the job. Finally, if the reward is not something of value to the person, for example, a few hundred dollars may not mean anything at all to a billionaire, then why would the person bother expending the effort? Of course, value here does not necessarily mean monetary and tangible items. A person can be motivated to perform a task for altruistic purposes, for non-monetary recognition, or purely for the satisfaction of overcoming a challenge.

The theory can also be expressed in mathematical terms, involving probabilities and values as shown in the Box 3-1.

**Box 3-1 Formula for Expectancy Theory**

> **Effort (or Motivation) = Expectancies (E) x Instrumentality (I) x Valence (V)**
>
> *Where*
>
> $E$ = *the probability of success (e.g., successful performance) given the effort,*
>
> $I$ = *the probability of receiving an outcome (e.g., pay increase, promotion) given the successful performance, and*
>
> $V$ = *the value of the reward/outcome to the individual.*

Thus, the theory posits that the higher E, I, or V, the greater a person's motivation level. (Of course, that is not to say there can be no other factors, such as perceived equity or personal illness, which affect a person's motivation. No model can be exhaustive of all potential factors of influence.) When there is more than one outcome of value, the effort associated with one outcome can be summed with the efforts associated with the other outcomes to provide a total effort score.

The formula in Box 3-1 is for illustration purposes. In day-to-day life, people are seldom expected to do all these calculations in detail. They do not usually have all the necessary information, nor do they always have time for such details. Yet, they may be taking expected values roughly into consideration in most of their activities without consciously knowing about it. Something as simple as which route to take at a fork road or how hard to play in a game may involve decisions, similar to the one demonstrated above, which people quickly think through.

## Goal Setting Theory

Another motivation theory is one advocated by Locke and Latham (1984). People are believed to be motivated if they have a goal that they are expected to achieve. A goal is a standard of performance expected of an individual. It can instill "purpose, challenge, and meaning" into work leading to "enhanced task interest, pride in performance, and a heightened sense of personal effectiveness" (Latham, 2004, p. 126). An often heard story is people underachieving because they are lost and do not know what to aim for. Hence, goal setting has been found to be very beneficial for organizations to enhance performance. To be effective, goals must be set appropriately. People may easily give up on their goals if what is expected of them is too high to attain.

Many organizations use goal setting as part of their performance appraisal. This lets employees know what is expected of them and provides a standard against which subsequent performance can be measured. These organizations may have guidelines suggesting the adoption of the (SMART) principles, outlined in Table 3-3 for the setting of goals and targets:

Who should be setting the goals? In an organizational setting, the often suggested approach is that the supervisor and the employee should jointly set them. The employee probably has personal development goals that will benefit both the employee and the organization of which the supervisor may not be aware. The supervisor knows of the organizational direction and goals and can translate these to the individual level so that organizational and employee achievement goals can be more aligned. More importantly, employees who are actively involved in the process will have a sense of ownership for the goals set and will often strive harder to achieve them. After all, they are responsible for the goals set. If they cannot achieve their goals, unless there are extenuating circumstances, it will be a reflection of either their poor performance or their poor goal-setting. Employee consultation and involvement has generally been shown to have a positive effect on employee buy-in of organizational initiatives.

**Table 3-3 SMART Goals**

| Specific | Goals should be specific to avoid unnecessary misinterpretation or guesswork. For example, a trainee has a specific goal of getting a 90% average mark in the next training course. |
|---|---|
| Measurable | Goals should be measurable, that is, a person needs to know if the goals have been achieved. Quantitative goals are usually easy to measure, but it does not necessarily mean that all goals need to be quantitative. Qualitative goals, such as a person with an anxiety disorder being able to walk through a crowded street without feeling panic or a Grade 1 student being able to write a few complete short sentences by the end of the grade, can be just as useful. |
| Attainable/Achievable | Goals should be challenging but set at a level that can be achieved. If set too low, the goal is meaningless if the target can be met regardless of the goal, and the process can even be insulting to some individuals. If set too high, goals lose any motivation they may have provided as there is no point in trying if success is not possible. |
| Relevant * | For goals to be useful, they must relate to something the organization cares about. That is why it is important for goals for individual employees to be aligned with that of the organization. |
| Timely and Time-Bound | Goals should be set in a timely manner and with a time specification. For example, if an organization wants its sales staff to increase sales by 50%, the time period, be it for the following year or for the following month, needs to be specified. |

* Some organizations consider the "R" in "SMART" to represent realistic. However, this overlaps with the "A" principle because having realistic goals means taking into consideration the constraints and ensuring that the goals are achievable. Hence, it may be more appropriate to consider "R" as setting relevant goals.

Once goals are set, can they be changed? There are two approaches to it. Some organizations prefer to leave the goals as is and allow explanations at the end of the performance period for the deviation from the expectation. Some prefer to change the goals as necessary because many things can change within the time set for performance (which is usually a year). Allowing goals to be revisited has the advantage of taking into consideration the changing circumstances to ensure goals are realistic and achievable, which in turn provides better motivation for the achievement of the revised goals. The drawback is the time required for the revision. The idea that goals can be changed any time in any direction can also adversely affect motivation. Imagine an employer telling its employees that due to the favourable market conditions, the sales goal is to be much higher than the initial one set a little while ago. The employees may feel that if they work harder to achieve the new goal, who knows when the employer will raise the bar again. Also, if the goals are lowered every time something happens, employees may rely on the goal adjustment rather than trying to work harder to achieve a goal that has become a little more difficult to achieve in the changed circumstance. Organizations must therefore be receptive to the changing circumstances and should adopt a balanced approach that provides some flexibility to adjust the goals justifiably and reasonably when needed in order to increase the motivational effect.

## Equity Theory

Equity theory, proposed by Adams (1965), is a social comparison theory, or as some may call it, a justice theory. Consider a situation where a student thought he had worked harder than most of the other students in his class and was quite happy to receive an 85% mark. A few days later, he learned that his mark was actually within the lowest quartile of the class. He began to feel upset because, despite his efforts, he was actually "below average." What happened here was not a change in his mark, but the outcome of making social comparison, which people tend to do all the time. According to the equity theory, people are concerned about the ratio of their job input to output (the outcomes from doing the job) and they care about the ratio in comparison with others. That is, people generally expect a higher output or a better outcome to be associated with a greater input. At the same time, they look at the outcome-input ratio of others to see if the equation in Box 3-2 is in equilibrium.

**Box 3-2 Formula in Equity Theory**

$$\frac{\text{Outcome self}}{\text{Input self}} = \frac{\text{Outcome other}}{\text{Input other}}$$

If the left-hand side is smaller than the right-hand side, it means that the outcome relative to the input is greater for the other person than for the individual self. In this case, an inequity is perceived by the individual. According to the theory, people will take actions to try to change this perceived inequity. For example, they may attempt to raise the outcome-input ratio by lowering their input (by doing less) or by trying to increase the outcome (such as pressing their employer for higher pay). They may also try to change their perception of themselves or their referent. Perhaps, through a reality check, they may come to realize that they have not actually worked as hard as they thought or that the referent's job was actually more difficult than initially thought. They may decide that the existing referent is not an appropriate comparison (because of too many basic differences) and to choose a different referent altogether. Finally, they may simply decide to go to work elsewhere in order to resolve the inequity once and for all (Robbins & Langton, 2001, p. 169).

Interestingly, when the left side of the equation is greater than the right side, people usually do not have a problem accepting the situation. It is unlikely that people will come forward and ask for a pay cut because they do not think the input level is worth the pay. This may be due to people generally looking out for their own self-interest. Moreover, people tend to see themselves in a better light than they deserve—a case of egocentrism. If students are told the median class mark is 80% and are asked before they receive their mark if they feel they perform above this mark, chances are the majority of the students think they do. In reality, the actual number of students doing better than the median mark should be equivalent to just half of the class. Hence, it is not surprising that people tend to overestimate their input or have too high an expectation of the outcome they deserve. Understanding this phenomenon, organizations may want to have more objective criteria to help individuals assess their input or outcomes so as to alleviate bias and subjectivity.

As equity theory involves a comparison with a referent, managers should consider who employees' common referents are. It can be someone in the same department doing similar work, someone in another department or branch office doing similar work, or it can be someone in another organization doing similar work. Hence, the equity issue can be internal or external. Internal equity involves internal consistency in the HR policies, for example, ensuring that people contributing equally are getting the same level of pay. External equity (the comparison with outsiders) can be more difficult to maintain because information on employees' external referents may be limited and whether they are totally comparable may be unknown. A lack of internal equity can lead to dissatisfaction about unfair treatment while a lack of external equity can easily lead to a loss of talent to other organizations.

## An Integrative Model

The above theories need not be mutually exclusive. Indeed, the various components of the different theories can be considered together. For example, to determine if a reward system is motivational to the people receiving it, Higgins (1982) suggests a simple integrative model of rational choice by combining the three above-mentioned process theories. It includes a few questions to be answered from the perspective of the people to be motivated:

- Is the reward based on my performance?
- Can I do the job satisfactorily?
- If I can do the job, what is the likelihood that I can get the reward?
- If I get the reward, what does it mean to me? How much do I value it?
- Will the rewards be distributed fairly?

The first four questions relate to the expectancy theory, the first two also concern the goal setting theory, while the fifth one comes from the equity theory. If reward is not based on performance, then the reward system itself does not serve a motivational purpose at all and organizations may need to look at other motivators. It is even possible that some people's performance is driven by factors that are unrelated to an organization's reward system, such as personal endeavour. Motivation can be related to many other organizational systems besides the reward system. For example, the way the work or job is designed will affect how certain employee needs, such as those for growth and self-actualization, are met.

Although the third question looks similar to the first question, a significant factor underlies it: trust. That is, even if the employee knows the reward is based on his or her performance and that he or she can do the job well, does the employee believe that management will give the reward when he or she has jumped the hurdle? Employees can be skeptical of management because the meeting of performance standards can be quite subjective at times. Is favouritism or discrimination involved? Does management have a hidden agenda of driving employees to work hard and then finding excuses to not grant the reward to save costs?

The fifth question adds the dimension of equity. Often, employees are concerned about whether the rewards are fairly distributed. Under the equity perspective, people tend to compare themselves with others and generally expect those contributing more to receive more. If at a time of a downturn everyone is taking a pay cut, including the bosses, and no one is bearing a disproportional share of the burden, then the cut tends to be seen as more acceptable. There are two dimensions to equitable distribution: *distributive justice* and *procedural justice*. A common problem with organizations is an emphasis on the former and an oversight of the latter. Distributive justice involves the substantive reward, such as the dollar amount, that is distributed. An employee will naturally be unhappy if he or she is doing the same work as others and has the same performance, but gets a lower reward amounts. Procedural justice deals with the process of the distribution, rather than the actual amount given. For example, employees need to know there is a system involving clear communication of expectations, good and unbiased measurements of performance, and appropriate feedback. Organizations that tend to keep things secret raise all kinds of employee doubt about the process. If the process that leads to the distribution is believed to be flawed, then the fairness of the substantive amount given will automatically be cast into question.

# THE INTRINSIC VALUE OF WORK AND THE CONCEPT OF SELF

Many organizations tend to over-emphasize the extrinsic side of rewards (something relating to the job context, such as salaries, bonuses, or nice offices) because their management believes in the rational economic person model. While extrinsic rewards certainly have their place—as Herzberg's theory suggests a lack of them can cause dissatisfaction—intrinsic rewards (something that relates to the job content) must not be underestimated.

Organizational management must understand that work can be an important part of an individual self. Because people identify with their work, it is not surprising to hear that some terminated employees or retirees suffer a loss of identity after they leave the workforce. When introduced to a person, people relate that person to his or her occupation or organization. It is just widely accepted as part of who the person is. People like to feel good about their self-image. Thus managers who understand this should be able to motivate employees by designing work that helps promote the self-image, something that conveys a sense of importance about the work done. Managers should also know that preying on the fears of employees (by threats of punishment, such as possible job loss, or by exercising constant control) does not motivate behaviour. Such tactics may also backfire because they threaten the employees' self-image. Employees who feel unappreciated and distrusted at work are not going to put in extra effort.

How a person sees him- or herself in terms of what he or she can accomplish has a major effect on behaviour. Weiner (1974) provides a framework on attribution theory that tries to explain why people do what they do by attributing cause to behaviours. It focuses on the interpretation of successes and failures based on whether the cause of the event is (a) internal or external, (b) stable or unstable, and (c) controllable or uncontrollable. It is assumed that people tend to attribute cause of successes to the self and cause of failures to outside factors in order to maintain their self-image. It is therefore important for management to establish proper assessment criteria and feedback processes that help determine the actual causes of success and failure so that contributing factors of success can be maintained or strengthened and root causes of failure can be addressed. If a person does not take responsibility for a failure when he or she should, there is little hope of improved performance. However, if an employee understands that the failure is due to the lack of his or her efforts, the person can be motivated to work harder next time. However, if a lack of ability causes the failure, simply working harder is not sufficient. The problem may be a lack of training and development provided by the organization. Managers must also be aware of their own attribution bias. If they often attribute unfairly the cause of success to the management rank and failures to the subordinates, a very demoralizing climate can be created. Similarly, if they tend to attribute the cause of success to past excellent performers or people they like rather than basing it on the real performance in the current situation, discontent may arise.

## MORE ON MACRO LEVEL MOTIVATION

It is important for managers to not only understand the various motivational theories and the meaning of work to the self-image as discussed above, but also to review or reflect further on some of the following macro-level questions:

- What do our employees want?
- What are we rewarding employees for? For example, are we rewarding for something that is within the control of the employees? Does the reward encourage group work or individual work? Do our incentives cater towards long-term employment or short-term productivity?
- What is our level of compensation as compared to the industry or other indicators? Is it meeting the needs of the employees and making them feel equitably compensated? Are we achieving both internal equity and external equity?

Motivation is all about the understanding of what drives human behaviour, which can be extremely complex even at the best of times. Even if some of the theories and models covered in this chapter sound straightforward, all of the relevant factors at play that may influence individual behaviour can never really be taken into account. Nonetheless, while the behaviour of individuals can vary widely in a given situation, the behaviour of a larger group of employees may be more predictable. Hence, it is reasonable for organizations to consider appropriate macro-level organizational policies to enhance motivation with the understanding that individual differences exist and that, while the policy may work for most employees, it may not work for each and every one. It may also be desirable in macro-policy-making that flexibility is built into the system to allow for the recognition of individual differences and the maximizing of individuals' potential contributions.

## FUTURE TRENDS

Although most of the motivation theories were developed decades ago, many have stood the test of time. For example, in a recent study to re-examine Herzberg's two-factor theory on the current organizational setting, intrinsic drivers (the motivators) were still found to be more important than extrinsic factors (the movers), such as financial outcomes (Bassett-Jones & Lloyd, 2005). Certain fundamental areas of human needs (such as social and security needs) remain rather stable over time, although how such needs are satisfied may have changed to some extent due to environmental changes. For example, social needs may no longer require constant face-to-face interaction, as the new generation is very comfortable interacting online. The meaning of security may have also changed in this new age since younger workers no longer expect to work for life with one employer. They feel secure if they believe they have the ability to secure employment with an employer (current or otherwise) as needed (Amar, 2004). The new generation of workers is discussed further in Chapter 10.

Two other trends can generally be identified that may affect future motivation and work design. One is the rise of the knowledge workers and the other is globalization. Amar (2004) advocates that as we move into a knowledge economy, there is a need for employees to be motivated to commit not only their efforts to the organization goals, but also their minds, because their talents, creativity, and tacit knowledge provide the organization with a competitive edge. He further suggests that this new generation of workers brings with them a different value system that tends to center on the self, family, and personal relationships. This may affect their needs in relation to the work-life balance. Because self-image seems to be particularly important for these younger workers, strategic use of motivation tools to positively reinforce the self-image may have greater success than the use of monetary rewards. These workers may also be keen to take on responsibilities and become successful so intrinsic rewards together with extrinsic rewards that provide a clear line of sight between the rewards and performance may drive their performance. Allowing the employees to design their own work and providing for lateral mobility (even if not upwards mobility due to flatter organizations) may also be beneficial for the employees' mind and their skill development. Creating a climate and organizational system that can convey management's appreciation of employee ideas is another good way of motivating workers to innovate and contribute.

With organizations getting more and more into the global context, due to such reasons as international expansions, partnerships, or outsourcing, managers are facing a much more diverse workforce than before. In Chapters 6 and 10, cultural diversity and issues relating to the international human resource flow are more thoroughly discussed. For the purpose of this chapter, it suffices to mention that work design should take into consideration cultural differences. For example, empowerment may be very attractive to some Western workers, but may be an alien term that can make workers uncomfortable in other country settings (Lee-Ross, 2005). Self-actualization is generally considered an important high-level need for employees in North America, but for Japanese employees growth and achievement for the group rather than the self are more important (Di Cesare & Sadri, 2003). The message here is that, in designing work for the purpose of motivation, one size may not fit all. The fundamental concepts underlying most motivation theories are usually helpful, but contextual differences and changes, such as in culture and other demographics, should be considered in their applications.

In sum, work design is an important contributing factor for employees' intrinsic motivation. Managers should consider the various factors in the motivational theories that are at play in the organization as well as the latest trends and developments in order to be able to design jobs that can best meet the needs and expectations of employees and drive their performance. Overall, work design is a major area of strategic human resource management because it can affect many other HR areas. If the job is not appealing to workers, recruiting and retaining the right people is difficult. Rewards and performance management also largely depends on the nature of the job. Therefore, work design should not be implemented in isolation of other HR policy considerations. An integrated approach aligning all HR areas is crucial for overall HR effectiveness.

# HRM in Action
## Quality Management at Honeywell

Honeywell Federal Manufacturing & Technologies (FM&T) has a clear mission "to design and deliver products, manage operations, and provide targeted services to advance national and homeland security objectives for the United States government and its allies." It provides many products and services for the national defense system. In 2009, due to its deep commitment to quality and impressive successes with various quality initiatives, it received the renowned Malcolm Baldridge National Quality Award for the Manufacturing sector. At that time, it employed over 2,700 employees and had an operating budget of $540 million. FM&T adopted an overall Management Assurance System that "identifies, implements, measures, and sustain the 'critical-to-quality' needs necessary for desired performance." Some of the more specific quality initiatives implemented at FM&T include:

- Enterprise Alignment Process to ensure the daily operations aligned with the balanced scorecard and the strategic plan
- Six Sigma Plus Continuous Improvement Model to integrate customer and business requirements in project designs and to improve processes and performance
- As part of Six Sigma, the DMAIC (Define, Measure, Analyze, Improve, Control) methodology was deployed throughout the company and shared with customers, suppliers, and collaborators
- External feedback including Voice of Customer surveys, benchmarking, ISO standards, Baldridge quality assessment criteria, etc. helped in prioritizing improvement opportunities
- VIRO filter system (Valuable, hard to Imitate, Rare, and Opportunity to exploit) to determine core competencies that the organization needed
- Change-management approach involving open door policy, workforce surveys, etc. to keep employees informed and engaged
- Employee Resource Groups provided networking opportunities for employees to leverage diversity and help in the development of diverse employees
- Health and safety awareness and interventions to encourage employees to report and even allow them to stop unsafe acts
- Career progression and training to provide employees with the necessary skills and development opportunities; an Electronic Learning Management system to manage organization-wide learning.

As a result, a business culture that focused on learning and quality improvements, as well as delivering results, was established. The organization's success was evident by its performance results in the 3-4 years prior to the award receipt, namely a 95% customer satisfaction, a 99.9% combined quality/reliability performance level for traditional customers, annual savings from productivity improvements and innovations in the range of $23.5 million to $27 million, annual energy conservation savings of 20%, and supply chain savings increase from $2 million in 2007 to $65 million in 2009.

Sources:
NIST. (n. d.). *2009 Malcolm Baldridge National Quality Award*. Retrieved January 31, 2012 from http://www.quality.nist.gov/PDF_files/Honeywell_FMT_Profile.pdf
NIST. (2009, May 21). *Application for the 2009 Malcolm Baldridge National Quality Award*. Retrieved January 31, 2012 from http://www.quality.nist.gov/PDF_files/Honeywell_Award_Application_Summary.pdf

## References

Adams, J. S. (1965). Inequity in social exchange. In L. Berkowitz (Ed.), *Advances in experimental social psychology* (Vol. 2, pp. 267–299). New York: Academic Press.

Amar, A. D. (2004). Motivating knowledge workers to innovate: a model integrating motivation dynamics and antecedents. *European Journal of Innovation Management, 7*(2), 89–101.

Bassett-Jones, N., & Lloyd, G. C. (2005). Does Herzberg's motivation theory have staying power? *Journal of Management Development, 24*(10), 929–943.

Boeree, C. G. (2006). *Abraham Maslow.* Retrieved May 8, 2008, from Shippensburg University, Psychology Department, C. George Boeree Homepage, Online Texts, Personality Theories website: http://webspace.ship.edu/cgboer/maslow.html

Dawson, S. (1996). *Analysing organisations* (3rd ed.). Basingstoke, UK: Palgrave Macmillan.

Di Cesare, J., & Sadri, G. (2003). Do all carrots look the same? Examining the impact of culture on employee motivation. *Management Research News, 26*(1), 29-40.

Greer, C. R. (2001). *Strategic human resource management: A general managerial approach* (2nd ed.). Upper Saddle River, NJ: Prentice Hall.

Hackman, J. R., & Oldham, G. R. (1980). *Work redesign.* Reading, UK: Addison Wesley.

Hammer, M., & Champy, J. (1993). *Reengineering the corporation: A manifesto for business revolution.* New York: HarperCollins.

Herzberg, F. (1968, January/February). One more time: How do you motivate employees? *Harvard Business Review, 46*, 53-62.

Higgins, J. M. (1982). *Human relations: Concepts and skills.* New York: Random House.

Latham, G. P. (2004). The motivational benefits of goal-setting. *Academy of Management Executive, 18*(4), 126-129.

Lee-Ross, D. (2005). Perceived job characteristics and internal work motivation: An exploratory cross-cultural analysis of the motivational antecedents of hotel workers in Mauritius and Australia. *Journal of Management Development, 24*(3), 253-266.

Locke, E. A., & Latham, G. P. (1984). *Goal setting: A motivational technique that works.* Englewood Cliffs, NJ: Prentice Hall.

Maslow, A. (1954). *Motivation and personality.* New York: Harper.

Maslow, A. (1971). *The farther reaches of human nature.* New York: Viking Press.

Maslow, A. (1998). *Toward a psychology of being* (3rd ed., R. Lowry, Ed.). New York: Wiley.

Mayo, E. (1960). *The human problems of an industrial civilization.* New York: Viking Press.

McClelland, D. C. (1961). *The achieving society.* New York: Van Nostrand.

Murray, H. A. (1938). *Explorations in personality.* New York: Oxford University Press.

Pyzdek, T. (1997). *Motorola's six sigma program.* Retrieved January 31, 2012, from http://www.qualitydigest.com/dec97/html/motsix.html

Robbins, S. P., & Langton, N. (2001). *Organizational behaviour: Concepts, controversies, applications* (2nd Canadian ed.). Toronto: Prentice Hall.

Schermerhorn, J. R., Jr., Hunt, J. G., & Osborn, R. N. (1997). *Organizational behavior* (6th ed.). New York: Wiley.

Schroeder, R. G., Kinderman, K., Liedtke, C., & Choo, A. S. (2008). Six sigma: Definition and underlying theory. *Journal of Operations Management, 26*(4), 536-554.

Taylor, F. W. (1911). *The principles of scientific management.* New York: Harper.

Vroom, V. H. (1964). *Work and motivation.* New York: Wiley.

Weiner, B. (Ed.). (1974). *Achievement motivation and attribution theory.* Morristown, NJ: General Learning Press.

 **Chapter 4**

# LEADERSHIP

## INTRODUCTION

Leadership is often a topic taught in organizational behaviour courses, but it is inseparable from strategic human resource management because a leader leads people, the human resources of the organization. When people say that they are leading a project or a process, they in fact mean they are leading a group of others in completing a project or process. Similarly, leaders are often charged with leading changes but the task really is leading people to work towards the new vision and objectives.

Almost everyone in organizations talks about leadership. However, does the word mean the same to everyone? Yukl (2001) states leadership is a confusing concept because it has been defined in various terms such as "traits, behaviors, influence, interaction patterns, role relationships, and occupation of an administrative position" (p. 2). After reviewing various leadership definitions, the one common assumption he finds is that it is "a process whereby intentional influence is exerted by one person over other people to guide, structure, and facilitate activities and relationships in a group or organization" (p. 2). He defines leadership as follows:

> Leadership is the process of influencing others to understand and agree about what needs to be done and how it can be done effectively, and the process of facilitating individual and collective efforts to accomplish the shared objectives. (p. 7)

It is important to note that leadership involves relationships not only within the group being led, but also outside of the group boundary. Groups inevitably interact with many others in an organizational setting: the group's sponsors; the bosses and peers of the leaders and members; other organizational groups that the group works with in performing its tasks; and external contacts such as customers and other outside stakeholders. Therefore, a leader must be able to manage all the various relationships involved, not just the relationships with the followers.

Even if the definition of leadership is generally accepted, how leadership actually works, who has the power of influence (e.g., should the leader retain all the power or should there be shared influence), how leadership is measured (by the outcomes or the process), and what constitutes effective leadership are still very controversial.

This chapter starts with a look at the main traditional types of leadership theories, namely the traits theories, style theories, and contingency theories, followed by an introduction to the concept of transformational leadership (versus transactional leadership) which is generally regarded as more appropriate for changing times. The roles of managers and leaders are examined and compared. The relationships of leadership with emotional intelligence, organizational culture, and power and influence are then addressed. The chapter concludes with a discussion of the topics of effective leadership and future trends.

## THREE TRADITIONAL THEORIES OF LEADERSHIP

According to Handy (1993), leadership theories usually fall under one of the following categories: *trait theories, style theories,* and *contingency theories.* Each of these theories seems to contain some element of truth, but they have their limitations in explaining the difference between effective and ineffective leadership.

### Trait Theories

The earliest approach to studying leadership revolved around the trait theories. These theories emphasize the individual rather than the situation. The theories hold that people with certain personal characteristics will make good leaders and organizations should be able to select good leaders on the basis of those characteristics. Generally identified important traits for leadership include intelligence, initiative, self-assurance, creativity, health, enthusiasm, sociability, integrity, courage, decisiveness, determination, and the helicopter factor, the ability to see the big picture (Handy, 1993).

Trait theories have been criticized because many studies found a great deal of diversity in leadership traits. For example, Geier (1967, as cited in Robbins, 1996, p. 414) identifies close to 80 leadership traits in 20 prior studies, but only finds five of them to be common across four or more of the studies. Traits are also difficult to define well and there is always subjectivity involved in the judgment (Gehring, 2007; Mullins, 1999). For example, does "decisiveness" apply to leaders who make quick decisions or to those who make firm decisions? Does intelligence mean cognitive, social, or emotional intelligence? Even though some traits may be generally associated with effective leadership, they are not a universal prescription for success. There is a lack of understanding of how the personal characteristics lead to leadership effectiveness. Some questions that arise from looking at these theories include:

- Is the relation of traits to leadership success really independent of the situation?
- What are the intervening variables or processes involved between traits and leadership outcomes?
- Are leaders born to be or can they be trained?

## Style Theories

These theories assume that leaders exhibit different styles, some styles being preferred by followers. Implicitly, if a leader has a preferred style, he or she may be able to motivate the followers to perform better. Styles can be described as falling within a continuum between the authoritarian (or structuring) and democratic (or supportive) approaches. Towards the authoritarian end, leaders use an autocratic system, exercising tight control, making decisions themselves, and simply telling employees what to do. Towards the democratic end, a participative system is used with authority for decision-making often delegated. In other words, powering sharing and subordinate empowerment are the key features of this style. This style is consistent with the strategic HRM approach discussed in Chapter 1 in which the paradox of control suggests that more power can potentially be gained by actually sharing power.

Evidence exists that democratic or supportive styles of leadership relate to subordinate satisfaction, lower turnover, fewer grievances, less inter-group conflict, and are generally preferred by subordinates, but the findings on the effect of leadership style on productivity are mixed (Handy, 1993). Also noted is that some people prefer to be directed and hence, do not mind having an autocratic leader. So, can leadership effectiveness really be understood without considering factors other than the leadership style?

This fundamental question leads to the next discussion on the contingency theories.

## Contingency Theories

Fiedler (1967) proposes that the most effective leadership style depends on the situation: the leader-group relationship, the task structure and clarity, and the power of the leader. For a well-defined task and a leader with strong power, the structuring or directive approach is more effective. Interestingly, for an ambiguous task and a weak leader, this structuring approach may also work well. However, if the leader is well-respected, the supportive approach is more effective when the task is ambiguous. According to this theory, organizations can structure their situational elements to give the leader a more favourable climate to work in.

Fiedler's theory is criticized as too simplistic in that it considers too few situational factors and that the findings from his studies on a limited range of groups may not be generalized to other settings.

The *path-goal theory* (developed by Evans (1970), and expanded upon by House (1971)) proposes that good leaders clarify the path for their followers and help them along the way to achieve their work goals. For example, the leader provides the coaching, resource support, and rewards to help and motivate followers towards their goals.

This theory identifies four leadership behaviours that might be used in different situations as described in Table 4-1 (Robbins & Langton, 2001, pp. 426-7; Schermerhorn, Hunt, & Osborn, 1997, pp. 322-3).

**Table 4-1 Leadership Behaviour and Situational Characteristics**

| Leadership Behaviour | Description and Situational Application |
|---|---|
| **Directive leadership**<br>Spells out what the followers should do and how to do it | Generally predicted to result in greater employee satisfaction when the task is ambiguous, especially when the followers have an external locus of control (i.e., believe they are not the ones in control of their own destiny) |
| **Supportive leadership**<br>Being friendly and concerned about the needs and well-being of the followers | Generally predicted to result in increased employee satisfaction when the work is highly repetitive and unpleasant or when the organization structure is bureaucratic. The idea is that the leadership is compensating for what is lacking in the job or environment such that the work is made more pleasant |
| **Participative leadership**<br>Focuses on consulting the followers before making decisions | Generally predicted to promote employee satisfaction, when employees are more open-minded and prefer having control over their own destiny |
| **Achievement-oriented leadership**<br>Sets challenging goals for followers and expects them to perform their best | Generally predicted to be more effective when the tasks are ambiguously structured and non-repetitive and the followers believe that efforts could lead to the desired performance |

One question that arises from these contingency theories is whether leaders can adjust their behaviour and style to the various situations.

Most of the traits, styles, and contingency theories mentioned above were developed when organizations were generally organized in the traditional hierarchical way. They tend to be concerned about guiding followers in the direction of established goals or clarifying tasks rather than about leading with a vision. The differences between these aspects are captured in the leadership literature discussions on transactional versus transformational leadership.

## TRANSFORMATIONAL LEADERSHIP

*Transactional leadership* must be discussed before the concept of transformational leadership is introduced to better contrast the concepts. Transactional leaders work within the existing organizational strategies, system, and culture, focusing on motivating individuals through an exchange relationship (with explicit agreements on expectations and rewards) and active management-by-exception, such as providing feedback when needed to ensure followers are on track (Vera & Crossan, 2004). This approach seems to assume that followers care about their self-interest and only perform for some explicit rewards. Such a relationship may generate compliance more than commitment or citizenship behaviour.

The origin of *transformational leadership* can be traced to Burns' (1978) study on political leaders. Since then, it has been expanded by Bass (1985) and others researchers. Contrary to transactional leadership, both the leader and the followers in transformational leadership are elevated to a higher level of values and motivation. The leader instills awareness and generates acceptance of the vision and purpose of the organization or group. He or she appeals to the followers' moral values and commitment, inspiring them to think with the leader and achieve what the leader envisions. This leadership approach is said to be able to transform followers' aspirations, identities, needs, preferences and values as they strive to achieve their full potential (Avolio, Zhu, Koh, & Bhatia, 2004; Lowe, Kroech, & Sivasubramaniam, 1996). Trust, integrity, and empowerment are common ingredients for such leadership. This approach relies more on the psychological contract than the explicit contract for motivation.

Transformational leadership is described along four dimensions (Bass 1985; Burns, 1978):

- *Idealized influence*
  The leader aspires to be the role model for the followers by appealing to them through charismatic ways, so that the followers will identify with him or her.

- *Inspirational motivation*
  The leader communicates his or her vision, convinces the followers of its significance, and provides a possible road map for its achievement.

- *Intellectual stimulation*
  The followers are challenged to think critically and creatively to achieve the vision or objective. The leader plays a key role in enhancing the followers' "self-efficacy, confidence, meaning and self-determination" through such approaches as coaching and mentoring (Avolio et al., 2004, p. 953).

- *Individualized consideration*
  The leader is concerned about the needs and concerns of the followers and understands that they may be different for different members. She or he listens attentively to the followers and provides the necessary support and encouragement to help them achieve their goals and potentials.

The guidelines for transformational leadership are neatly summarized by Yukl (2001):

- Articulate a clear and appealing vision.
- Explain how the vision can be attained.
- Act confidently and optimistically.
- Express confidence in followers.
- Use dramatic, symbolic actions to emphasize key values.
- Lead by example.
- Empower people to achieve the vision. (p. 263)

Bennis and Nanus (1985) also conducted an influential study through unstructured interviews with organizational leaders. The main insights tend to support the effectiveness of the transformational approach in that it is important to have a vision set and clearly communicated to generate commitment and trust amongst members. After more than a decade, Bennis (1999) still believes that a leader's main role is to provide meaning and direction (the vision to guide followers), trust (to ensure loyalty and reliability), hope and optimism (to provide the drive forward), and results (to generate confidence and sense of achievement).

The importance of vision has been well supported by many other authors and researchers. For example, Blanchard and Stoner (2004), after studying leadership for decades, conclude that

All world class organizations ... are driven by three critical factors:

- Clear *vision and direction* championed by top management
- Trained and equipped people focused on *implementation* of the agreed-upon vision and direction
- Established *recognition and positive consequences systems* that sustain the behaviors and performance that the vision and direction require (p. 21)

Basically, they argue vision and direction are "essential for greatness" because these allow people to make smart choices, to take the big picture into consideration, and to have a long-term perspective (p. 21). A vision that is shared by others creates "energy, excitement, and passion" (p. 23).

Closely related to transformational leadership is the idea of *charismatic leadership*. Charisma in this context refers to the exceptional leader's qualities (personality or abilities) *as perceived* by the followers. The followers idolize the leader and want to be just like him or her. Whether the leader is truly extraordinary is not the issue, as perception is the key. The leader possesses a certain personal appeal attractive to the followers, creating an emotional attachment that makes them willing to work towards the leader's goals.

Although charismatic and transformational leadership are similar in some ways, such as inspiring followers to work towards the leader's vision, there are significant differences, especially involving the influence process. Transformational leadership involves empowering subordinates and providing necessary levels of autonomy for them to make work decisions whereas charismatic leadership emphasizes dependence on the leader. Hence, charismatic leaders focus on their own image of exceptional qualities, which may only have surface value. The charismatic leader can easily abuse his or her power if members blindly follow the leader due to his or her personal appeal rather than real abilities or accept the vision as given without truly buying into it for merit. The goal accomplished may be more for the leader's self-interest and not necessarily what is best for the organization or group. Such a form of leadership is the hallmark of cults, but it is certainly found in the political arena and business organizations as well. Even if charisma has a positive effect on the organization, an organization relying heavily on this form of leadership can run into serious leadership problems when the leader leaves its employ. Overall, the relation between charisma and transformational leadership is summarized by a comment from Bass (1985), "Charisma is a necessary ingredient of transformational leadership, but by itself it is not sufficient to account for transformational process" (p. 31).

Before this section closes, it is important to mention that while transformational leadership has been very well regarded as an effective form of leadership, especially in changing times, transactional leadership is not always necessarily inferior. Indeed, studies have indicated that leaders can display both transformational and transactional behaviours in different intensities (e.g., Avolio, Bass, & Jung, 1999). Transactional leadership can contribute to a leader's effectiveness in performing certain roles, such as in coordinating, monitoring, and directing (Egri & Herman, 2000). Vera and Crossan (2004) further propose that transactional leadership can have its value in organizational learning, especially in stable environments, in matured firms, and in well-performing firms.

# A Functional View of Leadership

Leadership is not only an important area for academic research; it has significant implications for real-life organizations. Rather than simply focusing on theories and academic rigour in a well-controlled environment, people interested in the practical aspects of leadership instead examine and try to understand leadership behaviours in their functional roles in organizations. By observing or interviewing successful leaders and organizations, many authors are able to describe what leaders really do and what may contribute to effective leadership. One of the earlier studies came from Mintzberg (1973), who considers the leader role as one of the ten managerial roles listed in Table 4-2.

**Table 4-2 Ten Managerial Roles**

| Role | Description |
|---|---|
| Figurehead | Performance of symbolic responsibilities, such as heading ceremonies, signing important contracts, making official visits, etc. |
| Leader | Ensuring the follower group is motivated and provided with necessary support and guidance to achieve the group purpose through integrated efforts. |
| Liaison | Forming relationships with all the stakeholders and contacts outside of the managing unit which can be an important source of information and support for the unit. |
| Monitor | Keeping his or her ears to the ground and learning of various developments, both internal and external, that will affect the unit. |
| Disseminator | Receiving, analyzing, and passing on relevant information to the unit members to assist them with doing their work. |
| Spokesperson | Representing the unit to provide statements to people outside the unit. The audience can be others within the organization or as broad as the general public. |
| Entrepreneur | Initiating changes to capture opportunities for better performance. |
| Disturbance | Handling crises and conflicts as they arise which can involve unexpected events or clashes among people. |
| Resource Allocator | Deciding on the allocation of money, time, and other resources, which are often inadequate and in need of prioritizing, in order to make the best use of them to achieve the unit objectives. |
| Negotiator | Dealing with other parties when both sides want something from the other side (e.g., formal negotiations may involve contract negotiations with unions, customers, vendors, etc., while informal negotiations are often done on a routine basis with superiors, subordinates, and other unit managers). |

These ten roles can be further categorized as interpersonal roles (1-3), informational roles (4-6), and decisional roles (7-10). This list, however, does not really exhaust all the roles of a manager. For example, in a changing environment, the manager may need to play a change agent role as well. With so many roles to be performed by a person at the same time, managing role conflict is critical for effective performance. Understanding the role expectations of others and the role requirements arising out of the environment and the task at hand is important for reconciling the conflicts.

One of the ongoing debates on leadership—apparently started by Zaleznik (1977)—involves the comparison of leadership with management. While Mintzberg regards the leader role as only one of the ten managerial roles, many others argue otherwise and consider the two roles different. For example, Kanungo (1998, p. 77) identifies differences in the two roles, summarized in Table 4-3.

**Table 4-3 Leadership versus Management**

|  | Management | Leadership |
|---|---|---|
| **Time frame** | Day-to-day activities | Long-term objectives/strategies/plans |
| **Main role and work focus** | Act within existing culture/practice, administer standard practices, implement established plans | Provide vision and meaning, innovate and act as change agent |
| **Relationship with subordinates** | Supervising/monitoring behaviours often using the transactional approach, aiming at compliance | Motivating, empowering and inspiring, aiming at commitment |

Due to the above differences, some believe that leaders and managers are necessarily separate people. Others argue that it is possible for the same person to take on some leadership and some managerial roles. Kotter (1990) acknowledges the differences between the two roles but suggests that they are complementary, both are critical for organizational success. The key is to find the right balance between the two roles among the staff members and integrate them.

Collins (2001) also differentiates between leaders and managers and goes further to introduce a new higher level of leadership. Basically, he identifies five levels of contributions made by organizational members. A competent manager is at level 3 in the hierarchy chart. The manager "organizes people and resources toward the effective and efficient pursuit of predetermined objectives" (p. 20). An effective leader is at level 4, who "catalyzes commitment to and vigorous pursuit of a clear and compelling vision, stimulating higher performance standards" (p. 20). The highest level is the level 5 executives, who build "enduring greatness through a paradoxical blend of personal humility and professional will" (p. 20). While they must have strong professional will to succeed by catalyzing change for long-term results with unwavering resolve and accept appropriate responsibilities for poor results, they exhibit humility by taking a low profile approach, inspiring others to perform, preparing for successors, and properly crediting others for effective performance. Moreover, level 5 leaders are distinguished from level 4 leaders by the "first who" approach (p. 47). Level 4 leaders, using a "first what" approach, set a vision, form a road map, and then hire capable people to make it happen. Level 5 leaders focus on first getting the right people on the senior executive team, who then find the "best path to greatness."

> Level 4 leader:  First what ➝ Then who
> Level 5 leader:  First who ➝ Then what

Collins' introduction of the level 5 leadership concept may be especially applicable to the new era of the knowledge economy. Level 4 leaders do very well in a relatively stable environment. However, in the knowledge economy, where talent is a crucial organizational asset for success and where there is a shortage of competent executives, "first who, then what" is an appropriate new approach.

## EMOTIONAL INTELLIGENCE

Another recent branch in the leadership literature involves the concept of *emotional intelligence*. Goleman (1998), in research of over 200 large global companies, finds that effective leaders have a high degree of emotional intelligence (EI). EI in this context is the ability to recognize and understand the feelings of the self and others and to manage emotions in one's relationships in order to move people towards the organizational goals. That is not to say that technical skills and cognitive intelligence are not important. However, emotional intelligence seems to be even more important.

EI has five components (Goleman, 1998, p. 2), summarized in Table 4-4:

**Table 4-4 Emotional Intelligence Components**

| | |
|---|---|
| **Self-awareness** | The degree one understands one's moods, emotions, and drives as well as how they affect others |
| **Self-regulation** | The degree of control over one's mood swings and impulses |
| **Motivation** | The passion and drive to work towards a goal |
| **Empathy** | The degree one understands others' feelings and the skills in responding to others' emotions |
| **Social Skills** | The ability to build and manage relationships |

According to Goleman, EI increases with age and can be learned. Hence, organizations can focus their training efforts on enhancing this particular area. There are certainly tools and techniques to help one understand more about oneself and others. Coaching can also be used to help an employee raise his or her level of empathy through practice and feedback. EI is not only an important competency for leaders; it is probably as important for employees of various levels, especially those who have to provide front line customer service.

## LEADERSHIP AND CULTURE

Leadership cannot be thoroughly discussed without considering the aspect of organizational culture. The two are very closely related. The actions of the leader, in the sense of what is being emphasized, send cues to employees as to what is important to the organization. The culture being fostered by the leader has a strong impact on how things are done and what approaches are expected or acceptable.

Indeed, one of the most important tasks for a leader, especially a transformational one, is the *management of meaning*. According to Ready (1995), this task is about "orchestrating the process that engages the entire organization in crafting and identifying with the vision to create a compelling future" (p. 19). There is usually a range of messages a leader can convey about a situation, especially where uncertainties exist. The information the leader chooses to convey (the "what") actually shapes employees' perception of the situation and influences their actions. Similarly, the leader's choice of communication channels (the "how") influences the effectiveness of the transmission and what is actually received by the employees. The purpose of managing meaning is to ensure that employees understand the vision and organizational goals by proper communication of such. The ultimate challenge for the leader is to be able to help employees see where they need to go and how they can get there (see Path Goal Theory in Chapter 4). For a transformational leader, control is often exerted not by policies or rewards, but by setting the vision to be embraced by employees and by fostering an organizational culture that is supportive of that vision and guides employee actions accordingly. By empowering the followers to generate their commitment, the leader, who apparently has given up some power to others, actually ends up with more control because the control is now exerted through the self-regulation of many others. This is what the concept of the *paradox of control* is about.

Although messages can be conveyed by formal or informal means, *symbolism* plays a vital role in managing meaning. Symbolism is created through a variety of means, such as by telling stories of successes or failures, holding ceremonies for important events, and recognizing and awarding employees for certain actions or performances. Simply having a vision statement written somewhere is often not enough to drive employee commitment. The leader's own actions and values implicitly communicated through symbolic means generally say a lot more about his or her commitment to the vision. An example is in a crisis situation. A leader can use the situation to motivate employees to work harder because there is a common threat, a common enemy, or a common goal. However, if the leader chooses to convey the information in a pessimistic manner, with gestures that symbolize defeat and resignation, the situation is interpreted differently, in a negative way. This, in turn, adversely affects employee actions and probably organizational outcomes.

As indicated in Chapter 2, where Schein's 10 mechanisms for creating organization culture are discussed, three mechanisms that relate to leadership behaviour are particularly important as they send very strong signals about the organizational culture. They are "role modeling", "what leaders pay attention to", and "leader reaction to critical events." Further, leaders need to "walk the talk." If their actions and words are inconsistent, they will only create confusion for the followers that can result in a lack of trust in the leadership.

## POWER AND INFLUENCE

Most people will agree that power is essential for effective leadership. However, the word "power" is often associated with a negative connotation that is not warranted. Power can simply be defined as the potential to influence. In other words, it is a person's capacity to influence others to do as he or she desires, with influence being defined as "an interactive process in which people attempt to convince other people to believe and/or act in certain ways" (Rost, 1993, p. 157). Hence, having power or striving to gain more power does not mean a person has to be manipulative or abusive at all; there are many honourable ways of obtaining power. Moreover, effective leadership should involve the use of power to achieve goals that are mutually beneficial not only to the organization and leader, but also to the organizational members.

Generally, there are five main power sources (Handy, 1993), described as in Table 4-5.

**Table 4-5 Power Sources**

| Physical | The power of superior force |
|---|---|
| Resource | The ability to grant rewards and control resources |
| Position / Legitimate | The power due to the authority that comes with the position or role (usually related to the right of access to networks, information, and the right to organize work, relationships, and the work environment) |
| Expert | The power due to knowledge or expertise that others may not have |
| Personal | The power due to charisma or personal appeal |

Some of these powers are obviously associated with the organizational role (resource power and position power) while others are associated with personal characteristics. How much power one has over others ultimately depends on the perception at the receiving end. Even a formal job title does not necessarily guarantee absolute power as subordinates may or may not respect the legitimacy of the position. Similarly, two leaders at the same position level may not receive the same level of power because their personal characteristics and others' perception of power associated with them differ.

It has been suggested that physical power and position power tend to generate employee compliance, but the use of such sometimes leads to dissatisfaction. Expert power and personal power, on the other hand, generates more respect from followers and is associated with higher level of performance and satisfaction (Bachman, Bowers, & Marcus, 1968).

Caution is needed about the many possible sources of failure in acquiring and using power. For example, if a leader decides not to upgrade his or her education and skills or form networks to obtain information, then he or she is foregoing the chance to increase expert power. Abusing power by barking out unjustified orders or using fear tactics in a generally supportive culture can also backfire. Since power depends on the followers' perception, the sources of power must be known by others. Therefore, if a leader knows something important, he or she must demonstrate it; though not necessarily boast about it. Moreover, even if a leader possesses a certain power, follow-through especially in terms of rewards and punishments is important. In other words, having the power to control the rewards but never giving them out certainly does not sit well with employees who deserve the rewards. Similarly, the fear of punishment subsides if the threat never materializes.

As power is just the *potential to influence*, a leader may actually need to exercise influence in order to achieve desired results. There are many ways a leader can exert influence. Some common influence tactics are shown in Table 4-6 (see, for example, Yukl, 2001).

Of these tactics, rational persuasion is commonly used (Yukl & Seifert, 2002) and is often effective. Transformational leaders use tactics that generate followers' internalization of the task objectives, such as rational persuasion, inspirational appeal, consultation and collaboration. Most of the other tactics are associated with generating short-term compliance rather than long-term commitment.

### Table 4-6  Influence Tactics

| | |
|---|---|
| **Rational persuasion** | Using logic and/or facts to convince followers to support the leader's decision choice (e.g., statistical trends can be shown and financial data on various alternatives can be discussed) |
| **Inspirational appeals** | Appealing to followers' values or ideals (e.g., a leader may want to emphasize certain project or change outcomes that the followers think are particularly important to them, such as contributing to growth of self and others, bringing forth justice, providing benefits to the nation or community, etc.) |
| **Consultation** | Asking for suggestions for decision-making and sharing of action plans. As subordinates often know more about the specific work tasks and are the ones most affected by any changes, consultation tends to result in not only better decisions, but also buy-in from followers |
| **Ingratiation** | Giving praises or compliments to make the other person feel good (e.g., saying that someone is an expert in the area or is indispensable for the job may increase the chances that the person will be willing to help; but, if this is seen as manipulative or insincere, the tactic may be ineffective) |
| **Personal appeals** | Using charm or charisma to get the others to voluntarily go along, such as asking friends and colleagues for special personal favours |
| **Exchange** | Offering something the other party may want in return for something the leader wants (e.g., a leader may offer a subordinate a monetary reward for successful completion of a big project) |
| **Coalition tactics** | Making alliances with others to increase the degree of influence (e.g., a team leader seeks agreement and support from a member's boss in order to get the member to do certain things) |
| **Pressure** | Using threats and warnings to coerce someone to do as instructed (e.g., a leader can threaten to fire or demote a member who is not contributing satisfactorily to the leader's goal achievement) |
| **Legitimizing tactics** | Using position or authority to get compliance (e.g., a leader may remind others of his or her position, role, or mandate, such as, "As the Quality Control Manager, I must ensure that the product safety standards are enforced") |
| **Collaboration** | Working together as partners with a view to a win-win outcome through joint efforts (e.g., a leader may say that "we are in this together and I want you to have as much say in this as I do, and I will do whatever I can to help") |

## LEADERSHIP EFFECTIVENESS

What constitutes leadership effectiveness? How do we measure it? As may be expected, there is no single answer for it. Generally, outcome measures for leadership effectiveness include the performance and growth of the leader's group or organization; the group or organization's preparedness to deal with challenges; followers' commitment, satisfaction, and turnover; and personal development and psychological well-being of the followers (Yukl, 2001, p. 8). Sometimes, the leader's contribution to the group processes is considered another measure of leadership effectiveness. That is, whether the leader facilitates the team interaction, motivates the members, and brings out the best in them. It should be noted that within any of the above-mentioned dimensions, there is a long-term and a short-term perspective. It is not uncommon that people or groups will sacrifice long-term outcomes for short-term gain (and occasionally vice versa). Thus, it is important that the goals and objectives set be balanced and the means of goal achievement, such as whether other things have been compromised in the process, be considered too.

Lu (2004) suggests that effective leaders are basically those who (a) "know what to do with themselves", (b) "know what to do with their people", (c) "know what to do with the communication channels/environment within the organization", and (d) "have a holistic picture of what is going on within their organization" (p. 125). According to Kanter (1996), a leader not only has a vision for the group or organization, but is also able to translate it into actions for followers that yield results. An effective leader plays well the roles of facilitator, appraiser, forecaster, adviser, and enabler (Farren & Kaye, 1996). In the leadership measurement instrument developed by Alimo-Metcalfe and Alban-Metcalfe (2001), nine factors are identified for effective transformational leadership:

- genuine concern for others
- political sensitivity and skills
- decisiveness, determination, self-confidence
- integrity, trustworthy, honest, and open
- empowers, develops potential
- inspirational networker and promoter
- accessible, approachable
- clarifies boundaries, involves others in decisions
- encourages critical and strategic thinking.

Along a similar line, Edmonds (2000) proposes an integrated but much simplified model of effective transformational leadership based on prior studies (e.g., Bennis & Nanus, 1985). The five rules are

"Rule 1: *If you expect people to follow you there, you first must know where there is.*" This is about developing a clear, compelling, and appealing vision for the followers.

"Rule 2: *People are more likely to follow you there if you provide them with a map which is clear and easy to follow.*" A good leader must not only develop the vision, but effectively communicate it by words, symbolism, and behaviours so that everyone knows where he or she fits in and how to get to the visionary goals.

"Rule 3: *It is easier to get people to follow you there if that is where they want to go anyway.*" A leader's vision takes into consideration the talents, interests, goals, needs, and concerns of the followers and provides the link between the individual's motivation and the organization's objectives.

"Rule 4: *If you want people to learn to get there on their own, go with them rather than taking or sending them.*" This is about trusting the followers and providing the necessary autonomy for their development. Yet, the leader is there to oversee the progress and provide guidance and feedback along the way.

"Rule 5: *Before you can expect to lead others, you should be able to lead yourself.*" Effective leaders are good role models. They have a positive self-concept (i.e., they are confident, enthusiastic, and are comfortable with themselves and their roles), empathy for others, good inquisitive and listening skills, and a high but attainable standard set for their work. At the same time, they are also willing to accept mistakes and criticisms. (Section 4-7)

Having looked at various effective leadership descriptions, it is worth noting a few things that leaders should not do. According to Kotter (1995), leadership failures are usually a result of the following errors:

> Error #1: Not establishing a great enough sense of urgency ...
>
> Error #2: Not creating a powerful enough guiding coalition ...
>
> Error #3: Lacking a vision ...
>
> Error #4: Under-communicating the vision by a factor of ten ...
>
> Error #5: Not removing obstacles to the new vision ...
>
> Error #6: Not systematically planning for and creating short-term wins ...
>
> Error #7: Declaring victory too soon ...
>
> Error #8: Not anchoring changes in the corporation's culture ...
> (pp. 60-67)

As shown here, many different perspectives on measuring leadership effectiveness (or ineffectiveness) exist. Some focus on the outcomes aspects (what was achieved) while others focus on the leader's characteristics (how he or she behaves and treats others). In most situations, multi-dimensional measures provide a broader view, but they can give rise to their own challenges, such as how to determine overall effectiveness with widely varying scores across dimensions or criteria. The weighting of each criterion may depend on how well the dimension aligns with the overall objectives of the organization.

## THE FUTURE OF LEADERSHIP

When it comes to leadership, there does not seem to be any one approach that fits all. A lot depends on the persons involved and the situation, which tends to support the rationale of the contingency approach. The transformational leadership theory has also gained much popularity in recent years as more and more organizations realize that the command and control approach does not seem to be conducive to high performance. Despite its many merits, and there are many studies supporting its soundness, one should still be cautious in accepting transformational leadership as a universally appropriate approach. Indeed, it is suggested that effective leaders sometimes need to have a combination (in the "right" proportion) of transactional and transformational behaviours (Vera & Crossan, 2004). In fairly routine situations where immediate actions are needed, the transactional approach usually works well. However, when a future orientation is more important, the transformational approach is more appropriate.

With globalization, managing a diverse workforce from a distance and utilizing virtual teams become common occurrences. Leaders and managers must be sensitive to cultural differences and be cognizant of the challenges a virtual environment presents, such as the lack of physical cues and interaction that may hinder communication and cause difficulty in building rapport and trust. These require a unique skill set. Looking into the future, Hernez-Broome and Hughes (2004) identify a few trends that suggest a future leader needs the following characteristics:

- Collaboration skills and the competency to motivate and coordinate teams (which will certainly become more common in the future) in order to respond efficiently and effectively to uncertainties and changes.

- Have the ability to understand the global picture, think strategically in the global context, and deal with the global constituents on a wide range of issues—economic, political, legal, and social.

- Be savvy with technology, keep pace of technological changes, and be able to capture technology-related opportunities.

- Have integrity and trustworthiness, which has become more important in the post-Enron and WorldCom era.

As Barrett and Beeson (2002) suggest in their Conference Board study, the future leader must be able to effectively take on the roles of a master strategist, change manager, relationship builder, and talent developer. The master strategist provides the necessary vision and planning to prepare the organization for the future. The change manager captures future opportunities and deals with challenges that come the organization's way. The relationship builder creates external networks and alliances in the global setting and builds loyalty internally. The talent developer ensures the organization has the required talent to meet the new demands and challenges of the age of the knowledge economy and beyond. Despite all the controversies around the topic of leadership, there is little disagreement that leadership development and leader succession planning are critical factors for the success of future organizations.

# HRM in Action
## Leadership at Costco

Costco Wholesale Corporation (Costco) is renowned for its membership warehouses, which sell a broad category of merchandises to its business and individual customers at substantially lower prices than most stores. It maintains a low cost model by eliminating frills such as advertising, fancy decorations, or account receivable billing, not by short-changing its employees.

Jim Sinegal, a co-founder of Costco, served as the CEO from 1983 to 2011, leading the company through impressive growth to become the third largest retailer in the United States. At the end of 2011, it had around 600 warehouses, with 161,000 employees world-wide and 64 million member cardholders. Despite his success, Jim was well-known for his humbleness, integrity, and down-to-earth approach. His office, right in the middle of the hallway, could be easily accessed by anyone, and it had no walls or doors (he certainly went beyond an open-door policy to a no-door one). He would just use a simple folding table as his desk. He answered his own phone and sent his own faxes. Listening to employees and customers had become an important part of his life. He was just like a regular guy with a name tag that just said "Jim." He also liked to wear the Costco's basic dress shirt because he was proud of it and it suited his humble style. Unlike most other successful CEOs, his pay was modest and his own employment contract was reportedly only one-page long and even had a clause on his own termination.

More importantly, he treated his employees very well by providing above-average wages, good benefits plans (e.g., health insurance plans for even part-time employees) and internal advancement opportunities. To him, it was more important to build a loyal workforce for sustainable growth and profitability over decades than short-term profits. During the latest recession when many retailers slashed staff, Costco did not layoff its regular employees, and neither did it cut its health benefits, despite pressure from the Wall Street. The company continued to do well through the period.

Jim Sinegal was named by an investment firm Morningstar as its 2011 CEO of the Year for his exemplary corporate stewardship that fostered employee loyalty, drove operational excellence, and created great value for shareholders. He was also recognized as one of the "10 Examples of Tremendous Business Leadership" according to the American Express Open Forum as well as the Business Insider business news website. He continued to work as an advisor for the company for a year or so after his retirement in early 2012.

Sources:
Allison, M., (2012). Costco's colorful CEO, co-founder Jim Sinegal to retire. *The Seattle Times*. Retrieved February 7, 2012 from http://seattletimes.nwsource.com/html/businesstechnology/2016072309_costco01.html

Costco Wholesale. (2010). *Company profile*. Retrieved February 7, 2012 from http://phx.corporate-ir.net/phoenix.zhtml?c=83830&p=irol-homeprofile

Dearment, A. (January, 4, 2012). *Morningstar names Costco's Jim Sinegal CEO of the Year*. Retrieved February 7, 2012 from http://www.drugstorenews.com/article/morningstar-names-costcos-jim-sinegal-ceo-year

Hottovy, R. G. (January 4, 2012). *Morningstar's 2011 CEO of the Year redefined retail*. Retrieved February 7, 2012 from http://torontostar.morningstar.ca/globalhome/industry/news.asp?articleid=530261

Stanberry, G. (Feb. 25, 2010). 10 Business leaders you should strive to emulate. *Business Insider*. Retrieved February 7, 2012 from http://www.businessinsider.com/10-examples-of-excellent-business-leadership-2010-2

## References

Alimo-Metcalfe, B., & Alban-Metcalfe, R. J. (2001). The development of a new transformational leadership questionnaire. *Journal of Occupational and Organizational Psychology, 74*(1), 1-27.

Avolio, B. J., Bass, B. M., & Jung, D. I. (1999). Re-examining the components of transformational and transactional leadership using the multifactor leadership questionnaire. *Journal of Occupational and Organizational Psychology, 72*(4), 441-462.

Avolio, B. J., Zhu, W., Koh, W., & Bhatia, P. (2004). Transformational leadership and organizational commitment: Mediating role of psychological empowerment and moderating role of structural distance. *Journal of Organizational Behavior, 25*(8), 951-968.

Bachman, J. G., Bowers, D. G., & Marcus, P. M. (1968). Bases of supervisory power: A comparative study in five organizational settings. In A. S. Tannenbaum (Ed.), *Control in organizations* (pp. 229-238). New York: McGraw-Hill.

Barrett, A., & Beeson, J. (2002). *Developing business leaders for 2010* [Research Report No. R-1315-02-RR]. New York: The Conference Board.

Bass, B. M. (1985). *Leadership and performance beyond expectations.* New York: Free Press.

Bennis, W. (1999, Spring). The leadership advantage [Electronic version]. *Leader to Leader Journal, 12*, 18-23.

Bennis, W., & Nanus, B. (1985). *Leaders: Strategies for taking charge.* New York: Harper & Row.

Blanchard, K., & Stoner, J. (2004, Winter). The vision thing: Without it you'll never be a world-class organization [Electronic version]. *Leader to Leader Journal, 31*, 21-28.

Burns, J. M. (1978). *Leadership.* New York: Harper & Row.

Collins, J. (2001). *Good to great: Why some companies make the leap . . . and others don't.* New York: HarperCollins.

Edmonds, R. (2000). *Human resource management (HRMT-502) Study Guide* [Unpublished course materials]. St. Albert, AB: Centre for Innovative Management, Athabasca University.

Egri, C. P., & Herman, S. (2000). Leadership in the North American environmental sector: Values, leadership styles, and contexts of environmental leaders and their organizations. *Academy of Management Journal, 43*(4), 571-604.

Evans, M. G. (1970). The effects of supervisory behavior on the path-goal relationship. *Organizational Behavior and Human Performance, 5*(3), 277-298.

Farren, C., & Kaye, B. L. (1996). New skills for new leadership roles. In F. Hesselbein, M. Goldsmith, and R. Beckhard (Eds.), *The leader of the future* (pp. 175-188). San Francisco: Jossey-Bass.

Fiedler, F. E. (1967). *A theory of leadership effectiveness.* New York: McGraw-Hill.

Gehring, D. R. (2007). Applying traits theory of leadership to project management. *Project Management Journal, 38*(1), 44-54.

Goleman, D. (1998). What makes a leader? *Harvard Business Review, 76*(6), 93-102.

Handy, C. (1993). *Understanding organizations* (4th ed.). London: Penguin Books.

Hernez-Broome, G., & Hughes, R. L. (2004). Leadership development: Past, present, and future. *Human Resource Planning, 27*(1), 24-32.

House, R. J. (1971). A path goal theory of leader effectiveness. *Administrative Science Quarterly, 16*(3), 321-338.

Kanter, R. M. (1996). World-class leaders: The power of partnering. In F. Hesselbein, M. Goldsmith, and R. Beckhard (Eds.), *The leader of the future* (pp. 89-98). San Francisco: Jossey-Bass.

Kanungo, R. N. (1998). Leadership in organizations: Looking ahead to the 21st century. *Canadian Psychology, 39*(1/2), 71-82.

Kotter, J. P. (1990). What leaders really do. *Harvard Business Review, 68*(3), 103-111.

Kotter, J. P. (1995). Leading change: Why transformation efforts fail. *Harvard Business Review, 73*(2), 59-66.

Lowe, K. B., Kroech, K. G., & Sivasubramaniam, N. (1996). Effectiveness correlates of transformational and transactional leadership: A meta-analytic review of the MLQ literature. *Leadership Quarterly, 7*(3), 385-425.

Lu, X. (2004). Surveying the topic of "effective leadership." *Journal of American Academy of Business Cambridge, 5*(1/2), 125-129.

Mintzberg, H. (1973). *The nature of managerial work.* New York: Harper & Row.

Mullins, L. (1999). *Management and organisation behaviour* (5th ed.), Upper Saddle River, NJ: Prentice Hall.

Ready, D. (1995). Mastering leverage, leading change. *Executive Excellence, 12*(3), 18-19.

Robbins, S. P. (1996). *Organizational behaviour: Concepts, controversies, applications* (7th ed.). Englewood Cliffs, NJ: Prentice Hall.

Robbins, S. P. & Langton, N. (2001). *Organizational behaviour: Concepts, controversies, applications* (2nd Canadian ed.). Toronto: Prentice Hall.

Rost, J. C. (1993). *Leadership for the twenty-first century.* Westport, CT: Praeger.

Schermerhorn, J. R., Jr., Hunt, J. G., & Osborn, R. N. (1997). *Organizational behaviour* (6th ed.) New York: Wiley.

Vera, D. & Crossan, M. (2004). Strategic leadership and organizational learning. *Academy of Management Review, 29*(2), 222-240.

Yukl, G. A. (2001). *Leadership in organizations* (5th ed.). Upper Saddle River, NJ: Prentice Hall.

Yukl, G. A., & Seifeit, C. F. (2002, April). *Preliminary validation research on the extended version of the influence behaviours questionnaire.* Paper presented at the annual conference of the Society for Industrial and Organizational Psychology, Toronto, ON.

Zaleznik, A. (1977). Managers and leaders: Are they different? *Harvard Business Review, 55*(3), 67-78.

# GROUPS AND TEAMS

## INTRODUCTION

*Groups* are two or more people interacting with each other to achieve a particular purpose. Groups are common entities in organizations. They are formal or informal. Formal groups are those officially recognized by the organization to achieve a specific organizational objective. Informal groups emerge without such official recognition or function and are often formed for the purpose of enhancing personal relationships or special interests. Such groups coexist with formal groups, and they can have significant impact on both the work and relationship aspects of the organization.

*Teams* are usually seen as more than just work groups. According to Thompson (2000), a work group "consists of people who learn from one another and share ideas, but are not interdependent in an important fashion and are not working towards a shared goal. Working groups share information, perspectives, and insights, make decisions, and help people do their job better, but the focus is on the individual goals and accountability" (p. 3). On the other hand, a team is "a group of people who are interdependent with respect to information, resources, and skills and who seek to combine their efforts to achieve a common goal" (p. 2). Teams are expected to produce outcomes, members are collectively accountable, and interdependence and synergy are the key characteristics. Usually teams work in a larger social context (e.g., in an organization) alongside other teams, and resource flows among teams may be common.

Teams are a form of groups, but groups are not necessarily teams. Simply calling a group of people a "team" certainly does not make it a real team.

This chapter begins with a look at the purpose of groups or teams in organizations, the stages of group development, and the factors contributing to group effectiveness. Group dynamics such as the interaction pattern and decision-making

Note: An earlier version of some sections of this chapter written by the author was included in the *Human Resource Management Study Guide* (2007), Centre for Innovative Management, Athabasca University.

process are addressed, followed by an examination of the characteristics of different types of teams, including high performance teams. The chapter closes with a specific discussion on the importance of team and organizational learning.

## WHY ARE GROUPS OR TEAMS USED?

Katzenbach and Smith (1993) provide a number of reasons for using groups and teams. First, groups and teams bring together a mix of skills, knowledge, and experiences well beyond what individuals can provide. Hence, they respond to multifaceted challenges more effectively. Moreover, the synergy of efforts is greater than the sum of the parts. The internal communication and support system established within groups and teams also helps in their responsiveness to the changing environment or organizational needs. When clear goals are set, members can reinforce the team purpose with each other and generate higher commitment. At the individual level, groups and teams provide a social element that can make work more meaningful and enjoyable. They are beneficial to the members because they provide a sense of belonging or security that satisfies the members' social needs and opportunities for learning and growth that satisfies the members' higher-level needs. Also, they can help establish a person's self-concept and serve as a means for a person to seek support and assistance as well as to share knowledge or work. Members of groups or teams are much less likely to feel threatened by change due to their collective identity. As a result, they provide a great channel for fostering new ideas and innovations.

The special purposes groups and teams serve for organizations include the items described here (Handy, 1993, pp. 151-2):

- distribution of work
- management and control of work
- problem-solving and decision-taking
- information processing
- information and idea collection
- testing and ratifying decisions
- coordination and liaison
- increased commitment and involvement
- negotiation and conflict resolution
- inquest and inquiry into the past

Groups and teams are either temporary or permanent in nature. Temporary teams, such as a project team, are formed as necessary to carry out the work and then disband.

## STAGES OF GROUP DEVELOPMENT

Usually, groups go through different stages in their development that can be viewed as their life cycle. These stages are described in Figure 5-1 (Heinen & Jacobson, 1976; Tuckman, 1965; and Tuckman & Jensen, 1977).

**Figure 5-1  Group Development Stages**

|  |  |
|---|---|
| **Forming** | At this stage the group is basically a set of individuals who are trying to discover answers to some fundamental questions, such as the purpose of the group, what name the group should be called, what its composition should be, what the real tasks are, what is acceptable behaviour in the group, and how to define the group rules. |
| **Storming** | This stage is characterized by high tensions and in-fighting as members with different expectations voice their opinions, exert their influence, challenge the initial positions, and bring conflicts out into the open. Coalitions may form within the group depending on the group size and membership characteristics. Personal hostility may emerge, and fights over leadership or authority are not uncommon. This is an important stage in that effective handling of it usually leads to more realistic and acceptable goals, rules, and processes. |
| **Norming** | After expectations are clarified and conflicts resolved in the storming stage, the group enters this stage, realizing that it is a coordinated unit. There is a new sense of harmony, and the group's focus begins to shift to establish norms and practices. Keeping the group close together is often more important than actually getting the work done. |
| **Performing** | The group integration process is complete at this stage. It becomes mature, organized, and stable. It is able to handle complex tasks and produce results. |
| **Adjourning** | Many groups, such as task forces, are established to run for only a period of time. When the work is done, the group prepares for disbandment or adjournment until another opportunity arises that will bring the members together again. Sometimes, groups are disbanded before task completion due to member turnover, such as when critical members leave the organization. At this adjourning stage, the main goal is to wrap up the activities. Members may have mixed feelings at this stage: happy about their accomplishments, but sad about losing their comradeship. |

Not all groups move from one stage to the next as described in this model. Many circumstances can affect a group's progression, processes, and effectiveness. Some groups may become stuck at a certain stage. If the group cannot successfully handle a certain stage, such as the storming stage, it may be disbanded. Regression to a previous stage may happen (e.g., from norming back to storming) if new conflict-triggering factors surface.

## GROUP EFFECTIVENESS

A group is said to be effective when it scores high on the task performance and human resource maintenance (group relationship and interaction) dimensions. Not only does the group get the desired work done, it also maintains a good level of interpersonal relationships and the members are generally satisfied with their group experience. Many factors are at play in determining group effectiveness. Some of these factors, including task, group size, membership characteristics, resources and rewards, leadership style, and membership roles, are described below.

### Tasks

The nature of the task usually influences the type of work group required. Questions such as "How complex is the task?", "What needs to be accomplished?", and "What skills are required?" fall under this category. Highly complex tasks are harder to accomplish because of the varying skills required and the degree of cooperation needed. But complex tasks can also lead to greater satisfaction when accomplished. The importance or salience of the task as viewed by the organization and by the group members affects the level of individual group members' commitment and motivation. The degree of control (versus autonomy) that management exercises (or provides) along with their high expectation on the task also affects commitment and motivation. Likert (1967, p. 183) posits that along the leadership/management decision-making continuum from autocratic to participative, groups tend to work more effectively under the participative system (which he refers to as System IV in contrast to the exploitive-authoritative, benevolent-authoritative, and consultative systems). Clarity of the task also has an impact on the functioning of the group. The more structured the task, the less the ambiguity, the easier it is to get through the forming and norming stages. However, a more creative and cooperative group can handle a less structured task.

### Group Size

Large groups allow a greater scope of expertise in the membership, and more people are available to do the work. However, coordination is problematic once the group exceeds a certain size. "Free-ridership" is more common with larger groups. There is no magic number of members that will work well with each situation, but research literature indicates a group of five to seven members is a good size (e.g., Handy, 1993, p. 159; Schermerhorn, Hunt, & Osborn, 1997, p. 183).

Certainly, the optimal number may vary with the task complexity and the group membership characteristics.

## Membership Characteristics

The effectiveness of a group certainly depends on the qualifications and experience of its members. Complementary skills among members are important if performance outcome is a main goal. Complementary skills are generally categorized into the following main areas (Katzenbach & Smith, 1993):

- Technical or functional expertise

- Problem-solving and decision-making skills

- Interpersonal skills (e.g., communication skills, conflict management skills).

Sometimes resource constraints do not allow for membership selection to cover the entire set of skills required. In such situations, skill gaps need to be identified and development plans initiated. Expertise from outside the regular membership through, for example, seconded personnel or use of temporary consultants may be considered. While internal members have the advantage of knowing the organizational environment and culture, external members bring a fresh perspective in addition to their expertise.

A heterogeneous group has a greater chance of having the knowledge, skills, and talents required to complete the task. More perspectives are brought into the group that can lead to more creative and effective recommendations or solutions. However, such a group is also likely associated with higher conflicts, less cohesiveness, and less satisfaction. A diverse group may take longer to go through the various stages and processes as it takes time for members to understand each other and assess the varying suggestions put forth. On the other hand, members who come from similar backgrounds, with similar beliefs, values, and attitudes often form more stable groups and are more compatible with each other. Compatibility among group members is an important consideration, especially when the task is complex and good interaction among members is critical.

## Resources and Rewards

A group's success depends in part on the resources it is provided by the organization. Financial, human, and technological resources are important, and so are the support of management, the goals and vision provided, and good work methods and procedures. Rewards must be designed to facilitate the achievement of group goals rather than those based solely on individual performance.

## *Leadership Style*

The leader of a group can be a formal leader (one with a proper title and official authority) or an informal one (as generally recognized by the members). A leader plays a major role in determining where the group is going, how things are done, and how work is coordinated. All these have significant bearing on the ultimate effectiveness of the work group. The importance of leadership is demonstrated in the previous chapter and need not be reiterated here. The following questions, however, can help evaluate the team leader's performance (Katzenbach & Smith, 1993):

- "Has the leader adopted a team or working group approach?" (p. 146). For example, does the leader value member contributions in the decision-making process? Is group accountability emphasized over individual accountability?

- "Is the leader striving for the right balance between action and patience within the team?" (p. 147). For example, does the leader promote constructive conflict and provide members with challenges and opportunities for the good of the team and members' personal growth?

- "Does the leader articulate a team purpose and act to promote and share responsibilities for it?" (p. 147). For example, does the leader share the blame for failure? How good is he or she in identifying and overcoming team barriers?

## *Membership Roles*

Usually each member of a group plays a role, either formally or informally. That is, a set of expected behaviours is associated with each position in an organization or a group. Various problems occur when roles are handled inappropriately. *Role ambiguity* arises when a person is not sure what his or her role is and thus is unable to satisfy the expectations associated with that role. *Role conflict* occurs when a person has more than one role (which can be a role played outside the workplace) and satisfying the expectations associated with one role precludes or interferes with the ability to satisfy those associated with the other role. *Role overload* happens when a group member finds too much is expected of him or her. *Role under-load*, on the other hand, makes a member feel under-recognised and unfulfilled. Therefore, setting realistic expectations for each member is necessary for a group's success.

There are many roles the members can play in a group. Presented in Table 5-1 are the roles proposed by Ancona, Kochan, Scully, Van Maanen, and Westney (1996, p. 9) for effective group functioning.

**Table 5-1 Group Roles**

| Roles that build task accomplishments | Roles that build and maintain a group |
|---|---|
| • initiating<br>• seeking information and opinions<br>• providing information and opinions<br>• clarifying<br>• elaborating<br>• summarizing<br>• consensus testing (i.e., to see periodically if the group is close to a decision or if more time for discussion is necessary) | • harmonizing<br>• compromising<br>• gatekeeping (making sure everyone has a chance to voice his or her views)<br>• encouraging |

# INTERACTION PATTERNS AND DECISION-MAKING

Communication in a group takes various forms. All communication may be channelled through a central person, the leader, or the chair. Communication can be web-like, where everyone communicates with each other directly. The most ineffective form of communication is where each member communicates with only one or two other members with no central person playing a coordinating role. If the group is small and quick decision making is necessary, having a central person coordinate the ideas and make a decision works best. However, when issues are complex, the web style usually offers better solutions but the process may take longer. The web style, which encourages participation, tends to generate greater motivation.

How are decisions made in a group? Are decisions made based on majority or are they made just by the leader (or person of authority) or by a minority of the group members who dominated the discussion? Is unanimity required? Decisions made by one person are quick but group members may not feel ownership of that decision and therefore be less eager to support its implementation. Even decisions made by the majority have the drawback of ignoring minority voices. Unanimous decisions can be time-consuming and may not always be reachable. Decisions made by the minority are not desirable unless those minority members are experts on the topic in question.

There is no one best interaction pattern or decision-making method. It depends on the situation and the membership. However, to achieve good quality decisions, it is important that threats to group creativity, as identified in the following section, are properly addressed.

## GROUP CREATIVITY AND GROUPTHINK

Thompson (2003) identifies four threats to group creativities:

- *Social loafing*: members slack off because their individual contributions are less identifiable
- *Conformity*: also called groupthink (see below)
- *Production blocking*: members are not able to generate new ideas or be involved in deeper thoughts while listening to others at the same time
- *Downward norm setting*: the lowest performance denominator is allowed to be the benchmark. This is most likely to occur in the absence of strong internal or external incentives.

*Groupthink* arises when members are so eager to seek agreement with each other that minority or deviant views are suppressed and possible better alternatives are not given their proper consideration (Janis, 1982). Some of the symptoms of groupthink are

- group members so overconfident about the group and themselves that they are not afraid to take extraordinary risks;
- group members quick to rationalize evidence that challenges their assumptions;
- group members believing in the moral rightness of their group objectives such that they feel no need to further discuss or debate them;
- group members exerting pressure on those who raise the slightest doubt on the group's shared views;
- group members who hold different views tending to keep silent to avoid disrupting the harmony.

An environment that values diversity, creative thinking, constructive criticisms, and functional conflicts must be fostered to minimize the possibility of groupthink or other creativity threats. Members should feel comfortable raising different views or critically but constructively evaluating others' suggestions. Brainstorming and other similar methods are advocated to overcome groupthink. The common characteristics of these techniques are they allow for free suggestion of alternatives, withholding of judgment until the separate evaluation stage is reached, and the opportunity to build upon each other's alternatives. Other suggestions for promoting group creativity include diversification of the group; use of analogical reasoning (which allows for the application of knowledge in new situations); creating organizational memory (with common knowledge shared among groups, groups can have more time for creative thinking on areas that had not been previously addressed); use of trained facilitators; adopting high benchmarks; membership changes; and building a "playground" or innovative space with the view that non-conformist space may prompt non-conformist ideas and behaviours (Thompson, 2003, p. 107).

## TYPES OF TEAMS IN ORGANIZATIONS

There are many types of teams. Organizations or authors may categorize them differently. Some common types of teams are discussed here.

*Problem-solving teams* are teams where members share ideas and offer suggestions to remove problem areas and to improve quality, efficiency, and working conditions. They can be traditional manager-led teams where a manager or leader sets the goals and tasks to be accomplished and oversees the various activities of the team members. They can also be likened to a quality circle, which is usually a group of employees in the same area or department coming together on a regular basis to investigate causes of problems and make recommendations for changes. The team members usually do not have the authority to approve the changes.

*Cross-functional teams* are comprised of individuals from different work areas, often selected based on their expertise and knowledge in their respective areas. The members usually come from similar levels in the hierarchy. They are sometimes called *task forces* or *project teams* if they are temporary in nature, established to deal with a task or project. Some cross-functional teams are specifically responsible for process improvement. They have become much more common with the popularity of total quality management (TQM). Some cross-functional teams are more longstanding, as in the case of committees (e.g., health and safety committees, policy development committees). Steering committees can be a form of cross-functional teams as well. Usually, such committees are responsible for leading an area of development by providing guidance and direction.

*Self-managing, self-regulating, self-directing, self-governing, autonomous* and *semi-autonomous* are different terms that describe teams where members have a higher level of control and autonomy than those in traditional manager-led teams. These teams not only recommend changes, but also determine their implementation and are responsible for the outcomes. The members take on some of the responsibilities previously required of their supervisors in that they can plan and schedule their work, design how work should be done, and make other operational decisions. Fully autonomous teams can even handle their own members' staffing, performance evaluation, and compensation matters.

*Virtual teams* are a newer form of team where members work together or convene meetings via electronic means (such as networked computers and video-conferencing or teleconferencing). Many new software programs have been developed in recent years to facilitate this process. The advantage of such teams is that they can overcome distance, time, and space constraints. Also, it is often more economical and convenient for the members to remain in their regular office yet be able to interact with people far away. Virtual teams can work synchronously or asynchronously depending on the time zone differences and the task at hand. Synchronous discussions allow for immediate response and feedback and may facilitate quicker decision-making, while asynchronous discussions allow time for more reflection and thoughtful responses without the drawback of some members dominating the discussion forum. Due to the different setting, the group dynamics of virtual teams are often quite different from those of conventional face-to-face teams. In particular, the storming stage is less stormy if members take the time to think and reflect before responding. Virtual teams tend to be more task-oriented because the social element is missing to some extent. The lack of face-to-face contact may be a concern for some members who feel that there is less social rapport and less effective interaction. However, the effectiveness of virtual teams depends largely on the design of the method of interaction, the features and support of the software, the receptiveness of the members to new ways of work, and the degree of comfort in their use of technology.

Kirkman, Rosen, Gibson, Tesluk, and McPherson (2002) derive from conventional wisdom five major challenges for virtual teams, but find in their study of 65 cross-functional virtual teams in a high-technology firm that these can be overcome with appropriate measures:

- *Building trust*: rather than relying on social bonds, trust could be gained through member "reliability, consistency and responsiveness when dealing with teammates" (p. 71).

- *Optimizing process gains and losses*: proper training of both the leader and members in skills and process areas as well as having good software to facilitate communication and decision-making can create positive synergy (or reduce negative synergy).

- *Dealing with members' feelings of isolation and detachment*: selecting members who do not mind working virtually and giving them a realistic preview, maintaining continuous contact, or having occasional face-to-face meetings are some ways to address these concerns.

- *Finding members with the right balance of technical and interpersonal skills*: a proper selection process using behavioural interviewing techniques and simulations or based on current member recommendations (as they understand the fit) helps.

- *Assessing and enhancing member performance and development*: group communication archives and peer evaluations can be used for assessing member contributions while online resources can be explored for training and development.

The element of trust is worth particular attention because it is fundamental to collaborative teamwork. Lawley (2006) suggests that trust is built upon "perceived ability; benevolence; and feeling positive about other people in the group and the group's integrity" (p. 14). In her study of a mobile communications organization, she found that work at the set-up stage is very important for trust-building. This includes finding a common purpose for the team, selecting appropriate team members, and having leaders with good communicating, facilitating, and coaching skills. Moreover, a leader helps build credibility and reputation of the members by purposely sharing information on their roles, track records, and expertise.

## How to Achieve High Performance Teams

Irrespective of the team type, achieving good performance is usually a common objective. Buchholz and Roth (1987, p. 14) listed eight attributes for a high performance team:

1. Participative leadership
2. Shared responsibility
3. Aligned on purpose
4. High communication
5. Future focused
6. Focused on task
7. Creative talents
8. Rapid response

These characteristics are important for synergism, high energy input, and high performance output. Members on high performance teams usually feel empowered and highly committed towards the common goal.

All the suggestions provided earlier on enhancing group effectiveness are applicable to building a high performance team. In addition, attention should be paid to developing trust and team bonding in the relationship. As noted above, trust is a critical element in team relationships, especially due to the high level of interdependence among members and the collective accountability. Rapport and camaraderie provide positive feelings that enhance morale and solidarity and bond the team together.

## INDIVIDUAL, GROUP, AND ORGANIZATIONAL LEARNING

Groups and teams offer individual members a good chance to learn about group roles, group dynamics, and group synergy. Even if members cannot learn technical and functional expertise from each other, they can at least learn to understand and appreciate other members' work. Members can also learn from others, or through practice, problem-solving, decision-making, and interpersonal skills. Such experiences and skills are very useful for their future group or team involvement as well as in their day-to-day interaction with co-workers.

Learning does not only occur at the individual level, team-level learning occurs as well. What did the team do effectively? What areas could be improved upon? How did the team successfully complete its task? Answers to these questions provide valuable information for future teams in a similar environment. Team learning is defined as the "raising of the collective IQ of a group and capitalizing on the greater knowledge and insights of the collectivity" by Jamali, Khoury, and Sahyoun (2006, p. 343). It is a dynamic process involving the accumulation and modification of knowledge (Curado, 2006). Team learning assists in the development of a learning organization, one that "promotes continual organizational renewal by weaving in/embedding a set of core processes that nurture a positive propensity to learn, adapt and change" (Jamali, Khoury, & Sahyoun, 2006, p. 337). As Senge (1990) puts it, "teams, not individuals, are the fundamental learning unit in modern organizations … unless teams can learn, the organization cannot learn" (p. 10). Teams allow learning to spread faster and farther in the organization. Team learning enhances interpersonal relationships, leverages knowledge (especially tacit knowledge), improves team member competency, and contributes towards breakthrough thinking and organizational innovation (Bennet & Bennet, 2004; Kasl, Marsick, & Dechant, 1997). Team learning also has a significant indirect effect on organizational performance, including financial performance (Yang, Watkins, & Marsick 2004).

Watkins and Marsick (1993, p. 113) provide a list of questions for consideration in assessing the team learning process, conditions, and outcomes, including the following:

- How much opportunity do members have in defining the team objectives?
- How is team achievement valued over individual achievement?

- What is the level of support from top management?
- Can team members think more from the organization perspective than the departmental one?
- Do members consider all others members' perspectives in their analyses and decisions?
- To what extent is the team open to relevant outside information?
- Do members manage to transfer what is learned in the team to others in the organization?
- Are their available channels in the organization for conveying the team findings?

## CONCLUSION

Teams are an important part of many organizations and the phenomenal growth in their use is likely to continue as organizations become more fluid in structure and their challenges more complex and multi-dimensional. To capitalize on the use of teams, organizations must have a good understanding of the purpose of teams, the types of teams that can be formed, the team processes as well as their obstacles and enablers, and team effectiveness assessment. Moreover, to survive and flourish in the new economy, organizations need to recognize the significance of team learning. Efforts must be devoted to establish the appropriate conditions for team development and learning and to enable the knowledge and learning from effective teams to transfer to other parts of the organization.

# HRM in Action
## Teams and Employee Involvement in Boeing

Boeing Co. has long been a leader in the aviation industry, well-known for its manufacture of aircraft. It is also well-known for its use of innovative teams. In the late 1980s, self-directed work teams started to spring up as part of the total quality management and lean manufacturing initiatives. They have since become an integral part of the organization and the union has been an active player in this development.

At the St. Louis plant, two main types of teams emerged in the 1990s: Integrated Product Teams (IPT) and High Performance Work Organization Teams (HPWOT). IPTs were focused on design, engineering, and manufacturing development issues, involving engineering and manufacturing staff as well as suppliers and customer representatives. HPWOTs were more concerned about the work flow and other administrative issues. As both these types of teams were mainly self-directed in nature, the superintendent overseeing the teams no longer needed to be involved with planning or control, but assumed the role of a coach, facilitator, and resource/support provider. The teams selected their own leaders, managed their team work, assessed members' performance, and even directly dealt with suppliers and customers as needed. Data on team performance were tracked and provided as feedback to the teams themselves. Training was provided to both team leaders and team members to enhance both task skills and team interaction skills.

When an earthquake struck in February 2001, causing extensive destruction to buildings and a shutdown of the Boeing plant in Renton, Washington, employees, who were probably accustomed to a team culture, quickly formed themselves into teams, made the necessary decisions, and managed to relocate workstations and get things up and running within days. The company realized that people wanted to be involved and empowered, and engaged employees would drive top performance. Employee involvement also gave workers a strong sense of ownership, pride, and accomplishment, which not only benefit the employees, but also would go a long way in creating sustainable benefits for the organization. According to Harry Stonecipher, the President and CEO in 2004, "the more decisions that get made lower in your organization, the stronger your organization" (Procter, 2004).

As of February 2012, there were over 1,300 teams across the company's commercial jet programs and innovative teams are continuing to grow in number. Innovative ideas generated by teams and process improvements have probably contributed significantly to the reduction of final jet assembly time at Renton over the past decade from 22 days to 11 days. At Boeing, teams have not only been used for generating gains and reducing costs, safety teams have also been established to help foster a "safety first" mindset where employees would take both individual and collective responsibility for workplace safety.

Sources:

Boeing. (June 2009). *Safety in numbers*. Retrieved February 7, 2012 from http://www.boeing.com/news/frontiers/archive/2009/june/i_ids03.pdf

Clardy, A. (2001). *Teams at Boeing: Military aircraft production at the St. Louis Plant* [Working paper]. Retrieved February 7, 2012 from http://pages.towson.edu/aclardy/Working%20Papers/TEAMS%20AT%20BOEING.pdf

Kesmodel, D. (February 7, 2012). Boeing teams speed up 737 output. *Wall Street Journal*. Retrieved February 7, 2012 from http://online.wsj.com/article/SB10001424052970203436904577155204034907744.html

Proctor, P. (March 2004). Shared destiny. *Frontier, 2*(10). Retrieved February 7, 2012 from http://boeing.com/news/frontiers/archive/2004/february/cover.html

## References

Ancona, D. G., Kochan, T. A., Scully, M., Van Maanen, J., & Westney, D. E. (1996). *Managing for the future.* Cincinnati, OH: South-Western College Publishing.

Bennet, A., & Bennet, D. (2004). *Organizational survival in the new world: The intelligent complex adaptive system.* London: Elsevier.

Buchholz, S., & Roth, T. (1987). *Creating the high-performance team.* New York: Wiley.

Curado, C. (2006). Organisational learning and organisational design. *The Learning Organization, 13*(1), 25-48.

Handy, C. (1993). *Understanding organizations* (4th ed.). London: Penguin Books.

Heinen, J. S., and Jacobson, E. (1976). A model of task group development in complex organizations and a strategy of implementation. *Academy of Management Review, 1*(4), 98-111.

Jamali, D., Khoury, G., & Sahyoun, H. (2006). From bureaucratic organizations to learning organizations: An evolutionary roadmap. *The Learning Organization, 13*(4), 337-352.

Janis, I. L. (1982). *Groupthink.* Boston: Houghton Mifflin.

Kasl, E., Marsick, V. J. & Dechant, K. (1997). Teams as learners: A research-based model of team learning. *The Journal of Applied Behavioral Science, 33*(2), 227-246.

Katzenbach, J. R., & Smith, D. K. (1993). *The wisdom of teams: Creating the high-performance organization.* New York: HarperCollins.

Kirkman, B. L., Rosen, B., Gibson, C. B., Tesluk, P. E., & McPherson, S. O. (2002). Five challenges to virtual team success: Lessons from Sabre, Inc. *Academy of Management Executive, 16*(3), 67-79.

Lawley, D. (2006). Creating trust in virtual teams at Orange. *KM Review, 9*(2), 12-17.

Likert, R. (1967). *The human organization: Its management and value.* New York: McGraw-Hill.

Schermerhorn, J. R., Jr., Hunt, J. G., & Osborn, R. N. (1997). *Organizational behaviour* (6th ed.) New York: Wiley.

Senge, P. (1990). *The fifth discipline—the art and practice of the learning organization.* New York: Doubleday.

Thompson, L. (2000). *Making the team: A guide for managers.* Upper Saddle River, NJ: Prentice Hall.

Thompson, L. (2003). Improving the creativity of organizational work groups. *Academy of Management Executive, 17*(1), 96-109.

Tuckman, B. W. (1965). Developmental sequences in small groups. *Psychological Bulletin, 63*(6), 384-399.

Tuckman, B. W., & Jensen, M. C. (1977). Stages of small-group development revisited. *Group & Organizational Studies, 2*(4), 419-427.

Watkins, K. E., & Marsick, V. J. (1993). *Sculpting the learning organization: Lessons in the art and science of systemic change.* San Francisco: Jossey-Bass.

Yang, B., Watkins, K. E., & Marsick, V. J. (2004). The construct of the learning organization: Dimensions, measurement, and validation. *Human Resource Development Quarterly, 15*(1), 31-55

# Chapter 6

# HUMAN RESOURCE FLOW

## INTRODUCTION

Human resource flow (HRF) is about the movement of human resources into and out of an organization as well as within it. It involves full-time or part-time employees, temporary employees, or contract workers. As Pfeffer (1994) points out, people are the one main source of an organization's competitive advantage. An organization may have great business plans, but it needs the right people to carry them out successfully. Indeed, it needs the right people to be able to come up with great business plans in the first place. In short, the goal of HRF is to provide the organization with *the right people in the right positions in the right place at the right time*. Achieving this goal involves asking a number of questions: Who are the right people? How can the organization get them, keep them, and make the best use of their resources—the human capital? How should the organization deal with the people currently not at the right position, place, or time? Should an HRF decision be made by the HR department or the line department?

Many challenges arise in managing HRF, especially in a time when changes are often the only thing of certainty in organizations. In an unstable environment, forecasting is understandably difficult. The time and resources required are often not readily available unless there is top management commitment to the strategic roles of HRF. Rapid flow creates a chain of movements that can be quite disruptive to operations if not properly managed. Managers today have to deal with many issues that were much less common in the past, such as lean production, massive layoffs, contracting out, fast-changing job requirements, an aging workforce, and different worker expectations arising out of a new generation. As these issues are an integral part of line department operations, managing HRF is not a responsibility limited to the HR department. For an organization to be successful, line departments must fully cooperate with HR and contribute to the HRF management process.

In this chapter, the importance of strategic HRF and the need for HR planning are discussed first. Then various HRF processes are examined. These include the following, which are all discussed in this chapter:

- recruitment
- selection
- appointment
- promotion
- transfers and redeployment
- outplacement

The chapter also covers recent HRF challenges such as staff retention and international HRF. The role of unions in HRF is examined as well. The topics of orientation, training, and development, which are closely integrated with HRF, are covered in the next chapter.

## What is Strategic HRF?

Strategic HRF must be aligned with the organization's strategy. If an organization is to provide innovative services, then the HRF strategy must aim at attracting, retaining, and motivating people with creative talents. Strategic HRF should also consider the kind of organizational culture that is most appropriate for the organization and how HRF can help foster it. Many other considerations exist in strategic HRF. For example, what are the current versus future HR needs of the organization? Should hiring be focused on the job task or on personal attributes? What knowledge, skills, and ability (KSA) mix is required? What is the relative importance of technical competencies versus soft skills competencies? Should positions be filled internally where possible before external recruitment? What is and what will be the labour market situation and how well are the current HR policies attracting the quality of people needed? What changes must be made to the current policies to achieve the HRF goals in the future? Who should be involved in the HRF decisions and how much time and resources should be committed to it?

A major problem with organizations is effectively linking HRF strategy and the organizational strategy. In the past, the organizational strategy was often developed with little or no HR involvement. HR was then asked to develop strategies to support the organizational strategy. In such situations it is not surprising that the organizational strategy is not realistic given the HR constraints or that the organization's human resource potential is not fully capitalized. Further, if HR provides any negative views on the established organizational strategy, no matter how valid, they are regarded as a naysayer and unsupportive. As discussed in Chapter 1, HR and organizational strategies must be developed in line with each other, and HR should be a partner in organizational strategy development. The two types of strategies are integrated and the influence between them reciprocal. Thus, they cannot and should not be developed separately.

Broadly, the organizational HRF strategies can be categorized into four main patterns (Beer, Spector, Lawrence, Quinn Mills, & Walton, 1985, pp. 242-243).

1. *Lifelong employment*

   Typically this type of employment is long-term, with employees usually joining at the lower levels of the ranks and gradually moving up to higher levels. Jobs are generally secure, other than perhaps for just cause dismissals, and workers are not laid off during difficult times. As such, turnover is often minimal. This type of HRF pattern is more common in countries like Japan or certain European countries due to the cultural or legislative climate. Many North American organizations used to fall under this category back when the economic environment was a lot less competitive. Union organizations also tend to follow this pattern as job security is usually an important agenda for unions and employees.

2. *Up-or-out system*

   Under this system, employees have the opportunity to start at the low levels and move up through a predetermined career track. However, not everyone succeeds in doing so. Those who fail to show continuous competence to move up to higher levels are forced out of the organization while the others who make it over the hurdles are offered security terms such as tenure or partnership. Common examples of such firms are professional services firms and university faculties.

3. *Unstable in-and-out system*

   With this system, employees may be hired or fired at any level at any time, depending on the organization's needs. The economic condition of the organization, the market situation, the employee's performance and fit with organization, or any organizational changes are relevant factors. Employees are let go when there is a market downturn and any commitment of employment period is usually of a limited duration. Industries in highly competitive environments, such as retail and manufacturing, are most likely to use this flow pattern.

4. *Mixed pattern*

Many organizations do not neatly fall under any of the above categories as there may be different patterns adopted for different categories
of staff. For example, many organizations offer fairly secure jobs to their
core group of workers. That is, employees who are considered critical to
the organization are provided with permanent or indefinite employment
(lifelong employment system) whereas employees in other less critical position are hired or fired as needed (in-and-out system). Organizations that
start out with one flow pattern can also change to other systems over time.
The lifelong employment system, which was once a common system in
North America, has gradually lost its appeal to the in-and-out system as
market pressures mount.

How organizations select their HRF pattern really depends on the management philosophy, the organizational pressure and needs, and the organizational
strategy. There are organizations that perform well in any of the four systems and
organizations that fail in each of the categories.

## HUMAN RESOURCE PLANNING

Human resource planning (HRP) is a process in which the HR needs of the organization are analyzed and ways of meeting such needs are developed through
various HR systems or programs. The internal and external supply and demand
of labour on short-term and long-term bases are considered. Greer (2001, p. 162)
outlines the basic steps of HRP:

- interfacing with organizational strategic planning
- environmental scanning
- keeping track of the organization's human resource inventory
- forecasting HR demand
- forecasting internal and external HR supply
- comparing supply and demand forecasts
- developing action plans for labour shortages or surpluses
- providing input back to the overall organizational strategic plans

Organizations should pay attention to the preferred human resource flow
(HRF) velocity, which is the rate at which employees move across jobs. If the velocity is high, the rapid changes can result in a lot of disruptions. Hiring or training
of new employees or job incumbents may not be able to meet up with the demands

or requirements, and employees may feel an unhealthy level of stress and anxiety with the high degree of change and uncertainty. On the other hand, if the flow is too slow, employees may feel stuck at a position, which offers little incentive for them to continue to strive for excellence. Hence, the relationship between HRF velocity and HRM outcomes can be seen as an inverted U-shaped curve, with the most desirable situation resulting from a moderate level of HRF velocity.

HRP is often not done very effectively in organizations. Most of its positive impact tends to surface in the long run and it may be difficult to tie any direct benefit of HRP to the outcomes. Whenever there are time or resource constraints, people naturally focus their resources on issues of immediate concern, and long-run recruitment and development plans are deferred. If HR is not seen by top management as an important function just because it does not generate direct revenues, HRP is unlikely to be successful. Sometimes, simply looking at the reporting level of the HR department head provides a rough idea of the importance of the overall HR function and the strategic role it plays. If HR reports directly to the highest rank executive, chances are it has a much bigger influence on the organizational strategies and receives more support in developing appropriate HR strategies. If the HR department is subordinated within other areas like finance or operations, the significance of HR as a main contributor to competitive advantage may be overshadowed by other financial and operational concerns. Moreover, in order to have effective HRP, an adequate and current HR information system must be kept. The system should record employees' demographic data, skills level, career history, interests, and aspirations. The system should also allow for quick retrieval of information needed for management decisions, such as those related to turnover, succession planning, training needs, salary and benefits costs, and other HR related costs.

### Forecasting HR Needs and Succession Planning

Information from proper HR forecasting helps the organization identify the gaps in supply and demand and take active measures to address them. It also allows the organization to achieve greater flexibility in its future HR deployment.

Common forecasting methods include HR inventories, replacement charts, succession planning, and supervisory estimates. HR inventories usually involve keeping records of individual employees' personal and demographic information as well as their education, work experience, skill competencies, performance, and career potential. For effective use of such information in management or HR decisions, the information must be current and easy to retrieve in a useful format. Hence, a computerized HR information system that allows efficient searching, sorting, analysis, and presentation of a large volume of data is very helpful.

*Replacement charts* generally include potential replacements for each position of interest, together with information on the individuals' performance level and readiness for advancement. A replacement chart may look like an organization chart with additional information on the few top potential candidates for each position of interest. A sample partial replacement chart is shown in Figure 6-1.

**Figure 6-1 Replacement Chart Example**

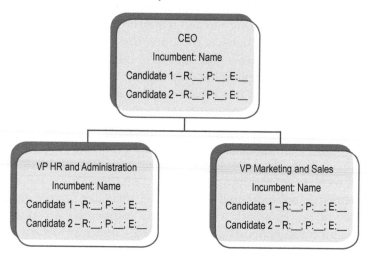

Legend for the codes:

**R:** Readiness for the position (1 = Ready now, 2 = Will be ready within 1 year, 3 = Will be ready in 2 years, 4 = Will be ready in 3 or more years, 5 = yet to be determined)

**P:** Performance (1 = Excellent, 2 = Very good, 3 = Average, 4 = Below average, 5 = cannot be determined)

**E:** Relevant work experience in number of years

Since replacement charts generally only contain limited information, some organizations may supplement them with replacement tables that keep more detailed information on all the potential candidates for each position of interest.

Succession planning extends beyond replacement charts and involves a longer term scope, with more focus on developing a pool of potential replacement candidates. With the aging population and more senior managers expected to retire in the not too distant future, succession planning is crucial to the smooth functioning of organizations.

Succession planning is done more often for the senior levels, as it is very time-consuming to examine the replacement for each position. However, rather than focusing entirely on the CEO level as was usually done in the past, organizations are now paying more attention to succession planning for the middle management level as part of the broader talent management initiative (Weinstein, 2006). A properly developed HR information system is very helpful in this regard, particularly for large organizations with many positions to plan for and numerous employee qualifications, performance, progress, and readiness to track. Succession planning should not be regarded as only an HR initiative (although HR can take on the role of educator and facilitator) because it requires leadership and commitment at the top levels to initiate a culture change if such planning is to become part of the normal business processes for which executives are to be held accountable (Ibarra, 2007; Weinstein, 2006). Cooperation and efforts of line managers as well as buy-in from employees are also critical factors for such planning success.

Heiden (2007) summarizes the benefits of succession planning as follows:

- reducing risk of not having people for critical jobs
- increased productivity
- improved morale
- better engagement and development of employees
- better alignment of organizational goals and employees' career goals.

Despite the general recognition of the importance of succession planning, especially at a time of possible looming labour and talent shortages, many organizations still do not have a succession plan. In a 2006 survey conducted by the Society of Human Resource Management 58 percent of responding organizations claimed they had succession plans but only 29 percent had formal plans (Heiden 2007). In small- and medium-sized enterprises as few as 10 percent of owners have a formal succession plan, 38 percent have an informal one, while the majority have none at all (Bruce, 2006). More recent findings from the Korn/Ferry Executive Survey in 2010 still reveal that succession plans for the CEO position was not in place for a majority of the global respondents (only 35 percent of respondents were prepared), even though it was considered critical for corporate governance (Korn/Ferry International, 2010). This indicates the need for organizations to seriously consider adopting the initiative and to ensure all related areas such as employee development, learning and talent management, and performance management are well aligned and integrated.

For more junior levels, especially for career paths that have a high turnover, it is not worth the effort to figure out exact succession or replacement plans since candidates in the potential pool may not be there for long and external recruitment is likely to be required. In this situation, organizations may simply use rule-ofthumb formulas such as one supervisor for a certain number of front line employees to predict their needs for some general positions.

Sometimes, rather than planning the succession for each position, organizations estimate the aggregate numbers of current and future workers for each job category by using a *transition matrix* (or Markov model). A transition matrix makes use of historical data patterns to predict the probability of movements across jobs from one period to the next. This allows the organization to estimate its internal supply of labour for various jobs. Such a matrix may contain information as shown in Table 6-1.

In this matrix, the numbers under Time Period 2 illustrate how many workers are expected to move into the column job category from the respective row categories over that time period. For example, looking at the column for Job Category 3, 16 workers are expected to remain in that category over the period, one is expected to move in from Job Category 2 and 10 from Job Category 4, giving a total predicted internal labour supply of 27 workers for this category in Time Period 2. Looking at the row for Job Category 2, for example, there are currently 10 incumbents, with one expected to move to Job Category 1, one to move to Job Category 3, and one to leave over the time period. The numbers in the highlighted diagonal cells of the matrix represent the number of workers staying in the job categories. With the predicted internal labour supply known, the organization can estimate the gaps and make action plans for recruitment of new workers or training of current workers to take on the necessary job positions.

Forecasts can be made using more complex techniques such as computer simulation, regression analysis, linear programming, and operation research methods. Detailed discussion of these is outside the scope of this book. However, these methods usually require the specification of a number of parameters, either as predictors or constraints, and proper measurement of them. Expert forecast is also a way of forecasting the HR demand. For example, the Delphi technique involves having experts provide a series of input, with each round of new input based upon feedback from all other participants in the previous round.

When internal supply exceeds demand, plans to reduce the surplus are necessary in the long run. Attrition is used if the organization can afford to take a longer adjustment time. While it may be more costly to keep extra people, the positive effects include lesser impact on staff morale and better opportunity to ensure tacit knowledge of departing staff is captured and transferred during the longer handover period.

When demand exceeds internal supply, an organization must recruit new members.

**Table 6-1 Transition Matrix Example**

|  | | Time Period 2 | | | | |
|---|---|---|---|---|---|---|
| **Time Period 1** | Current No. | Job Category 1 | Job Category 2 | Job Category 3 | Job Category 4 | Exit |
| Job Category 1 | 5 | 4 / 80% | 0 / 0% | 0 / 0% | 0 / 0% | 1 / 20% |
| Job Category 2 | 10 | 1 / 10% | 7 / 70% | 1 / 10% | 0 / 0% | 1 / 10% |
| Job Category 3 | 25 | 0 / 0% | 5 / 20% | 16 / 64% | 0 / 0% | 4 / 16% |
| Job Category 4 | 50 | 0 / 0% | 1 / 2% | 10 / 20% | 25 / 50% | 14 / 28% |
| Total | 90 | 5 | 13 | 27 | 25 | 20 |

## RECRUITMENT

Recruitment is the process of finding new employees for the organization. It involves identifying the main sources of potential candidates and taking action to get them to apply for the job. There are many questions to answer and steps to take before the recruitment process starts.

What type of employees does the organization want to hire? Is the organization interested in hiring for a specific current job or hiring individuals with competencies that can meet the organization's current and future needs? Is the new employee to fill an existing vacant position or a new position? Existing positions become vacant due to staff turnover such as resignation, retirement, promotions, or transfers. Staff turnover does not always have to be seen as a negative situation. It provides a good opportunity to review the overall staffing needs and to make necessary changes to the vacant job position—more easily done when no existing incumbent is involved. Therefore, organizations should not always rush to fill a vacant position based on past job requirements. An up-to-date job description and job specification is a good start for a job-based recruitment.

A *job description* provides information on the tasks of a position and focuses on the job, not the person performing the job. It usually includes the reporting relationships, the tools and equipment involved, and the expectations of the job (the job standards). On the other hand, a *job specification* emphasizes the requirements of the job holder and addresses the areas of skills and competencies needed for the job. Both of these documents are developed through the process of *job analysis,* which is a systematic study of the job—its characteristics, dimensions, skill requirements, and relation to other jobs or positions. There are many ways to collect information for analyzing jobs. Previous documents about the job, if available, can be reviewed. Questionnaires or interviews can be conducted with existing employees and the people with whom they closely work, such as supervisors, colleagues, subordinates, suppliers, and clients. Observation of the work done by the incumbents is another means of indicating the tasks and skills required. Production reports, automated work-tracking systems, time sheets, and other written records of job activities (such as critical incidents) by the job holder provide further useful data. Job analysis is very helpful to organizations, especially in the areas of recruitment and selection, job classifications, and salary determination.

For decades, the job analysis approach has been widely adopted by many organizations in determining staffing needs. Now organizations are facing constant changes and challenges; layoffs, restructuring, multitasking, and lateral movements are common occurrences. Organizations now find traditional job analysis too rigid a tool and keeping job analysis information current too difficult. Some organizations are also learning that flexibility is the key to success in this environment and that they fare better by focusing more on the overall potential of individuals to perform well in the organization rather than the job skills for a particular job. Hence, the competency-based approach is gaining attention.

Belcourt and McBey (2000) define competency as "any knowledge, skills, trait, motive, attitude, value, or other personal characteristic that is essential to perform the job and that differentiates superior from solid performance" (p. 126). Core competency, on the other hand, is defined as "characteristics that every member of an organization, regardless of position, function, or level of responsibility with the organization, is expected to possess" (p. 126). Examples of competencies are initiative, problem-solving skills, industry or technical knowledge, communication skills, customer service orientation, resource management, drive for achievement, and the list can go on. In general, competency-based models consider not only the requirements for the immediate job, but also the overall fit with the organization. They focus more on the person than the job task. Organizations can certainly take both the person and job dimensions into consideration; they are not mutually exclusive. The challenge is for the organization to strike a balance in their emphasis. Is the recruitment to meet the short-term or long-term requirement? Is the position more technical in nature or one that requires an employee with a broad range of general characteristics?

### *Internal or External Recruitment*

Once the organization knows what kind of people it needs, the next consideration is where to find them. Should they be hired from inside or outside? Both approaches have their advantages and disadvantages. Emphasizing internal promotions sends a message to employees that there are good advancement opportunities and that they are valued. Internal employees also have a better knowledge of the culture, policies, and processes of the organization. Internal replacements occur faster and are less expensive. On the other hand, internal promotions may set off a chain of movements, each resulting in another position needing to be filled. The major drawback from hiring from within is the lack of "new blood." For organizations that need innovative thinking and where existing staff do not have the competencies required, hiring from outside is preferred. Hiring an external person with the right skills can save a lot of training time, especially for technical training. The decision to hire from within or from outside often relates to the organizational and overall HR strategies. Many organizations have a general policy to look for suitable candidates inside the organization first before advertising outside if a suitable candidate is not found. Some organizations advertise both internally and externally at the same time to shorten the time span for recruitment. Others just do an external search, especially when there is no suitable internal talent.

If the decision is to recruit from outside, the next question is how it should be done. What will be the appropriate channels for recruitment? Common avenues include referral from existing employees, recruitment through colleges and universities, job advertisements, and employment agencies and headhunters.

The choice usually depends on the level of the position and the types of skills required. Newspaper advertisements tend to have the broadest reach and generate a large number of applicants, but sorting through them is time-consuming. Many of the applicants do not really possess the types of competencies required. Online recruitment advertisements (especially through social media networks) are beginning to play a significant role as more and more job seekers turn to the Internet. If recruiters can pick the appropriate network, one that is for the specific profession or occupation, they will have a better chance of reaching the target audiences and receiving good quality applications. Referral from employees is the least expensive and the chances of finding a trustworthy person who can fit in are usually better, but the organization is less likely to benefit from diversity. Recruitment from colleges is most appropriate for more junior and technical positions while headhunters are generally used for senior executive positions where a limited number of suitable candidates are targeted.

### Employment Equity Considerations

In Canada, the Employment Equity Act (1995) aims at promoting equality and the employment opportunities of minority workers in organizations under federal jurisdiction. Specifically, clause 2 of the statute states its purpose is "to correct the conditions of disadvantage in employment experienced by women, aboriginal peoples, persons with disabilities and members of visible minorities by giving effect to the principle that employment equity means more than treating persons in the same way but also requires special measures and the accommodation of differences." Every year, federally legislated organizations with over 100 employees are required to provide a report on the appointment, promotion, and termination statistics of various categories or ranks of workers by each of the four identified minority groups. The statistics in the report indicate if certain minority groups are underrepresented. Where that is the case, numerical goals for increasing representation are needed. Measures taken and action plans for promoting equality are also required for reporting. Similar legal employment protection for various minority groups is available in the United States. It is called *affirmative action* instead of *employment equity*.

Employment equity differs from *pay equity*. The former is concerned with employment opportunities and access to positions (e.g., hiring, promotions, and terminations), while the latter (at least in Canada) basically relates to equity in pay between the genders. Pay equity is presented in more detail in Chapter 8.

Does employment equity lead to *reverse discrimination*? This has always been a controversial question. Does giving minority groups particular treatment mean discrimination against the majority? The Act does not require employers to hire people who do not meet the job requirements: hiring decisions are still based on merits. It does not mean employers should blindly hire anyone just because they are in a minority group. Rather, the goal is to find ways to attract appropriate minority applicants to the job and remove barriers for their employment so they have an equal chance of getting suitable jobs. For example, directly targeting recruitment advertisements to certain groups or providing additional information sessions for them can be used when regular channels do not readily reach them or when regular advertisements do not send a sufficiently strong message about the organization's equal opportunity efforts. Organizations should also consider removing barriers for minority workers, especially the disabled, by providing reasonable accommodation.

### Reasonable Accommodation

For employees with disability or religious belief, employers are often required by law to provide reasonable accommodation. Reasonable accommodation means that the employer must provide facilities or ways for these employees to overcome barriers related to the performance of their work. For example, the employer can move furniture around to widen the corridor for an employee who uses a wheelchair. For employees who cannot work on certain days due to religious belief, shifts can be scheduled to allow a day off on those days. Generally, employers need to accommodate where it does not cause undue financial hardship. Providing a ramp for wheelchair access is a reasonable accommodation, but it may not be reasonable if a part of the building has to be torn down to install the ramp. This reasonable accommodation requirement extends to potential employees in that qualified job applicants should not be turned down just because of their disability or religious belief when reasonable accommodation would allow them to do the job properly.

The need for reasonable accommodation for disability applies to more than people with physical disabilities; the needs of people with mental disabilities, temporary illnesses, addictions, and obesity also must be considered.

## Communication to Potential Employees

It is important for organizations to provide truthful and relevant information about the organization and the job to the job applicants. Here are a few essential areas to consider for inclusion in a job advertisement. (Some organizations prefer to give more detailed information in subsequent stages of the recruitment and selection process, such as during selection interviews.)

- *About the organization and the position*: Who are we and what are our vision, mission, and strategies? What do we value? What is the organizational culture like? What is the purpose and role of the position being advertised?

- *The psychological contract*: What should the potential employee expect of the organization and of the position? Would the position be a term position or one of indefinite term? What will be the organization's commitment to the new employee? Will there be training and development offered to foster a long-term relationship? What will likely be the employee's career path within the organization?

- *What abilities and skills are needed for the position*: What are the competencies and KSAs required for the job? What levels of experience, education, and training are needed? What other qualities, characteristics, and personal attributes are essential for success in the job?

- *What will likely be offered to the successful candidate*:
  o *Salary and benefits* – As discussed in Chapter 3 regarding motivation, money is an important hygiene factor even if it is not a motivator itself. For people who do not know the organization and its structure, the salary range usually signals to some extent the level of responsibilities of the position. Naturally, higher pay attracts better quality applicants. The decision for the organization is the level of quality needed. For some positions, an average worker is fine and thus it is not necessary to pay higher than the average market rate. But for some critical positions, the organization may be willing to pay well above the market rate to attract the best candidates.
  o *Intrinsic rewards* – What growth, advancement, and learning opportunities does the position provide? Is the work challenging? Does it involve a variety of tasks? Will the incumbent be working independently? Will he or she have team support?
  o *Other terms and conditions* – These include the hours of work, the work location, break times, frequency of pay, and other logistical or administrative aspects.

- *What process should be followed*: Is a detailed resume or a simple application form expected? Where will the applications be sent or delivered? Will email or faxed applications be welcome? Usually, the complexity of the process should decrease with the level or rank of the position. For example, for part-time entry-level positions the process should be as simple as possible or no one will bother to apply.

Proper communication helps potential job applicants understand the job and greatly reduces the number of mismatched applications, saving time and effort for the potential candidates and the organization's personnel. A good job advertisement also helps to build the organizational image and branding. For example, most customers are inclined to shop with an ethical organization than an organization that uses sweatshops.

## SELECTION

After identifying the pool of potential candidates for the job, the next step is to ensure the most suitable person is selected. Many selection methods are available and involve collection and analysis of biographical data, tests, or interviews.

### Biographical Data

Data available through the job application form or the resume provides a quick and simple means of screening. The person responsible for the screening must understand the requirements of the job and what to look for in the data on which to base the inclusion or exclusion decision. This technique is often used first to screen out the least suitable candidates and to achieve a reasonable number of potential candidates on the shortlist for further selection. Electronic screening of applications is particularly cost effective when there are a large number of applicants.

### Tests

Tests are useful for screening but their use is not without controversy. To ensure tests are useful and not arbitrary, irrelevant, or even discriminatory, they must be reliable and valid. Reliability refers to consistency of the test results. That is, the test result of an individual should not vary from day to day or from occasion to occasion. Neither should the test result vary just because the test is administered by another person. Validity refers to measuring what is intended to be measured. If a test is not reliable, then it cannot be valid. However, a reliable test is not necessarily a valid one. Consider the example of an applicant being asked his or her favourite colour. The answer is likely to be consistent from test to test and thus the question is reliable, but if this colour preference has no relation to his or her ability to perform the job, then the question, and any like it, is not valid. Obviously, or-

119

ganizations want tests that have good predictive validity, meaning the results are good for predicting such areas of interest as future job performance or job tenure. Correlation analysis between the test scores and subsequent performance (or other factors of interest) can be done after the employee has been employed for a period of time to determine if the test is valid for use in future selections. Alternatively, where organizations cannot afford to wait for a period of time to determine the validity of a test measure, correlation analysis on existing employees in similar positions can be conducted to see if their test scores relate to the criteria of interest (e.g., performance). These empirical methods that explicitly correlate test data with the criteria of interest to the organization are used to establish what are commonly called *criterion-related validity*.

Other types of validity are *content validity* and *construct validity*, which are especially useful when empirical data is not available for analysis. Content validity refers to how well the test components directly reflect the actual job characteristics. For example, a test on reading and writing skills has content validity for an editor job. However, it is not always easy to establish a direct link between the contents of the job and the test, especially when the job content cannot be clearly defined operationally. In such cases, more indirect measures are used that focus at the construct level of the traits and characteristics required for the job. For example, an intelligence test has construct validity for a scientist or an inventor position.

Many types of tests are available for employee selection. They are usually classified as follows:

- *Knowledge, skills, and ability (KSA) tests*

  These tests measure the existing level of KSA of the applicant. If hiring a typist, a typing test is a valid test to conduct. Similarly, a test of applicants' technical knowledge is needed when hiring for a technical position. However, the validity of such tests is less easily demonstrated for more complex positions. For example, managerial skills are not readily revealed by a simple test.

- *Aptitude tests*

  Aptitude tests are intended to measure a person's potential to take on the new tasks. These do not test the current KSA per se but instead focus on the ability to learn.

- *Personality tests*

  These psychological tests are intended to measure a person's attitudes, interests, values, temperament, and orientations. For example, it may be useful for an organization to know if the candidate for a sales position has an eagerness to succeed and a pleasant personality. However, since these are basically self-reported tests, there is no assurance that the candidate will be honest in answering the questions. They can intentionally bias the results by selecting answers they feel will be seen favourably by the organization. That is not to say that these tests cannot be valid, but care must be exercised in adopting and utilizing them. If the test is provided by an external vendor, some objective data should be requested to prove the validity of the test.

* *Intelligence tests*

  These tests are intended to measure the intellectual ability of individuals on logical, verbal, or abstract reasoning. In the past, most intelligence tests focus on general intelligence, usually indicated by the intelligence quotient (IQ). Recently, emotional intelligence (EI), which concerns the understanding of one's own emotions as well as the emotions of others and acting in response to such an understanding, has been hailed as an important competency, especially for leaders (see Chapter 4 on Leadership). EI is closely related to social intelligence which emphasizes the social relations dimension. As a result, tests on EI are gaining attention.

Organizations that intend to use tests to screen applicants must not only ensure the tests are valid, they should also be aware of the impact of the tests on the applicants. For example, there are some individuals who personally do not believe in certain types of tests, especially personality tests, and may view such tests as irrelevant or even intrusive. Having too many tests can also deter people from applying for the job or continuing with the recruitment and selection process, especially for relatively junior low-paying positions because potential candidates may not feel the process is worth their efforts.

With the advent of HR technology, many of these tests can now be administered by the candidates themselves as part of the initial screening process. This can provide the organization with a more manageable and yet more qualified applicant pool for selection consideration.

## Interviews

Most organizations use the interview method to help in their hiring decision. Interviews often provide two-way communication. Members of the organization have the opportunity to meet the candidates and ask any questions that help them in making their decision. At the same time, each candidate obtains more information about the organization and the job to help him or her decide whether to join the organization should his or her application be successful.

A common form of interview is the *structured* type. The interviewer or the panel of interviewers prepares a list of questions in advance that are asked of all candidates. This ensures that the essential aspects are covered and that all applicants receive the same basic treatment. However, many organizations like the flexibility of asking additional questions as appropriate, depending on the responses to the initial set of questions. In that case, the interview takes the form of a semi-structured interview.

Although interviews provide relevant information on the KSA of the individual, more often interviewers hope that the interview will help their assessment of how the individual fits with the organization. However such an assessment is not always reliable considering that the candidate is likely on his or her best behaviour, which does not always reflect his or her true nature. Interestingly, the general belief is that interviewers tend to form their decision within minutes of seeing the job applicant, long before many questions have been asked. That is why job applicants often care much about first impression management. While interviews do not guarantee that the most truthful information is presented, experienced interviewers using appropriate questions and techniques can often solicit additional valuable information. For example, using behavioural type of questions, the candidate is asked to describe a situation where he or she handled a challenging matter in his or her past job. Alternatively, the candidate is given some hypothetical situations, which are usually quite reflective of the actual job, and asked to provide a response on the action to be taken. The advantage of asking about past behaviours is that they can sometimes be confirmed with referees. If the candidate is lying, he or she is usually unable to answer subsequent probing questions satisfactorily.

Interviews, just like any other selection methods, can be biased. Interviewers may carry with them their own prejudices. For example, interviewers may prefer people who are like them although such people are not necessarily the best types of candidates to fill the position in question. Interviewers may also not be trained well and may not know exactly what to look for. Hence, the effectiveness of the selection process is quite dependent upon the selection of the interviewer or panel of interviewers. To avoid problems with individual bias, organizations often resort to using multiple interviewers, especially for more important positions. Since the decision is based on the panel's view rather than an individual's, the chances of bias are reduced as interviewers keep each other in check. By discussing the merits of each individual, initial biases may be subsequently reduced. If the interviewers are experienced and well trained, the inter-rater reliability in the selection of the most suitable candidate should be reasonably high.

Interviewers must also be very careful not to ask illegal questions. Questions that ask for demographic information unrelated to the job requirement are prohibited by human rights legislation in most developed nations. Such questions cannot be asked in interviews or any other parts of the selection process. For example, the Canadian Human Rights Act, applicable to organizations under federal jurisdiction, prohibits discrimination based on race, national or ethnic origin, colour, religion, age, sex, sexual orientation, marital status, family status, disability, and conviction for which a pardon has been granted. All the provinces in Canada have similar provisions applicable to organizations in their respective jurisdiction. While interviewers may not ask whether the applicant is married or has children, they may ask if the applicant will be available to work overtime if needed because the latter does not ask about marital or family status and is intended to see if a bona fide occupational requirement can be met. Rather than asking the origin of the applicant or how old the applicant is, the applicant may be asked if he or she is legally eligible to work with the organization. Personal information such as age and family status needed for company documentation (e.g., for insurance coverage or CPP deductions) should be obtained after the person is hired. This can prevent allegations that the information was gathered for discriminatory screening.

In summary interviewers should pay attention to the following:

- Be aware of personal bias.

- Prepare in advance (e.g., attend necessary training; coordinate with other panel members; review the job specification and description).

- Make the candidate feel welcome and comfortable (as this may be the interviewers' future colleague).

- Be willing to listen to both the candidates' responses and the comments and feedback from other interviewers on the panel (one learns more by listening than by talking).

- Do not ask leading questions; the best information is usually obtained from freely provided information.

- Do honestly answer questions that the candidate would like to know about; do not oversell the organization (even if the candidate appears very suitable, overselling leads to unrealistic expectations that can cause dissatisfaction in the long run, and in the worst case, may affect the outcome of lawsuits in the event of wrongful dismissal for misrepresenting the job security issue).

- Do not ask illegal questions.

- Write notes to help with the decision and document the reasons for the decision. (Memory tends to fade after a while and may not always be reliable after a long series of interviews. Moreover, in the event the decision is being challenged, such as by management members or the human rights court, the document can provide a proper defence.)

## *Reference Checks*

Suitable candidates identified up to this stage may undergo reference checks. Usually, such checks require the candidate to name a few referees who can provide information on their work or academic abilities. Almost invariably, such references provide favourable information for the candidate (or they would not have been named in the first place). While references from the current employer are very helpful, such references are not always available especially if the applicant does not want the current employer to know about his or her application before the appointment is finalized. Consideration must also be given to the situation where a biased reference is provided, either because the current employer is not happy about the employee leaving or the employer is too keen to get rid of the employee. Therefore, the true value of reference check is not always without question. Many employers are beginning to fear the legal implications of giving references. If an employee was terminated and a negative reference (or no reference) is provided, lengthening the time the person needs to find alternative employment, the employer may be liable to pay a higher amount for reasonable notice. However, if negative performances are not indicated and the new employer relies on the overall favourable reference for the hiring that turns out to be detrimental, the previous employer may be liable for the new employer's damage, especially if knowledge of the negative performance facts would have prevented the damage. So providing a truthful and objective reference as needed is advisable.

Some organizations also perform other reference checks such as credit checks. Such checks must be shown to be genuinely related to the job position. For example, it may be reasonable for bank applicants but not so for a filing clerk in an educational institute where there is no money or items of cashable value to be handled through that position.

## APPOINTMENT

After the selection decision is made, the organization is almost ready to make an employment offer. Even though the general terms and conditions associated with the job are mostly predetermined, the specific details (e.g., where salary is to be commensurate with experience or working hours can be flexible) need to be determined and negotiated. Prior to the formal appointment, some organizations provide a realistic job preview for the candidate. That is, the candidate meets with fellow coworkers and sees how the work is done in the real setting. If the actual working conditions are not appealing to the candidate, it is to the mutual benefit of both parties to know this prior to making a firm commitment. Realistic job previews can also be done during the interview phase if preferred.

Some organizations require employees to sign an agreement regarding the organizational code of conduct, which may include promises to not divulge confidential company information and to use company property as prescribed. Employers have the prerogative to make HR rules and policies by which employees must abide. However, these rules must be reasonable, properly communicated, and consistently applied. In other words, an employee cannot be punished for violating a company rule when the same action by another employee is condoned.

To assist new employees in settling into the job, the organization may want to provide an orientation program as well as ongoing training and development. These topics are discussed in Chapter 7.

## PROMOTIONS AND TRANSFERS

With changes in the business environment and management philosophy, many organizations seem to have moved away from tall hierarchical structures to flatter structures. Promotions up the career ladder, which once was presumed to be the natural path, are no longer a norm. There are a few HR implications for such changes. First, organizations cannot afford to reward employees with promotions all the time as there are limited positions at the higher level. The limited career advancement opportunity may also prompt employees to seek greener pastures. Nowadays, people tend to change jobs, even careers, much more frequently than in the past. Flatter organizations also mean that each supervisor may have to oversee a larger number of subordinates and proper delegation of responsibilities may be necessary for effective performance.

Organizations always have to strike a good balance between external recruitment and internal promotions. While external recruitment provides new talent that is not available in-house, new employees do not have the same degree of firm-level knowledge, especially in understanding the organizational culture. Moreover, external recruitment can affect staff morale if existing employees who are qualified to do the higher level job are bypassed. Similarly, if there is more than one employee applying for a job, the unsuccessful candidates may have concerns about justice. Hence, transparency in the process and open communication are crucial to ensuring good employee understanding of the reasons for the appointment decision. In other words, employees care not only about substantive justice (the distributed outcome) but also the procedural justice (the distributive process). These concepts are covered in Chapter 3 on Motivation. For the area of promotion, *substantive* or *distributive justice* means that the decision is seen to be based on the merits of the applicants: the most qualified applicant gets the job. As for *procedural justice*, communication of properly set criteria and using well-qualified and respected panels of decision-makers usually enhance the perception of it.

Very often employees in an organization do not have all the necessary information on job applicants to be able to determine if there is distributive justice. However, the perception of procedural justice gives them the confidence that the decision outcome is a fair one; that it comes from a fair process. On the other hand, even if a decision is made in a just way, poor management of the perception of procedural justice can result in the belief that the decision is biased.

Lateral transfers occur for many different reasons. Employees may apply to move to a new vacant position at the same level or organizations may initiate the redeployment based on need. Transfers can also occur for training and development purposes to allow employees to gain more experiences in various job tasks. Transfers to positions that offer good development opportunities may indeed be used as a reward for good performance. As with promotion, how employees are selected for the transfer, whether the transfer is generally considered as favourable or unfavourable from an employee's perspective, needs to be done in a way as perceived to be fair.

Occasionally, employee demotion needs to be considered. Demotion refers to the move of an employee to a level of lower responsibility. Sometimes it occurs due to the personal preference of an employee for a better work-life balance. It can also occur if an employee is not performing up to par, despite proper training and support being given. As demotion is a very sensitive issue, it must be handled with extreme care. Failure to do so may lead not only to employee dissatisfaction, but also to potential legal suits, such as a suit on constructive dismissal. Further information on this aspect is discussed under the termination and performance management areas.

## INTERNATIONAL HRM

With many organizations having branches in various parts of the world, international HRM has become a rather important topic. A key strategic HR decision in international business involves staffing of the subsidiary in other countries. Staffing options include the following (Dowling, Schuler & Welch, 1994; Perlmutter, 1969):

1. *Host-country nationals* (HCNs) – This is a polycentric approach in which each foreign subsidiary is considered unique and deserving of autonomy. Hence, key positions in the subsidiaries are filled by people in those countries who know the local culture and environment well.

2. *Parent-country nationals* (PCNs) – This is an ethnocentric approach in which the parent-country employees are considered most suitable to hold the key positions in the subsidiaries because they know the corporate culture and parent country environment well and their success in the parent company is expected to translate into success in the subsidiary in the foreign country.

3. *Third-country nationals* (TCNs) – This refers to the hiring of individuals from countries other than the parent or host countries for the key positions in the subsidiary, some of whom may have worked in a subsidiary in another country before. This is sometimes associated with a geocentric approach, one with a global perspective, in which the most qualified person gets the job, irrespective of the country of the individual.

Each of the above options has its advantages and disadvantages. HCNs may know how to conduct business in the local environment but may not fully understand the corporate vision, structure, and policies. Communication between the subsidiary and the parent company may be compromised, especially if there are language and cultural barriers. PCNs, on the other hand, allow the parent company to have a high degree of control of the subsidiary situation but the key staff's very limited knowledge of the host country situation may make it difficult for the subsidiary to attract clients and grow the business. TCNs are supposed to have a variety of international experience but, as countries can be quite different from one to another, the experience may only be transferable to some extent.

Many organizations may use some kind of mixed approach. It is not uncommon that the PCN approach is used to start up a subsidiary. Organizations with a high level of firm-specific knowledge or unique corporate vision may particularly find it necessary to send expatriates to the host country to help establish the subsidiary framework and directions as well as to train the successors. Over time host country employees start to fill some key positions as they gain more knowledge about the organization.

## Transfers of PCNs

Issues of *expatriation* and *repatriation* involve not only the employees, but also their families. Environmental factors such as the economic, legal, societal, and cultural climate; organizational factors such as management philosophy, existing policies, and skills inventory and gaps; and employees' personal concerns are all relevant factors to consider in an international transfer decision. The importance of the various issues differs depending on the location of the transfer. In countries where the exchange rate fluctuates steeply or where the cost of living is substantially different from the parent country, determining a fair compensation is difficult. It is commonly expected that an employee will not suffer any economic losses or decrease in the quality of living as a result of an out-of-country transfer. From the legal perspective, many countries have different labour laws and standards. For example, human rights, the existence of which is often taken for granted in many developed countries, may not be of concern in the less developed nations (e.g., child labour is not viewed as a serious issue). Gifts to business contacts, that may be considered bribes in some countries, may well be an expected custom in others. Expatriate employees also have to go through proper immigration or visa application procedures to ensure that the right to work in the country in question is obtained. Societal concerns stem from the expectations of the host country citizens. Some people do not like the idea of having foreigners coming in to tell them what to do, while in other places people from the parent country are seen as having the expertise to help with the country's growth and development.

Cultural problems are often the most difficult to overcome because culture is ingrained into every aspect of work and life for the expatriate and his or her family. Compared to the spouse and children, the expatriate himself or herself often has less trouble adapting to the new environment because he or she (a) is very busy with the new work, (b) has colleagues in the new workplace to familiarize him or her with cultural issues, and (c) has other expatriate colleagues to keep him or her company or advise him or her of issues of concern. Often, the spouse finds himself or herself without similar support. He or she may have given up a good job just to be with the expatriate in the transfer. Without a supportive network, it is difficult for the expatriate's family to overcome the obstacles. Any family issues can easily affect work performance. Therefore, prior to any international transfer decisions, good information exchange must happen to ensure that the employee and his or her spouse are aware of the potential changes. Culture sensitivity training, language training, and training on understanding the various environment dimensions of the new workplace are necessary, not just for the employee, but also the spouse as well. Some organizations go as far as providing support to the spouse in seeking a meaningful job in the new place or in finding a suitable school for the children. Expatriates should also be provided with a good understanding of what is expected of him or her in the new country as a new resident and as a new manager or colleague. For example, what is the tax law like? Can they say things freely without concern about political reprisal?

To help understand cultural differences, Hofstede (1980) highlights four main dimensions of the differences:

*Power Distance*: It is the degree people in a country accept unequal power and respect people of higher authority. Countries like China have a high power distance where the leaders or people of the older generation are often highly regarded, whereas countries like the U.S. have a low power distance as equality is a valued principle.

*Individualism versus Collectivism*: Does the society emphasize the rights and interests of individuals or the collective group? Relationships tend to be "looser" in individualistic cultures as people are more concerned about each person's own right and individuality. Most cultures in the Orient are generally regarded as more collective than the North American culture, which is known for individualism.

*Uncertainty Avoidance*: How well is uncertainty and ambiguity tolerated in the society? In countries with high uncertainty avoidance, one may expect to have more rules and laws to maintain structure and order. It will generally be risk-averse and less tolerant of diversity in opinions or actions. Countries like Japan, where people are generally expected to follow a number of rules and traditions, rank high in this dimension whereas countries like Denmark, which has a high degree of freedom in many aspects, rank low in this dimension.

*Masculinity versus Femininity*: This dimension arises from the inherent differences between the genders. It can also be described by terms such as the career success and the quality of life dimension. The male gender is linked with assertiveness, competition, money, and success-orientation while the female gender is related to caring, nurturing, building relationships, and having a good quality of life. Thus cultures that emphasize these different aspects may be described in masculine or feminine terms. The Japanese and North America cultures are generally regarded as masculine whereas places like Norway and Sweden are considered more feminine.

A fifth dimension was added later to this list (Hofstede, 1993; Hofstede & Bond, 1988):

*Long-Term versus Short-Term Orientation*: This refers to how the people in a country generally perceive the importance of achieving long-term or short-term fulfillment and the degree people adhere to traditional work values (hence, this dimension is also called *Confucian Dynamism*). Places like Hong Kong and Japan rank high as they tend to emphasize hard work, investing for longer term benefits, and saving money for future needs. The Chinese tradition also tends to consider education (a Confucian virtue) as a key investment for future success. Youngsters are also taught not to spend every penny earned. This is quite in contrast with the North American culture where many students have to earn their way through the university and, with the widespread use of credit cards, spending in advance of the payday is considered a common experience.

Finally, in 2010, a sixth dimension was added, based on Michael Minkov's *World Values Survey* data analysis (Hofstede, 2011, p. 16; Hofstede, Hofstede, & Minkov, 2010):

*Indulgence versus Restraint*: This refers to the extent people in a nation freely allow the pursuit of gratification of needs and basic human drives. Countries with a high score on indulgence (e.g., generally those "in South and North America, in Western Europe and in parts of Sub-Sahara Africa") tend to place emphasis on the enjoyment of life through gratification while countries with a high score for restraint (e.g., generally those "in Eastern Europe, in Asia and in the Muslim world") tend to have stricter social norms that may suppress or regulate such gratification.

A good understanding of culture according to these fundamental dimensions may help an expatriate appreciate the differences and adapt more easily to the new environment.

In sum, organizations can prepare expatriate staff for an international transfer by alleviating uncertainty and anxiety through such actions as providing culture-transition training, housing, child care, spousal employment assistance, personal services, extended home and vacation leaves, travelling allowances, and better salaries and benefits including currency protection and tax equalization (Guzzo, Noonan, & Elron, 1994).

## Repatriation

No expatriation should be considered without a corresponding consideration of repatriation and the long-term plan for the parent-host relationship. Many organizations do not plan well into the future and are too optimistic to think about "what if it doesn't work out?" Once the expatriate's parent company position has been filled, it may not be easy for him or her to return to it or a comparable position, especially if that position is very senior and carries with it a very specialized knowledge in a field or profession. If the transfer is only for a limited term, then proper succession planning is really crucial, as there can be a chain of displacements and redeployment involved. Expatriates with children also need to plan for their education. Some may want to settle down in the new country for at least a period of time, while many just want to gain a few years of overseas experience and return to their home country. An open communication discussing the terms of repatriation is needed. Some repatriation options may need to be committed upfront in order to entice the initial transfer.

Upon an expatriate's return to the home country a re-orientation is at times required, especially if the individual has been away for a long time and has not often visited the parent company office during the expatriate term. Occasionally, repatriation may be initiated by the company and not the employee. In such cases, the employee may not be happy to be back. If he or she may have settled down well in the foreign land or married a host country citizen; or the quality of life in the foreign place is actually better than the home country situation. In such situations, the organization needs to understand the concerns and motivation of the individual and try to address them in the most helpful and equitable manner.

## HUMAN RESOURCE OUTFLOW

HR outflow refers to the process of employees exiting the organization. It can be due to retirement, resignation, expiry of contract term, dismissal for cause, and termination or layoffs for reasons such as restructuring.

### Retirement

Retirement is usually a situation that allows planning on the part of both the employee and the organization. Employees about to leave the organization can act as a mentor or coach to their potential successors to pass on as much tacit knowledge as possible. The retiring employee can also be asked to help build the organization's explicit knowledge base by writing handover notes, procedures manuals, software programs, or other documents and to capture and highlight some of the best practices learned through his or her experience.

Retirement can be a strategic component to consider for an organization. In an economic downturn, some organizations offer early retirement options to all or selected employee groups. Such options often involve some financial incentives, such as a lump sum payment or little or no reduction of pension benefits. Early retirement has the advantage of bringing down the employment size without involuntary termination of employees and can occur much faster than using natural attrition to downsize the workforce. The downside to it is that employees who accept the offer may be the more productive ones, who are likely to be able to find comparable employment easily, or who may want to start self-employment. If this is not done with careful planning, key employees with special expertise may leave. Various scenarios must be considered before the offer and any conditions clearly communicated.

On the other hand, organizations may be in a situation where they need more employees than they can find. With an aging population, retirement of the boomers may lead to further shortage of skilled manpower. Rather than lose an employee outright at one point in time, some organizations provide a transitional phase for retirement: bridge retirement or phased retirement which allows the employee to continue working at reduced hours for a period of time. Such an arrangement can help the organization meet the labour demand, allow training time for successors, and help the retiring employee go through an important change in life by providing a good adjustment period.

Retirement arrangements are sometimes curtailed by *mandatory retirement* in collective agreements or employer policies. While mandatory retirement is prohibited in the United States, mandatory retirement (normally at age 65) was quite a common practice in most Canadian jurisdictions until recently. By the end of 2012, all Canadian jurisdictions except New Brunswick are expected to have banned this practice (Carlson, 2011) because it can be considered age discrimination, which violates human rights principles and more specifically the Charter of Rights and Freedoms. Some provinces, though, have provisions for certain exceptions, such as when it is supported by bone fide occupational reasons. This may apply to cases where the occupations have a very high demand on physical or mental strength (CBC, 2010). Still, proving such may be difficult and it awaits to be seen how further cases will develop in the foreseeable future.

## Resignation

Many workers no longer expect to have a job for life. Instead, people tend to change jobs, employers, or even careers quite a few times. When demand for labour in the market is high, top employees and specialized professionals are often "headhunted" to go elsewhere. Competitors offer better pay and incentives to lure away even junior employees. Employee retention can present a serious challenge to organizations if they do not prepare for such market demands and labour competition. Often, organizations have to do the right things all along to retain their employees rather than trying to make a last minute effort when an employee has indicated the intention to leave. Good ongoing efforts to motivate employees by treating them fairly both tangibly and intangibly, fostering a good working relationship based on trust and open communication, and providing a good working environment as well as opportunities for growth and accomplishment are just some of the essential ways to prevent employees from going elsewhere. Organizations or industries in particularly volatile markets should be even more cognizant of the unpredicted changes and establish various labour contingency plans.

When employees want to leave the organization, it is very beneficial for the employer to understand why employees choose to leave. A properly conducted exit interview provides such information and sheds light on whether there is anything the organization needs to do to prevent other employees from feeling the same way and leaving the organization in the future. For example, if it is revealed that quite a few departing employees have obtained jobs that pay double the salary for the same levels of responsibilities, a review of the compensation may be needed. Similarly, if employees are generally dissatisfied with some working conditions, such as safety concerns, those would certainly need to be addressed.

## Dismissal

The terms *dismissal* and *termination* are at times used interchangeably. However, termination of employment is initiated by either the employer or the employee whereas dismissal is initiated unilaterally by the employer. Dismissals can be for just cause or otherwise. In *just cause dismissals*, also called *summary dismissals*, the employee, due to his or her wrongdoing, is not compensated in monetary terms for the loss of employment nor is any notice of termination required.[1] A number of grounds may constitute just cause: wilful misconduct, gross misrepresentation of qualifications, gross incompetence, and breaching of safety, confidentiality, or other important company rules (see Palmer and Palmer (1991) for more information on just cause dismissals and other forms of discipline, especially related to the union setting.) However, employers must be very careful about any dismissal situations and do things the proper way. For example, if an employer feels an employee is grossly incompetent, it is unlikely that the employee can be dismissed without first being warned of the substandard performance, being given proper training to help him or her achieve better performance, and being given the opportunity to demonstrate improvement in his or her performance (such as by providing a reasonable time frame). If an employee has violated some important company rules, the employer often needs to go through a process called *progressive discipline*, in which the first offence results in a verbal warning and subsequent offences lead to more progressive forms of discipline, such as written reprimand, followed by suspension, and finally dismissal. That is not to say that employers cannot fire someone for a first time offence under any circumstances. If the offence involves something of very serious potential consequences, such as a pilot being caught drunk while on duty, a just cause dismissal can be justified given that the violation can cause death or bodily harm to others.

---

1  In some countries, such as New Zealand, redundancy due to operational need can be a just cause for dismissal. This is, however, not the case in Canada, in which termination due to redundancy still requires a reasonable notice or pay in lieu of notice.

In discipline cases, it is of utmost importance that the employee being disciplined is given the opportunity to tell his or her side of the story, that there is due process to handle such situations. Employees disciplined must also be informed as to the consequences of subsequent violations, so there are no surprises. Good documentation of the offences and disciplinary measures taken must be made. Organizations often end up paying huge sums of money awarded in wrongful dismissal suits not because the employee does not deserve to be fired, but because proper disciplinary records have not been maintained. The worst case scenario for HR is when there is poor communication between line departments and HR and no proper poor performance records have been kept. By the time HR hears about a dismissal situation, it may already be too late to take any remedial action.

Different countries have different legal provisions for terminations other than for just cause. The U.S. largely embraces the employment-at-will concept, which means that employers can hire and fire anytime they wish without being concerned about wrongful dismissal suits, other than in very limited situations such as when it violates some other human rights or public policy legislation. Canada, on the other hand, recognizes all employment as indefinite unless otherwise specified (e.g., term employment). Notice of termination or wages in lieu of notice is required if the employer's unilateral termination is not for cause or where cause has not been established. The employment standards legislation in various jurisdictions provides the minimal standard of termination notice, which tends to increase with tenure. These are usually applicable to only employees below the management level.

Collective agreements between employers and unions and individual employment contracts can have provisions exceeding the minimum standards as provided by legislation. For example, for very senior positions the "golden handcuff" kind of contract may require both parties to provide notice or wages in lieu of notice up to one or two years for termination of the employment relations. Even in the absence of a notice of termination clause, such a clause can still be implied and acted upon in the common law court in Canada for non-unionized organizations. (For union settings, instead of bringing the suit to the courts, the employee has to bring the grievance to the union, which may escalate it to final binding arbitration as necessary.) Awards as high as two years or so of notice, or wages in lieu, have been given in some situations. Here are some factors of consideration cited in court decisions in giving the awards (Lam & Devine, 2001):

- tenure of the employee
- level of the position
- age of the employee

- difficulty of the employee in finding alternative employment
- manner the employee was treated in the dismissal (that is, whether the termination was acted on in bad faith)
- hiring circumstances (whether the employee, even if terminated while on probation, was lured into the employment with insincere promises of stable employment and career opportunities)
- other mitigating factors (such as whether the employee has been actively in search of work to reduce the potential income loss)

Particularly worth mentioning are two landmark cases on wrongful dismissal regarding the treatment of the terminated employees. In *Wallace v. United Grain Growers Ltd.* [1997], the Supreme Court of Canada explicitly extended the reasonable notice period to compensate for the emotional trauma and mental stress the terminated employee had gone through in a situation where the termination for just cause dismissal was not proven and the employer had treated the employee callously in the termination process (Humber, 2006). This sparked a number of lawsuits in the following decade seeking extension of the notice period under the *Wallace* factor as well as controversy on whether such an extension in place of a separate claim for damage is indeed appropriate. The *Honda Canada Inc. v. Keays* [2008] case finally clarified the Supreme Court's latest position by separating the claim for mental distress or other damage from the reasonable notice that was simply to compensate for lost earnings (Rudner, 2008). Irrespective of the channel of claim, it is clear that bad faith manner of dismissal would result in increased cost for the employer. Even without these legal precedents, employers should still treat employees fairly and with respect as this can be regarded a fundamental aspect of the psychological contract between the employer and employee and a critical element in the proper management of an organization's valuable human resources.

### Constructive Dismissal

Constructive dismissal is a wrongful dismissal situation where an employer unilaterally changes one or more fundamental terms and conditions of employment that adversely affect the employee in a way that the employee feels he or she must quit the job rather than accept the changes. In such situations, it is important for the employee to indicate his or her concerns as soon as possible. If the employee silently takes on the new terms, he or she will probably be unsuccessful in later suing for constructive dismissal. Basically, constructive dismissal protects employees from being in effect forced to resign by the employer. It ensures that they at least get appropriate notice or compensation for their job loss that results purely from the employer's action. The court considers this type of situation as a dismissal rather than a regular resignation.

There is no hard and fast rule on what constitutes constructive dismissal. The unilateral change that deviates from the original employment contract must be significant enough that the employee feels he or she has no choice but to leave. One reasonable question to consider is whether the change is so large that the employee probably would not have taken the job in the first place had the new terms and conditions been in place at the time of employment. Demotion, substantial decrease in salary, a significant change in the job nature, a relocation involving an unreasonable distance, and a marked change in working hours are among possible reasons for a constructive dismissal suit. While employers can always provide a notice period or pay in lieu of notice that is generally adequate under common law to initiate the change (as if it were a case of termination), this approach is rather time-consuming or expensive. To prevent unnecessary constructive dismissal suits in a constantly changing environment, employers need to be careful in communicating employment terms and conditions and need to build in some flexibility in their employment contracts. Managers also need to be aware of not only the legal obligations regarding dismissals, but also the moral commitments as well, especially if an organization values its employees. A good organization simply does not force its employees out without providing adequate notice or some kind of support.

## DOWNSIZING AND RESTRUCTURING

To most people, downsizing simply means the reduction of the workforce. Cameron (1994a, 1994b), however, provides a broader definition that downsizing refers to intentional changes by organizations to reduce resources or resource use. It involves a set of activities aimed at not just reducing expenses, but also improving efficiency, productivity, and competitiveness. Both workforce size and work processes are involved. He further identifies three strategies organizations used for downsizing (1994b):

1. *Workforce reduction* focuses on the staff head count, using methods such as attrition, buy-out packages, early retirement, layoffs, etc. Some methods take longer while an across-the-board cut is quick. However, the latter approach can have many undesirable repercussions. For example, it is difficult to predict or decide on who will go. Without corresponding work redesign, remaining workers have to take on extra work, easily leading to burn out or necessary work just falling through the cracks. Workforce

reduction may also violate the implicit employment contract, leading to lower morale and poor staff commitment.

2.  *Work redesign* focuses on reducing work as well as reducing staff. Functions, tasks, and hierarchical levels are eliminated or consolidated to achieve greater efficiency. This is usually a medium term strategy since the redesign takes time.

3.  *Systemic change* focuses on changing "the organization culture, and the attitudes and values of the employees" (p. 199). This is an ongoing continuous improvement process that takes long-term commitment and involves everyone in the organization trying to simplify everything, often through bottom-up changes.

In terms of change approaches, Freeman and Cameron (1993) identify three general types:

*   *Change in work* – job tasks eliminated, combined, or changed
*   *Change in technology* – automation of work to reduce labour needs; better material and information management using technology
*   *Change in structure* – use of effective teams; eliminate hierarchical levels; consolidate departments/units

Cameron (1994b) finds that across the board cuts to staffing tend to be associated with organizational dysfunction while effective downsizing firms tend to invest on systemic planning; focus on participation, communication, and increased employee efforts; implement gradual changes; and emphasize a quality culture. In sum, critical factors to successful downsizing include "employee involvement, teamwork, communication and information sharing, rewarding, appraising training, articulating a vision and administrating downsizing in a trustworthy and fair manner" (p. 210). Similarly, Cascio (2005, p. 48) suggests that organizations wanting to restructure responsibly should take the following steps:

1.  Carefully analyze the need and impact of restructuring.
2.  Consider the benefits of stability versus the benefits of change.
3.  Communicate with employees and seek their input in advance of restructuring: "Sometimes workers have insightful ideas that may make layoffs unnecessary."
4.  Not use quick downsizing to fix a long-term problem.
5.  Ensure the process and decisions of layoff are perceived to be fair and consistent.
6.  Keep communicating about new developments.

7. Ensure the firm continues to be attractive to survivors and prospective new hires.

8. Train employees to adapt to the new ways of doing things.

9. Review and modify various HR systems to ensure they are aligned with the new organizational strategies and direction.

Additional factors to consider in a downsizing situation are legal constraints, union presence, and survivor syndrome. When massive layoffs are intended, advance notice to a government department or the organization's employees may be required in some jurisdictions. In union settings, collective agreements negotiated may have provisions on the steps the organization must follow before layoffs can take place. This may involve consulting or informing the union and providing necessary compensation to employees for outplacement. Seniority rules may apply as to who will be selected to go (often the most junior members). Complications can arise in such a setting if the junior members in a job category tend to be in a more specialized unit. A more senior member does not necessarily have the job-specific knowledge or skills to take on the job. Also, is bumping allowed? That is, if a position is identified as redundant, can the incumbent bump another more junior member in another job or unit? If so, there will be substantial chain effects, causing major work disruptions. If the downsizing process is not done properly, grievances may arise, leading to not only further administrative concerns, but also more anxiety and frustration for the employees. Hence, in situations like this, rather than working against the union, it is a good idea to get their involvement by having open honest communication regarding the organizational challenges, the need to downsize, and what ways can be used to achieve the goal.

Most organizational downsizing focuses on the leavers rather than the survivors. There is usually the assumption that the survivors are more than happy to be remaining and will try their best to work hard to stay on. While this may be true to some extent, research has found that *survivor syndrome* is common as an aftermath of downsizing. Survivors may feel anxiety, guilt, anger, or relief (Brockner, 1986). They may be anxious of their chances of staying in the next round of layoffs. They may feel guilty because they think they do not deserve to stay while their friends and colleagues are laid off. They may feel angry and betrayed because they know employees' years of loyalty and hard work are not reciprocated by management in terms of proper reward or job security. To prevent or alleviate the situation, management must be sensitive to the remaining employees' emotions and try to revitalize the workforce. Emphasizing procedural justice in the layoff process and maintaining good and advance communication with employees (both leavers and survivors) can likely reduce the negative emotions of the survivors. Treating the leavers well and offering them outplacement assistance also sends a message to the survivors that the organization is a good employer and will care for them in the event that they cannot be retained at some time in the future for economic or other reasons. Indeed, if done well, downsizing can be seen as an opportunity for greater competitiveness and for future growth and success.

## UNIONS AND HRF

Unions, where present in the workplace, have various impacts on the HRF, some of which have been briefly mentioned above. For the purpose of union survival and prosperity, unions often try to negotiate union security clauses in their collective agreement with the employers. There are three general types of union security clauses, namely, *closed shop*, *union shop*, and *agency shop* provisions. A closed shop provision requires the employer to hire only union members for the bargaining unit jobs. (Such provisions are lawful in Canada, but are forbidden in some countries.) A union shop provision allows the employer to hire anyone but the new employee must join the union either upon employment or within a certain period of time. An agency shop provision, also called the *Rand formula* in Canada (named after Judge Rand who made a judicial decision in this regard back in the 1940s), allows employees in the bargaining unit to not join the union but requires them to pay full or partial union dues nonetheless. This is because the union, as the exclusive bargaining agent of the entire unit, needs to represent all employees (union or non-union) of the unit and agency shop provisions prevent the injustice arising from free-riding. If a closed shop provision is in place, the pool of potential recruits available to the employer is limited to members of a union. In situations where the union is reputable for screening qualified workers, such as in some professions, this may not be a drawback at all. It can even ascertain the level of qualifications and expertise of the job candidates. In union shop or agency shop settings, it is important for the employer to advise potential job applicants of the union setting and the associated commitments new employees need to make in terms of union membership and dues.

Clauses in the collective agreement also affect promotion situations. It is not uncommon for unions to negotiate seniority clauses for promotions to reward employees' long service. There are three general types of such clauses (Palmer & Palmer, 1991, pp. 493-497):

- *Sufficient ability seniority clause* – This clause is worded in such a way that the employer is required to promote the most senior person amongst all applicants who have met the qualifications necessary for the job. In other words, it does not matter who is the best in performing the job.

- *Relative ability seniority clause* – This clause is worded so that seniority is only the governing factor in situations where the candidates' qualifications are considered equal. In other words, ability is the main concern and seniority is only a tie-breaker.

- *Hybrid clause* – A hybrid clause lists a number of factors, usually including both qualifications and seniority, as criteria for promotion consideration. The employer must provide reasonable consideration of all the factors and the proper weight attached to them.

Understandably, where criteria are not stated clearly, the interpretation of these clauses can give rise to many disagreements between employers and the unions. In particular, the hybrid clause can be subject to many challenges. Even when the criteria are clearly stated, measurement of qualifications and ability or even seniority (e.g., if an employee has worked in part-time or casual capacities or across different bargaining units) is still open to argument.

Unions can also be a watchdog for unfair disciplinary decisions, including dismissals. Collective agreements often contain specific provisions that spell out the disciplinary process (such as progressive discipline) and the levels of penalties. In situations where a collective agreement disallows termination other than for just cause and a dismissal happens that was not warranted, an arbitrator can substitute lesser penalties or even require the employee be reinstated. Such arrangements are quite different from those in the non-union setting where monetary compensation is usually the remedy for loss or damage.

As discussed above, unions can play a vital role in layoffs. Collective agreement provisions may require advance notification or consultation or specific order of layoffs (e.g., by seniority). Even absent such provisions, it is still a good idea to have the union involved in such major decisions. This ensures any good alternatives the union and employees put forth are properly considered and that the rationale for the layoff is well understood so implementation is as least disruptive or harmful as possible.

## STAFF RETENTION CHALLENGES AND STRATEGIES

As the baby boomer generation retires, one of the major challenges organizations face is the attraction and retention of competent staff. In this new economy, knowledge workers are often recognized as key employees to drive organization success. Because much of an organization's knowledge is tacit or unrecorded knowledge residing with the employees, the organization can ill afford losing such valuable assets. The retention issue is of particular concern in booming economies where labour shortages are likely to be more severe.

Withers (2001) indicates that retention strategies must respond to worker values. Such strategies include the following:

- proactively providing workers a better work-life balance
- promoting a sense of deeper cause (make work more meaningful)
- creating opportunities for growth and development
- treating employees more as partners rather than a factor of production
- initiating coordinated efforts to build a workplace community (with more interaction)
- building or rebuilding trust through ethics and fairness.

Along similar lines, Mathis, Jackson and Zinni (2008, pp. 55-60) provide a more elaborate list of drivers of retention as shown in Table 6-2:

**Table 6-2  Drivers of Retention**

| Characteristics of the employer | Culture and value (e.g., provides good work environment, treats employees well) Management and leadership: clear vision and effective management Job security |
|---|---|
| Work design | Matching employees with jobs Time flexibility and other job arrangements or benefits for better work-life balance |
| Career opportunities | Training and development (including, for example, mentoring) Career planning and opportunities for advancement |
| Rewards | Competitive pay and benefits (considering both external and internal equity) Good performance management system (with procedural and distributive justice) Recognition (through both tangible or intangible rewards) |
| Employee relationships | Supervisor and management support Positive co-worker relationships Fair, inclusive, and non-discriminatory workplace |

There is no single road map to retention success, but the above framework provides food for thought in this area. As many of the points mentioned have long-term implications (e.g., trust-building), staff retention should be an ongoing concern and not just a one-time initiative in response to the business cycle or a temporary labour market fluctuation.

## CONCLUSION

As HR is likely the most important resource to an organization, HRF, which helps to obtain and retain valuable employees and place them in the right positions, is a critical organizational process. It requires careful and thorough planning as well as fair and proper administration of each component of the process. It is not sufficient to just recruit and select the right person. To maximize the contribution by the individual, proper orientation as well as training and development must be provided and promotion or growth opportunities offered as appropriate. Organizations face a number of challenges in the HRF area that must be proactively addressed. These include globalization (which prompts the need for international HRF), keen market competition (which tends to emphasize lean production through downsizing), and labour shortage (which demands good retention strategies). Ongoing attention to government regulations, such as changes to mandatory retirement and other human rights provisions, and case law is necessary to be responsive to the legal environment. In a union setting, as most HRF decisions have a direct effect on the employees and likely involve the collective agreement provisions, involving the union in major HRF decisions is a wise choice to ensure better buy-in and smoother implementation of changes.

# HRM in Action
## International HRM at Siemens

Siemens is an integrated technology company with over 400,000 employees in about 190 countries. Managing such a big workforce worldwide is not a simple task. Its global strategy and approach are briefly described along the following few areas:

*Centralization/decentralization*: Siemen's strategy can generally be considered geocentric and transnational, with interdependent global units well connected and coordinated through a Corporate HR department and a network of HR councils. Although there is strong central control, local adaptations are allowed as warranted. More importantly, regional and local HR staff and top managers are involved in developing global HR policies.

*Talent management*: To leverage employee talent from all over the world, Siemens adopts a global integrated system/platform for various HR initiatives, including goal and performance management, compensation management, career development, succession planning, and recruitment management. In particular, the global recruitment platform supports cross-border recruitment and deployment based on the company's worldwide recruiting standard and a defined recruitment process. Worldwide training and development programs are also established to help employees develop skills in business learning that can be applied to their specific region and be used for managing/collaborating across border. Just in the 2010 fiscal year, over 2000 employees participated in Siemen's Core Learning programs involving seven areas of core competence: Sales/Account Management, Manufacturing, Research & Development, Human Resources, Project Management, General Management, and Procurement/Supply Chain Management/Logistics. Moreover, easily accessible training is offered through an online global learning portal with more than 1,000 options including leadership excellence, business, and product training courses.

*Diversity management*: At Siemens, diversity is considered a factor for success and it wants its employees to reflect the diversity of its customer base. It has a Chief Diversity Officer for global diversity management and a diversity balance scorecard that focuses on tracking and analyzing diversity-related data. Fundamental employee rights are standardized across the world, but flexibility is built-into their HR policies to meet employees' diverse needs, such as to provide a good work-life balance.

Sources:
Farndale, E., & Oaauwe, J. (2005). *The role of corporate HR functions in multinational corporations: The interplay between corporate, regional/nation and plant level* [Centre for Advanced Human Resource Studies Working Paper Series, Paper 477]. Retrieved February 10, 2012 from http://digitalcommons.ilr.cornell.edu/cahrswp/477
Marks, O. (June 8, 2009). *Siemen's global success factors cloud.* Retrieved February 10, 2012 from http://www.zdnet.com/blog/collaboration/siemens-global-successfactors-cloud/617
Mueller, H. (2001). *Developing global human resource strategies* [Discussion paper for European International Business Academy 27th Annual Meeting]. Retrieved February 10, 2012 from http://hemueller.de/files/eibaihrm.pdf

## References

Beer, M., Spector, B., Lawrence, P., Quinn Mills, D., & Walton, R. E. (1985). *Human resource management: A general manager's perspective.* New York: The Free Press.

Belcourt, M., & McBey, K. (2000). *Strategic human resources planning* (2nd ed.). Toronto, ON: Nelson Thomson.

Brockner, J. (1986). The impact of layoffs on the survivors. *Supervisory Management, 31*(2), 2-7.

Bruce, D. (2006, October). *SME succession: Update* (Canadian Federation of Independent Business Research Report). Retrieved July 6, 2007 from http://www.cfib.ca/success/pdf/succession-2006-10.pdf

Calson, K. B. (2011, December 18). Tories ends forced retirement, decades of 'age discrimination'. *National Post.* Retrieved January 17, 2012 from http://news.nationalpost.com/2011/12/18/tories-end-forced-retirement-decades-of-age-discrimination/

Cameron, K. S. (1994a). Investigating organization downsizing: Fundamental issues [Guest editor's note]. *Human Resource Management, 33*(2), 183-188.

Cameron, K. S. (1994b). Strategies for successful organizational downsizing. *Human Resource Management, 33*(2), 189-211.

Cascio, W. F. (2005). Strategies for responsible restructuring. *Academy of Management Executive, 19*(4), 39-50.

CBC. (2010, October 18). *Mandatory retirement fades in Canada.* Retrieved January 17, 2012 from http://www.cbc.ca/news/canada/story/2009/08/20/mandatory-retirement-explainer523.html

Dowling, P. J., Schuler, R. S. & Welch, D. E. (1994). *International dimensions of human resource management* (2nd ed.). Belmont, CA: Wadsworth.

Employment Equity Act, Consolidated Statutes of Canada 1995, c. 44.

Freeman, S. J., & Cameron, K. S. (1993). Organizational downsizing: A converging and reorientation framework. *Organization Science, 4*(1), 10-29.

Greer, C. R. (2001). *Strategic human resource management: A general managerial approach* (2nd ed.). Upper Saddle River, NJ: Prentice Hall.

Guzzo, R. A., Noonan, K. A., & Elron, E. (1994). Expatriate managers and the psychological contract. *Journal of Applied Psychology, 79*(4), 617-626.

Heiden, S. (May 2007). *Leveraging successful succession planning.* Retrieved June 7, 2007 from Talent Management, Succession Planning website: http://www.talentmgt.com/succession_planning/2007/May/318/index.php

Hofstede, G. H. (1980). *Culture's consequences: International differences in work-related values.* Newbury Park, CA: Sage.

Hofstede, G. H. (1993). Cultural constraints in management theories. *Academy of Management Executive, 7*(1), 81-94.

Hofstede, G. (2011). Dimensionalizing cultures: The Hofstede model in context. *Online Readings in Psychology and Culture, Unit 2.* Retrieved May 1, 2012 from http://scholarworks.gvsu.edu/orpc/vol2/iss1/8

Hofstede, G. H., & Bond, M. H. (1988). The Confucius connection: From cultural roots to economic growth. *Organizational Dynamics, 16*(4), 5-21.

Hofstede, G. H., Hofstede, G. J., & Minkov, M. (2010). *Cultures and organizations: Software of the mind* (3rd ed.). New York: McGraw Hill.

Humber, T. (2006, November). How Wallace changed the wrongful dismissal landscape. *Canadian HR Reporter* [Canada's Employment Lawyers Directory], 14.

Ibarra, P. (2007). The myths and realities of succession planning. *Public Management, 89*(1), 24-27.

Korn/Ferry International. (2010, December, 21). *Korn/Ferry survey reveals more interest than action in CEO succession planning among top companies.* Retrieved May 1, 2012 from http://www.kornferry.com/PressRelease/11916

Lam, H., & Devine, K. (2001). Reasonable notice for wrongful dismissal: Court versus human resource decisions. *Relations Industrielles/Industrial Relations, 56*(2), 365-390.

Mathis, R. L., Jackson, J. H., & Zinni, D. M. (2008). *Human resource management* (Canadian ed.). Toronto, ON: Nelson Thomson.

Palmer, E. E., & Palmer, B. M. (1991). *Collective agreement arbitration in Canada* (3rd ed.). Toronto, ON: Butterworths.

Pfeffer, J. (1994). *Competitive advantage through people.* Boston: Harvard Business School Press

Perlmutter, H. V. (1969). Some management problems in spaceship Earth: The megafirm and the global industrial estate. *Academy of Management Proceedings, 12,* 59-87.

Rudner, S. (2008). Courts adopt 'moderate' approach to HR. *Canadian HR Reporter, 21*(14), 3.

Weinstein, M. (2006). What's next? Finding success in succession planning. *Training, 43*(7), 40-44.

Withers, P. (2001). Retention strategies that respond to worker values. *Workforce, 80*(7), 36-41.

*Chapter 6*

 **Chapter 7**

# Training and Development

## Introduction

Recognizing that employees are a crucial asset to the organization, organizations need to provide their valued employees with good ways of furthering their knowledge and skills. This can be done through proper training and development to increase their human capital. Training and development is often mutually beneficial to both the organization and the employees. The organization will likely get better performance while the employees can have better career progressions. Moreover, there may be legal obligations for organizations to provide necessary training to ensure the employees can do the current job, especially if the training needed is firm-specific and not general training that can be obtained elsewhere by the employee. If an employee loses a job due to being unable to perform the job well, but has not been given the proper training and opportunity to improve, there may be grounds for a wrongful dismissal suit. Also, as employers have a vicarious liability for employees' fault in the event the employee harms a third party, adequate training to ensure safety to both the employees and the people with whom they interact is paramount.

With job security and life-long careers becoming less common in today's economy, employees are more concerned about their overall employability. The new generation may be more interested in working for organizations that provide them with knowledge and skills that will make them employable, whether it is with the current firm or another organization. Although there is the economic argument that organizations providing general and transferable training will risk losing the trained employee if that person decides to leave the organization, not providing training valued by employees would make the firm a much less attractive place to work. Hence, training and development is an important tool for attracting and retaining talent for the organization. Rather than refraining from offering general training and development for fear that it will benefit a competitor when a trained employee leaves, an organization should focus more on being a good employer so that employees would not want to leave.

More importantly, training and development signals to employees their value to the organization. If the organization is willing to spend money and time on their development, it indicates the organization's intention to care for the individuals and treat them as an asset to the organization. Organizations need not only financial capital to flourish, but also human capital. Training and development is one of the ways to increase human capital for the organization. This investment increases productivity via better knowledge and skills as well as higher staff morale and commitment.

This chapter starts out with a discussion on orientation, followed by a look at training and development. The essential considerations in deciding on training and development programs, including needs assessment, suitability of types of programs, instructional design aspects, and program evaluation, will be covered. As training and development cannot be addressed only from the organization's perspective, this chapter will also look at career planning for employees and their career anchors.

## ORIENTATION

Once an employee is hired, he or she needs to be given the opportunity to learn more about the company, be introduced to people, and become familiar with the work culture. This process of acquainting the new employee is the orientation program. Some organizations have a well-developed program (such as the Japanese-style orientation) with formal sessions held to provide the history, vision, and mission of the organization; the culture of the organization; the general expectations of employees; and the terms and conditions of employment. Tours of the various departments may be arranged and colleagues are introduced. On the other hand, some organizations have no orientation at all. The employee is assigned a seat and given tasks as they arise. The employee learns the system by trial and error or by taking the initiative to ask. Many organizations have a less formal kind of orientation, usually involving HR explaining some terms and conditions, a supervisor having a brief meeting to discuss the work required, and then a colleague who introduces the employee to other workers. The employee may be left with manuals to look through on the first few days of work and told to ask questions as needed, or a "buddy" of a similar rank or position may be assigned so that the employee feels comfortable having someone to guide him or her along.

The way the orientation is conducted sends a strong signal to the new employees about the culture of the organization, how important employees are in general, and, in particular, how the addition of him or her is valued. An employee who is left to figure out the work tasks and environment on his or her own may feel lost and unwelcome. Loading a person with tons of reading materials on the first day is likely to be ineffective. Organizations need to think about what the most important things are for an employee to know on the first day or two of work, which probably include what the job is really about, who the employee will work with, what are the normal work hours, where people tend to go for lunch, and so on. Organizations must be cognizant that if the new employee has been applying for multiple jobs and been given multiple job offers, a poorly conducted orientation can lead to the new employee disappearing within days of employment with a resulting loss of valuable time and costs in recruitment.

## TRAINING AND DEVELOPMENT PROCESSES AND PROGRAMS

Training and development are two closely related terms. Both are important for employees to perform a job well. Yet, training is focused on teaching the specific skills required of the job, especially the current job. Development is not specifically related to current job skills but focuses on providing the employee with learning that can be applied to their future jobs or careers. Organizations that emphasize training but not development have a short-term focus. A lack of development plans leaves employees, who may want to take on other positions and move to higher levels of responsibilities, and the organization as a whole unprepared for future needs.

While organizations tend to acknowledge the importance of training and development, in tight financial situations or when crisis looms, these areas, particularly the development area, are usually the first to be cut. Organizations that do not spend sufficient resources on these areas get into a vicious cycle of not having the appropriate competencies for the jobs, causing their performance to suffer which leads to further financial crunch and fewer resources for needed training and development. Organizations that provide training and development on an ad hoc basis without a well-developed program or genuine top management support are most likely to neglect training and development in bad times.

### Needs Assessment

The first step in determining the needed areas of training and development is through a needs assessment. This can be done informally or formally. The job incumbent, supervisors, colleagues, clients, HR department, consultants, and experts in the field are all possible sources of information for determining the current and future needs of the position. The difference between the skills required and the existing skills the job incumbent possesses represents a gap that can be addressed by proper training and development. A point to emphasize is that organizations should not overlook the importance of involving the employee in the training and development decisions as he or she is closest to the work and can often provide the most insightful feedback. Having the employee involved also leads to better buy-in of the training and development programs. It cannot simply be assumed that all employees will wholeheartedly embrace such programs. Training and development may encroach on the employee's time and work habits, with a result that certain ways of doing work need to change. Many people tend to resist changes because it leads to uncertainty, insecurity, and possibly more efforts, at least in the short run while one is learning the ropes. As Lewin (1952) points out, change involves three steps:

- unfreezing (when people dissociate with their old way of thinking or doing things)
- change (when people learn how to do things differently)
- refreezing (when people accept the new way of doing things as the standard practice)

Getting employee buy-in may help with the unfreezing stage, but it is far from sure that the other two stages will proceed successfully. Even if someone has been taught the new methods, how much is retained and how much is applied to the job after the training often depends on the need to use the new methods and the encouragement received.

### Career Planning and Career Anchors

It is not adequate to just do a needs assessment from the organization's perspective. Employees have their own growth and development goals too, in order to advance their career. Employees' own career planning is very much related to HR planning, especially in the area of succession plans and internal promotions. Good employers will help meet employees' needs and their career aspirations, so that they will have happy and committed employees who can and are willing to take on higher level responsibilities at the right time.

Career planning is the process in which an employee's current career status or stage, personal values and orientation as well as qualifications (such as skills, knowledge and abilities) are assessed; his or her career goals identified; and action plans made to help achieve the goals through appropriate career development activities.

*Career stages* for working adults can generally be categorized according to their age (Dessler, Cole, Goodman, & Sutherland, 2004). At the *exploration stage* (ages 15-24), people tend to change jobs and explore various occupations to try to find one that is most suitable for them. At the *establishment stage* (ages 24-44), people tend to build up their expertise in the job or field. At the *maintenance stage* (ages 45-65), people tend to want security in the job or area of work. At the *decline stage* (ages over 65), people may be faced with the need to have reduced levels of responsibilities. These ages or stages are certainly not set in stone, but rather are provided as a general guideline to help with career assessment and planning. People may enter the workforce at different times, and there may also be multiple entrances and exits to the workforce as required by other life choices, such that the age-stage match will need to be adjusted.

*Career anchors* are the main concerns or values (something one is not willing to give up) related to one's career. Schein (1996) discussed eight main anchors that drive one's career choices, as follows:

- autonomy/independence
- security/stability
- technical-functional competence
- managerial-function competence
- entrepreneurial creativity
- service/dedication to a cause
- pure challenge
- life style.

These anchors signify what things are important for the individual and so have a major influence on career choices, planning, and development pursuits. Similarly, Holland (1973, as cited in Dessler, et al., 2004, p. 201) identified six vocational orientations or preferences for individuals that have important implications on what types of jobs will best suit them. These are provided in Table 7-1.

**Table 7-1 Vocational Orientations/Preferences**

| Orientation | Jobs/Preferences |
| --- | --- |
| Realistic orientation | Jobs that requires physical skills and strength |
| Investigative orientation | Jobs that involves cognitive abilities |
| Social orientation | Jobs that involves Interaction with others |
| Conventional orientation | Jobs that are structured, with well-established rules |
| Enterprising orientation | Jobs that involves influencing others |
| Artistic orientation | Jobs that are creative, expressive, and individualistic |

Knowing the current competencies one has as compared with those required for the future career roles is just as important as knowing one's career stage and value or orientation. Knowing the competency gap can steer one into the proper development path.

## Types of Training and Development Programs

Training and development can be done through formal or informal programs. These can take several forms:

- Formal classroom education and training
- Mentoring by supervisors, more senior members, or professional experts (ad hoc or ongoing)
- Job rotations and temporary assignments where individuals are exposed to a variety of jobs
- Job enrichment where individuals are given additional work at higher levels of responsibilities. This is also called vertical loading. (Note that this is different from job enlargement which provides only horizontal loading to the person's job without increased level of responsibility)
- Seminars and conferences
- Formal workshops for career planning and development.

Not surprisingly, most training and development experience occurs on the job or through mentoring, rather than in formal educational settings. Greer (2001) indicates that mentoring has many advantages, including "providing viable role models, candid feedback, instruction, insights into the company's policies, advice, and other support" (p. 243). Mentoring also helps the "protégés gain visibility and responsibility" and provides the mentor with a sense of fulfillment.

Training and development programs can also be categorized according to their purpose. Table 7-2 provides some common examples.

In terms of the instructional design and method of delivery of training and development programs, a wide range exists. For example, lectures and presentations are good for providing some background materials. Group discussions allow for sharing of knowledge and experience. Case studies provide the opportunity to analyze complex real-life situations and to develop strategies and action plans. Role plays prompt participants to put themselves in others' shoes and to remove self-bias. Simulations, by putting participants in a situation like a real-life one, are particularly good for interactive learning in a safe environment and are applicable in some technical situations, such as flying an aircraft, or in soft-skills training, such as negotiations and decision-making.

**Table 7-2 Types of Training and Development Programs – Examples by Training Purpose**

| | |
|---|---|
| **Leadership and Management Development** | For senior level employees or employees with good potential for advancement |
| **Technical Training and Development** | For employees whose current or future jobs involve technical functions |
| **Diversity/Cross-cultural Training** | May include cultural sensitivity training, language training, etc. |
| **Soft Skills Training** | Examples are communication skills, negotiations skills, problem-solving skills, etc. |
| **Team Training** | Training on team interaction and problem-solving skills and the management of team roles and team dynamics |
| **Apprenticeship** | Usually for entry level positions to skilled trades |
| **Internship Programs** | For students to learn real-life experience |

With computers being a part of almost every worker's life, computer-based or e-training is becoming increasingly popular. Such training can be provided as a paced program where participants must complete certain modules at a certain time, or it can be unpaced, allowing participants the flexibility of completing the modules at their desired rate. E-learning can be a cost-effective tool as there will not be the need for classroom space and travelling time and costs. With advances in technology, what can normally be achieved through traditional classroom settings can now mostly be done online as well. Indeed, online training programs may have certain learning advantages, as it may allow the learner to choose the best learning time to participate and can provide more time for reflection if an asynchronous and unpaced delivery mode is used. Developments of more effective collaborative online tools have also helped to facilitate group work in the virtual environment.

How should organizations choose their training and development programs? Which ones are more effective than others? It is important that organizations know what areas of training and development are needed. As discussed earlier, a needs analysis is a good start. Internal or external training and development programs have their advantages and disadvantages. Internal programs may require special expertise that may not be available. Maintaining training space is also costly if not fully utilized. Training sessions that pull staff members away from their work at the same time can be disruptive to the day-to-day operation. The main advantage with internal programs is their customization to the needs of the organizational situation. Staff members may also feel at ease during training as they know each other. External programs can be either more costly or less costly than internal programs. Training and development of general skills and knowledge are more cost efficient if done by external programs where employees have a wider choice of providers and time frames more suitable for them. If an organization needs more customized programs, it can approach an outside provider for such specific arrangements. Some providers only offer off-the-shelf programs while others are quite willing to create customized programs at an additional cost.

## Effectiveness of Training and Development Programs

To evaluate the effectiveness of a program, the content of the program and its ability to meet the needs gap must be considered. Training effectiveness generally includes the short-term and long-term perspective. A participant's improvement in skills and knowledge can be objectively tested using a suitable pre-test and post-test. Evaluations and testimonials from participants about the value of the program can be obtained. The longer term perspective concerns the retention and applicability of the training skills and knowledge to the actual job after a period of time has elapsed since the employee completed the training. There can always be a knowing-doing gap as well as issues of retention. Therefore, employees should be provided the opportunity and encouragement to apply what they have learned in a timely manner.

More and more organizations are demanding that the effectiveness of training and development programs be provided in monetary terms, such as the *benefit-cost ratio* (BCR) or *return on investment* (ROI). The BCR simply divides the benefits from the program by the cost for the program, while the ROI requires the cost be subtracted from the benefits before it is divided by the cost (Phillips, 1996). A simple example is a training program offered to a group of term employees that costs $100,000 and gives rise to a productivity increase of $150,000 over their term of employment. In this case, the BCR is 1.5 (i.e., $150,000/$100,000), while the ROI is 50% (i.e., $150,000 - $100,000 x 100%). Of course, it is not always easy to clearly determine the benefits and cost of programs, especially more complex ones that extend over a period of time. Direct and indirect costs and benefits in relation to areas like output, quality, time, and customer satisfaction should be captured and, where possible, measured by analyzing historical data, getting input from the employees involved and their supervisors, seeking expert opinion on an estimated value or cost, or doing external research for related value or cost data (Phillips & Phillips, 2002). A main benefit of ROI is the ability to demonstrate to senior management the value of the training programs to justify continued commitment to them or to help management in prioritizing the programs. It also allows management to hold managers accountable for meeting the training objectives.

The use of ROI, however, is not without problems. Many factors affecting performance outcomes can come into play. For example, higher capital investment and better technology can improve productivity at the same time investment in employee training is made. So, it is important to isolate the effects of the HR programs. Some techniques for doing so include: having control groups for comparison with the training groups; using trend lines for projection for comparison with actual data; and referring to stakeholders' estimates or research study findings of the outcome specifically related to the HR program (Phillips & Phillips, 2002). It should be noted that not all benefits can be readily quantified as the conversion may require too much subjectivity or too many assumptions be made that may jeopardize the overall accuracy and credibility of the ROI. Such items are called intangible benefits and they include improved public image, increased employee commitment, and lower stress. These qualitative data are just as important and deserve the same degree of attention as the quantitative data (Phillips & Phillips, 2006). Indeed, as Ulrich and Smallwood (2005) identify, organizations should focus more on the intangibles—the "hidden value of a firm" or "the shareholder value not determined by financial results"—and the ways HR can help to create such intangible value in a sustainable way.

## CONCLUSION

Training and development is as important to the organization as it is to the individual employees. It provides the organization with the right employee competencies at the right time and allows individual employees to further their knowledge and skills to handle their existing job tasks or take on a future role with bigger responsibilities. The determination of the training and development programs needed should start with a needs assessment of knowledge or skill gaps in the organization as well as what employees want in terms of their growth and development. The type of programs to be provided will depend further on an analysis of the pros and cons of the various program types and the resources available. Finally, the effectiveness of the training or development program(s) provided should be evaluated based on some established criteria.

---

# HRM in Action
## Training and Development at Federal Express (FedEx)

FedEx is one of the leading companies in time-sensitive delivery services, with a core philosophy of "people – service – profit". It means people come first. With good employees, good service comes next and it will be followed by profits. As having competent people is a key to success, the company places great emphasis on investing in training and developing its employees, particularly its executives and managers.

Leadership training and development is extensive. Employees entering the management ranks must attend their in-house Leadership Institute (founded in 1984), which helps participants to think critically on complex issues, particularly involving leading people. The curriculum involves lectures, simulations, reflective journals, and active experimentation (applications of learned concepts to practice). The instructors, the "management preceptors", are carefully selected from internal outstanding leaders to serve at the institute for a couple of years, where they can share their expertise with other managers. As part of the leadership-training continuum, week-long leadership classes are required of managers whenever they are advancing to a more senior rank. Managers around the world are flown to headquarters for specific training as needed. Recurring training is also offered to managers every 18 months, even if they are staying at the same level. General personal development programs are also provided. For example, the company partners with an external provider so that employees can learn experientially about self-awareness, trust, leadership, and team skills in an outdoor natural setting. Overall, managers are required to have forty hours of training per annum for their development, fifteen of which need to be related to the "people" aspect. Leaders and managers are also expected to learn from the customers. For example, they would call their customers for input and may even take calls at the call centre to directly interact with customers.

To advance into management ranks, an employee must go through the leadership evaluation and awareness process (LEAP), which consists of a "Is Management for Me?" training class. Then, the employee has to demonstrate in a profile report his or her competence in nine dimensions that the company considers critical for leadership, namely, "charisma, individualized consideration, intellectual stimulation,... courage, dependability, flexibility, integrity, judgment, and respect for others" (Day & Halpin, 2001, pp. 42-43). The report, together with the manager's report and peer evaluations. will be assessed by a LEAP panel.

---

Sources:
Fedex. (n. d.). Retrieved February 18, 2012 from http://www.fedex.com
Day, D., & Halpin, S. M. (2001). *Leadership development: A review of industry best practices* [U.S. Army Institute for the Behavioral and Social Sciences Technical Report 1111]. Retrieved February 18, 2012 from www.au.af.mil/au/awc/awcgate/army/tr1111.pdf
FranklinCovey. (January 2008). *FedEx: A testimonial to the 7 habits.* Retrieved February 18, 2012 at http://franklincoveyresearch.org/catalog/CFR070835_FedEx_SucSto__r1.0.1_.pdf
Peterson, G. (2006). *Inside FedEx Express* [Secretary of Defense Fellowship Program report]. Retrieved February 18, 2012 from http://www/ndu/edu/sdcfp/reports/2006Reports/FedEx05.doc

## References

Dessler, G., Cole, N. D., Goodman, P. M., Sutherland, V. L. (2004). *Fundamentals of human resources management in Canada.* Toronto, ON: Prentice Hall.

Greer, C. R. (2001). *Strategic human resource management: A general managerial approach* (2nd ed.). Upper Saddle River, NJ: Prentice Hall.

Lewin, K. (1952). Group decisions and social change. In G. E. Swanson, T. N. Newcomb, & E. L. Hartley (Eds.), *Readings in social psychology* (Rev. ed.), New York: Holt.

Phillips, J. J. (1996). ROI: The search for best practices. *Training & Development, 50*(2), 42-47.

Phillips, J., & Phillips, P. (2002). How to measure the return on your HR investment: Using ROI to demonstrate your business impact. *Strategic HR Review, 1*(4), 16-21.

Phillips, J., & Phillips, P. (2006). Return on investment measures success. *Industrial Management, 48*(2), 18-23.

Schein, E. H. (1996). Career anchors revisited: Implications for career development in the 21st century. *Academy Of Management Executive, 10*(4), 80-88.

Ulrich, D., & Smallwood, N. (2005). HR's new ROI: Return on intangibles. *Human Resource Management, 44*(2), 137-142.

# REWARDS MANAGEMENT

## INTRODUCTION

Rewards management is an important management area because it has significant implications on costs to the organization and sends important messages to employees as to how the organization values them. Rewards are usually used by organizations to achieve a number of objectives, such as motivating employees, attracting and retaining employees, and focusing employees on tasks that the organization considers important, at a reasonable cost. Therefore, rewards management should be well integrated with other areas of human resource systems. Moreover, aligning the rewards system with the organizational goals and ensuring a fit with the management philosophy and organizational culture is a key to organizational success. For example, an organization that values talent is likely to pay more than minimal wages and to provide long-term benefits that encourage talented employees to stay. However, it is not uncommon for organizations to fail to reward employees appropriately. Workers often complain about being overworked and underpaid. Organizations may also be using wrong criteria for rewards. For example, an organization that claims it emphasizes quality but rewards employees for production volume and speed is unlikely to reach its quality objective. An organization that wants to increase cooperation among employees cannot do so successfully if it emphasizes individual rewards rather than group or organizational level rewards. Similarly, an organization that gives a bonus for full attendance to boost productivity may end up with sick workers coming in and spreading their illness, adversely affecting the unit's overall productivity. Indeed, this latest phenomenon of workers coming in while sick (for fear of loss of bonus or salary, of being seen as not hardworking, or of having too much to do to afford taking a day off) is termed a problem of *presenteeism*.

Money is the first thing that usually comes to people's minds when they hear about rewards. Do rewards necessarily mean money? Is rewards management the same as compensation management? Although the words *compensation* and *rewards* are often used interchangeably, some authors (e.g., Long, 2002) view them differently. Compensation refers generally to the monetary aspect (the pay and the tangible benefits) and carries a transactional connotation in the sense that work is an unpleasant task that needs to be compensated. When viewed this way, compensation is only part of rewards. Rewards include the non-monetary aspect used to indicate to employees the appreciation of their contributions. Therefore, a reward can be a simple thank you, a pat on the shoulder, or a recognition award that tangibly is worth no more than a piece of paper, but intangibly worth a lot more. A promotion or, sometimes, just better or more challenging job assignments can be a reward too. Hence, rewards are anything that is of value to employees, and they are extrinsic or intrinsic. Rewards of intrinsic value are those that address the employees' higher needs, such as their self-actualization needs, by letting employees experience growth and a sense of accomplishment.

Rewards management and performance management are very closely related topics. Performance management is covered in the next chapter. It is, however, necessary to clarify at this time that rewarding for performance is only one of the many elements of the rewards system. For example, in a seniority-based rewards system or a skills-based pay system, performance is not necessarily a rewards criterion, although in some seniority-based systems pay increments can be withheld for very poor performers.

This chapter starts with an overview of rewards philosophy used to guide rewards decisions. This is followed by an introduction to the various pay approaches, namely, job-based, seniority-based, performance-based, and skills-based. Next, common types of rewards based on different levels (individual, group, and organization) are discussed. Some major determining factors in rewards management such as internal and external equity as well as legislative requirements are then addressed. The chapter closes with a discussion of the various types of employee benefits that constitute a significant part of the rewards system.

## REWARDS PHILOSOPHY AND PRINCIPLES

Organizations often face financial constraints and conflicting demands in its rewards management. What should take priority and how should limited resources be allocated to employees? This is why a rewards philosophy outlining the main reward principles is needed to guide rewards decisions. The following are questions to ask in determining the main reward principles:

- What should the reward mix be: monetary versus non-monetary rewards, salary versus benefits, and base salary versus incentive pay? The flexibility of the system when the need for changes arises depends largely on the reward mix.

- What should the base for the rewards system be: job-based, seniority-based, performance-based, or skills-based? If it is performance-based, should it be based on individual performance, group performance, or organizational performance, or performance at a combination of levels?
- Should the organization pay top wages, average market wages, or minimal wages?
- How should the system be administered (e.g., to ensure distributive and procedural justice)?

There are no simple answers to the above questions, but a rewards manager must be cognizant of the organizational objectives, management philosophy, organizational culture, labour market condition, employee expectations as well as the financial and other constraints in designing the reward system.

## PAY APPROACHES

There are two general views for determining employees' pay. One is that it should be based purely on the job characteristics without regard to any factors related to the incumbents. For example, consideration is given to the level of difficulty of the job tasks, the skills and experience required, the unpleasantness of the working conditions, the risks involved in performing the job, and the employment security associated with the job. In its strictest form, everyone doing the same job is paid exactly the same. The other view is that the pay should be determined by the incumbent employee characteristics, by considering aspects such as the employee's qualifications (education, experience, skills, and other personal characteristics deemed favourable for the organization); tenure or seniority; or contributions and performance. Very often, organizations adopt a hybrid approach, in which the pay scale is based on the job while the employees' pay within the scale depends on individual factors.

## Job-Based Pay

The determination of job-based pay usually involves a job evaluation system, whereby jobs are analyzed, rated, ranked, or given a point score to determine their relative importance in the organization and their corresponding worth in terms of pay. Common job evaluation systems include:

- *Job classification* – Descriptive job grades are established in a hierarchical order. Jobs are then evaluated by comparison with the grade descriptions and slotted into a job grade accordingly. An organization may have one job classification system for all the jobs or multiple job classification systems for different occupational areas (e.g., sales or production jobs) or classes of jobs (e.g., managerial or clerical). Examples of the factors considered are knowledge required for the job, operational or people skills, and the need for decision-making. Within each factor, descriptions of the various levels are explicitly provided. The higher the job grade, the higher the requirement related to the factor. Clear specification of factors and their levels is not an easy task, nor is the selection of a representative set of factors applicable to all jobs involved in the organization or in an occupational group. Moreover, a detailed set of grading rules needs to be established to address how a job should be classified overall if it falls under different levels for different factors.

- *Job ranking* – Jobs are compared to each other and their relative importance to the organization or department is determined. The "judges" assigned the task may come up with their own criteria for the ranking. Understandably, ranking within a department is a lot easier, especially in a traditional hierarchical type of organization. However, ranking across occupational areas can be tricky, more so without clear criteria. When many jobs are involved, ranking by the comparison method can be quite impracticable. Even when the ranks are established, the differentials between two consecutive ranks are not known nor are they constant. Hence, attaching a fair money value to the ranks can be difficult. This method has also been criticized as being rather subjective and arbitrary.

- *Factor comparison* – This can be considered an extension of the job ranking method in that key factors are explicitly used to determine the ranks. For selected key jobs, their total wage rates are allocated across the factors, and for each factor the money value assigned must be in accordance with the ranking for the factors, thereby ensuring internal equity. With the master rate schedule developed, a new job can be ranked by these factors and appropriate money values assigned to each factor. The pay level would then be the sum of the money values of all the factors. The method can be quite complex and involves substantial time and cost.

- *Point method* – A number of relevant factors are predetermined and points are assigned to each factor in the evaluation of each job. For example, the factors for white collar jobs used by the Hay Group—a consulting group well known for their use of the point method in evaluation—are: know-how, problem-solving, and accountability as well as working condition, where its use is appropriate (Skenes & Kleiner, 2003). The job worth is then expressed as the sum of the factor scores. A monetary value, probably derived from market surveys and analyses, is then determined for the score. Often, jobs of similar scores are grouped into a job grade for ease of administration. Compared with other methods, this one seems to be more objectively based and is generally more accepted by employees. It also allows for comparison across different types of jobs, such as between an engineer and a human resource professional, because they are based on a common scoring system. The main drawback is the time and cost involved.

For all the above methods, the starting point for the evaluation is the preparation and review of the job description, which determines the relative worth of the job to the organization. The translation into pay usually involves a further step of looking at the market situation, such as by conducting surveys or using existing compensation survey information. There is often a range of pay to consider given the market information. The choice of the appropriate pay level will depend on the management philosophy as well as the financial resources of the organization. An innovative firm may pay top salaries to recruit and retain invaluable talents while a fast-food chain that does not generally care much about specific skills or qualifications may just pay minimally.

## Seniority-Based Pay

This form of pay system, which links pay with tenure, is more common in traditional organizations and government departments. It is also more entrenched in union settings as some unions take the view that other pay approaches give rise to more arbitrary and biased pay decisions by management. Often, employees are given a salary increment every year, either at the anniversary date of their employment or promotion or at a date set by the organization for all employees, such as the start of the calendar year or the fiscal year. The advantages of this system are that the criteria for increase are clear and it is relatively easy to administer. There is no need for individual employee negotiation. The main criticisms for this pay system are its rigidity in dealing with a constantly changing environment, its overemphasis on retention, and the disregard of the level of contributions made by the employees. People doing exactly the same job may be paid very different amounts purely because of their tenure. For jobs where experience is not a very essential factor for effective performance the cost effectiveness of this pay approach can be quite low. Sometimes, organizations adopt a modified seniority-based pay system in which increments are withheld for poor performers and double increments are given to top performers. Occasionally, employees with meritorious performance are given exceptional increases beyond the salary scale maximum. For these organizations, the performance factor is introduced into the pay system that is primarily seniority-based.

## Performance-Based Pay

The underlying rationale for performance-based pay is consistent with the expectancy theory (Vroom, 1964). According to this theory, the expectation of performance-related rewards motivates employees if the employees believe that the expected performance level is achievable, the rewards will be granted upon performance, and the rewards are viewed as valuable to them. In using money as the reward, it is assumed that employees value extrinsic compensation. Whether money is truly motivating is subject to theoretical as well as empirical debate. According to Herzberg's two-factor theory (Herzberg, 1968), while money is an important hygiene factor without which people are dissatisfied, it is not a motivator. Maslow's hierarchy of needs theory also suggests when the lower needs are met, factors that meet the higher level needs, such as social needs, self-esteem needs, self-actualization needs, become the motivating forces (Maslow, 1954). On the other hand, it seems generally accepted that people making more contributions deserve a higher pay, and according to equity theory, people tend to compare the ratio of the outcomes of their contributions to the input effort with that of others (Adams, 1965). Empirically, the results were mixed. Performance-based pay has certainly worked well in raising performance for some organizations but not necessarily so for others.

There are two main types of performance-based pay. One is *merit pay* and the other is *incentive pay*. Merit pay involves either a salary increase or a merit bonus for recognition of good performance in the past period. The amount of the increase or bonus is not specified prior to the performance period, although employees may have formed some kind of expectations from past practices. Incentive pay, on the other hand, involves telling employees in advance what they will get for a certain level (or various levels) of performance, so that employees have the drive to aim for the target. Incentive pay is common in sales jobs in the form of commission. Incentive pay can also be in the form of base pay increase, incentive bonuses, profit-sharing, or gain-sharing. (Profit-sharing and gain-sharing are two different concepts that are covered later in the chapter.)

Although performance-based pay, in particular merit pay, seems to be very commonly used in North American organizations, it presents a number of issues of concern.

- *Long-term versus short-term perspective*

  It is not unusual that long-term performance can be sacrificed for short-term gain or, occasionally, vice versa. Since the line of sight for the reward is considered important to motivate employees, many performance pay plans involve a relatively short perspective. So, even if the organization's performance improves with the pay plan, it is still uncertain how things will unfold in the long run. There is also the argument that organizations need to continuously provide the monetary reward in order to continue the motivation. However, in some situations, there comes a point when it is difficult to improve performance much further and the incentive plan no longer works effectively. Moreover, as people tend to view past levels of monetary rewards as entitlements because they are used to getting these rewards, once the rewards are not given out, either due to performance level improvements not being sustained or the organization's financial constraints, the negative impact on employee morale can be quite substantial.

- *Measurement problems*

  It is difficult enough to measure individual employee performance due to the many dimensions involved. When it comes to measuring group or organizational performance, on which some performance pay plans are based, the problem becomes much greater. If there is a problem with measuring performance or effectiveness, how can performance pay plans be appropriately designed? Moreover, many factors other than employee performance contribute to an organization, group, or unit's performance, such as external environmental factors, changes in technology, and changes in capital investment. Without the ability to delineate the effects of various contributing factors, how does management know whether performance pay plans actually work and are responsible for the improvements?

- *Over-emphasis on extrinsic reward*

  The focus of most incentive plans on monetary rewards sends the message to employees that extrinsic rewards are most important. People who are just interested in the money are attracted to such plans, more so than people who are intrinsically motivated, resulting in the organization failing to develop a sense of commitment among employees that is often a key to sustainable success. Employees who become focused only on what is tangibly rewarded may ignore other areas that have an indirect effect on the organization's ultimate effectiveness. In other words, only things that get rewarded get done. For example, if employees are rewarded for productivity, other areas such as quality, cooperation, and sharing of knowledge may suffer. Employees may also think of ways to beat the system, which sometimes involve less than ethical means. Consider a situation where employees are rewarded for sales or service revenues. They may talk their customers into buying something more expensive than is needed, even at the risk of the product being returned at a later date. They may also be tempted to provide erroneous information to customers in order to generate a higher level of sales or service revenue. One can usually tell upon walking into a store whether it is paying employees by commission or flat salary. In some cases, employees working under the commission system actually ask customers whether they are planning to make a purchase that day, and if not, the employees walk away. These actions usually drive customers away and harm the reputation of the company.

- *Adverse effect on cooperation*

  Incentive plans have the potential to discourage cooperation, especially those rewarding individual level performance. Why would anyone help out colleagues or share knowledge with them when only individual performance matters? This is especially so when rewards are only given to the top performers; employees are pitted against each other resulting in overall sub-optimal performance for the unit. Incentive plans are also often the reason for contention between the sales and production departments. If sales people are paid by commission for sales volume, they may do everything possible to generate sales, even to the point of promising unreasonably short delivery dates or customization that may not be agreed to by the production people. Increased conflicts and decreased trust can greatly impact the organizational culture and drive employees apart from each other.

- *Employee preference and perceived inequity*

  Many jobs do not have a direct measurable outcome. For example, staff in support areas, such as human resources or finance, may feel left out of incentive plans based on commissions or bonuses for sales or production employees reaching certain objective targets. This creates a sense of inequity for some employees and negatively affects morale. On the other hand, some risk-averse employees prefer stable wages rather than incentive plans to take uncertainties out of their wages.

- *Costs*

  Substantial costs can be involved in designing, implementing, and maintaining the performance pay system. In order for a performance pay plan to be effective, it needs to be of sufficient value to result in a difference in behaviour. However, organizations must ensure that the cost involved does not exceed the benefits obtained from such a pay plan. It is also important to remem-

ber the non-monetary aspects of costs. A negative effect on the organizational culture can be even more costly to the organization than the tangible costs involved.

When incentive plans are to be implemented, the question arises whether the base pay should be reduced. Not many employees willingly support a base pay reduction. If no reduction is made, is there sufficient room to create an incentive difference without driving up the organizational cost too much? Moreover, performance plans, once implemented, are quite difficult to change in the long run because any adjustments potentially affect the pay of some employees, who will likely object to it. If the adjustments make everyone's pay no less than what it was under the old system, it means the pay is forever going upwards. This can be problematic for the organization if it is not outweighed by increased productivity.

Despite the cautionary points raised above, performance pay plans can work but they need to be properly designed. In this age of rapid changes where employee commitment, teamwork, and knowledge sharing are crucial for organizational success, individual performance pay plans may not be the most appropriate. Instead, group-based incentive plans address many of the problems discussed above. Of course, no system is perfect. Group-based performance pay systems may be seen as less within an individual's control and subject to free-riders taking advantage of others' contributions. Some group-based incentives are discussed later in the chapter.

## Skill-Based or Competency-Based Pay

The skill-based pay system recognizes the importance of individual skills and knowledge to the organization. So, rather than paying for the job or for performance or tenure on a specific job, the pay is associated with the employee's qualifications. Pay increases are granted when employees demonstrate mastery of extra skills (e.g., higher skills level or broader skills scope) or attain some additional recognized qualifications that are important to the organization, such as completion of training programs. The main premise for this pay approach is to pay people for what they can do for the organization, not just what they have done or are doing. It is future-oriented and focuses on development. For people with jobs the effectiveness of which is hard to quantify or where results are unlikely to be seen in the short term (such as developing drugs for the treatment of a certain disease), this pay method may be superior to the performance-based one. Employees working on projects where transferable skills are critical for project success are also suited for such a pay arrangement.

Since this pay method is purely person-based, it sends the message to the employees that they are an important resource to the organization. Encouraging self-growth and development is also consistent with satisfying employees' higher level needs (see Maslow, 1954). It tends to support an organizational culture of teamwork, cooperation, and learning, where talent is valued and employee involvement welcomed. With employees mastering not just a deeper level of skills in their job area, but also a wider range of skills applicable to other areas, this pay method provides much more functional flexibility for the organization because it facilitates cross assignments and multi-tasking.

As with any pay system, some disadvantages are associated with skill-based pay. First, it is not always easy to identify all the skills relevant to the organization's effectiveness and assign an appropriate dollar amount to it. Additional skills gained by employees may not be usable immediately and some skills, especially technological ones, become obsolete after a period of time. Also, employees are not able to keep up their skills if they do not have the opportunity to practice them. In other words, organizations may be incurring additional cost for little or no benefit in return. Moreover, there is a limit as to how many skills relevant to the organization an employee may want to learn and for which organizations will pay. Hence, an employee's pay can reach a cap after mastering a number of skills and can no longer be used to provide further incentives for individual learning. Another potential problem is that employees may come to expect a lot from the organization in terms of training and development upon which their pay is contingent, and those who do not get their chance for the training or development may be resentful.

Competency-based pay is very similar to skill-based pay and can be seen as a broader form of it. Such a pay approach tends to apply more to professional and managerial ranks. Competencies generally refer to "any knowledge, skills, trait, motive, attitude, value, or other personal characteristic that is essential to perform the job and that differentiates superior from solid performance" (Belcourt & McBey, 2000, p. 126). Hence, competency-based pay recognizes a broader range of criteria than do skill- or knowledge-based pay, such as more general cognitive abilities and behaviours. Zingheim, Ledford, and Schuster (1996) provide some examples of competencies considered important by organizations, such as, customer focus, communication, team orientation, technical expertise, results orientation, leadership, adaptability, and innovation. These examples show that "competencies" is quite a vague and general term and can mean different things to different people. Hence, tying pay to competencies can be a challenge. Despite this drawback, competency-based pay has gained much popularity in recent years as organizations increasingly recognize the need to use their human resource assets to gain a competitive advantage. After all, jobs at the senior ranks are more strategic and macro in nature, and there is no easy way to directly measure the job performance especially in light of all possible confounding factors. Therefore, paying by competency measures is no less desirable than by other measures. The competency focus also emphasizes not just the ends but also the means, and its multi-dimensionality better reflects the diverse nature of managerial jobs.

## Adopting an Appropriate Pay System

Different pay systems have their own merits and drawbacks and there is no "one size fits all" approach. The choice of the system depends largely on the organizational objectives and its management philosophy, as well as the types of jobs involved. It is not uncommon for organizations to adopt different pay systems for different job types. Chen and Chen (2004) propose a framework of the pay approach within an organization based on two main dimensions: *explicitness of job worth* and *competitive advantage of human resources*. Explicitness of job worth is considered high if the job involved is easily analyzed through job evaluation. Competitive advantage of human resources refers to the skills required of a position and how much they contribute to the organization's competitive advantage over other firms. These dimensions, as shown in Table 8-1, are used to determine which of the four pay approaches is appropriate.

**Table 8-1 Choice of Pay System**

|  | Explicitness of Job Worth | Competitive Advantage of Human Resources |
|---|---|---|
| **Job-based pay** | High | Low |
| **Seniority-based pay** | Low | Low |
| **Performance-based pay** | Low | High |
| **Skill-based pay** | High | High |

Hence, it is not surprising to find high performance organizations tend to favour performance-based pay or skill-based pay, while traditional organizations with stable environments and jobs tend to favour the job-based or seniority-based pay approaches.

The above pay approaches usually involve individual-level pay plans, based on the individual's job, seniority, performance, or skills. However, performance-based pay can also be determined at the group level or organization level. Some common group-based and organization-based incentive plans are discussed in the following sections.

# GROUP-BASED INCENTIVES

Group-based incentives take many forms. Basically, incentives are provided for the group members upon the achievement of certain group goals or if the group outperforms others. The group can be a small task group, a unit, or a department. Incentives are often in tangible form, usually involving money or an explicit promise of rewards valued by members, such as better work assignments. Common group-based incentives include pooled performance pay plans and gain-sharing plans.

## Pooled Performance Pay Plans

Under such plans, a group of employees are rewarded a variable pay amount based on the performance of the entire group. Such performance is often based on the total sales revenue of the group or on the total volume of goods produced by the group. Members of the group share the pooled performance pay, often equally. These types of plans encourage teamwork and are particularly important when members' jobs are so integrated that they need to work together to generate an overall high level of performance for the unit. As with any group-based incentives, such plans can be subject to free-rider problems, especially when the group is large and free-riders are not easily noticed or identified.

## Gain-Sharing Plans

Gain-sharing is often confused with profit-sharing but they refer to different plans. Gain-sharing aims at directly reducing costs while profit-sharing focuses on increasing profits. In gain-sharing employees, often in groups, suggest a variety of cost-saving measures for the organization. Examples are a reduction of waste, a change to using more efficient resources, or a process improvement that speeds up the process and creates fewer bottlenecks. Cost is an aspect often seen as more within the employees' control than profit so the line of sight to the gain-sharing reward is relatively clearer than for profit-sharing. Still, many people are involved and many factors affect production cost. Therefore, the motivation of the incentive is still not as great as under an individual plan, but there could be fewer of the undesirable effects often associated with individual plans.

The most well known type of gain-sharing plan is the *Scalon plan*, named after its developer. The original Scalon plan looks at the reduction in labour cost, which is expressed in terms of percentage of sales value of production. The gain is then shared between the employees and the organization by some predetermined formula (such as a 50-50 split). Some modified forms of the plan involve cost reduction beyond the labour cost (Belcher, 1996) because, as discussed above, cost reduction can involve many different areas, not just the labour area.

Gain-sharing plans work especially well when the organization encourages a culture of participation. Employees not only get extrinsic rewards due to the incentive plan, but are also intrinsically motivated to develop improvements to work processes because their suggestions are valued, they feel they can take ownership of their work, and their creative cost-saving measures give them a sense of achievement. On the other hand, if an organization is implementing gain-sharing purely to provide monetary incentives without paying attention to employee involvement, the gains are not always the most beneficial to the organization. Such an approach tends to attract recommendations from money-minded individuals whose cost-saving suggestions may compromise other areas not specified in the gain-sharing criteria.

For gain-sharing plans to work effectively there must be trust and cooperation between management and employees. Employees must believe that management is sincere in their desire for employee contributions, that their recommendations will be taken seriously, and that management will share the gains. One potential drawback of gain-sharing plans is that ideas may run out at some point in time, leading to little or no pay out, which can be discouraging for employees especially when they have received much larger sums before when there was plenty of room for improvement. Gain-sharing can also be challenging to implement in a dynamic market where products or services become outdated easily.

## ORGANIZATION-BASED INCENTIVES

In organization-based incentive plans, individuals receive a variable pay portion based on the organization's overall performance. Such incentive plans either cover all employees in the organization (as everyone is believed to have contributed to the organization's success) or a select group such as the executives (whose contributions are believed to specifically tie in closely with the organization's performance). Common organization-based incentive plans include profit-sharing plans and employee stock plans.

### Profit-Sharing Plans

Profit-sharing plans work on the basis of distributing a certain percentage of an organization's profits (often net profits) or profits above a specific preset target to employees according to some predetermined formula (which may be distributed equally to all involved or may relate to the level of an employee's salary or position). The plan can apply to certain employee groups or all employees in the organization who have been with the organization for some duration of time. Profit-sharing plans are supposed to align employee efforts with the profit-maximization goal of the organization. The symbolic message sent to employees is that everyone is in this together and employees are as deserving as shareholders or upper management in obtaining a portion of the profits. However, whether such plans are really effective in motivating employee performance towards profit maximization is still questionable. Most critics of such plans present the following arguments of the plans' weaknesses:

- Numerous variables affect an organization's profitability, most of which are not within the employees' control, such as external market condition. Hence, efforts do not necessarily translate into profits.

- The line of sight between employee efforts and profits is not clear to many employees. Does an employee on the assembly line putting in screws see the direct effect of his or her work performance on profitability? The more indirect and unclear the line of sight, the lesser the motivation effect.

- Employees can easily free-ride on others, leading to inequities and overall lower performance. An employee may think that the effect of one person's effort on profitability for a whole organization is negligible and slacking by a few is easily masked by the efforts of others. Hence, there is no need for any particular individual to pull his or her weight. However, if too many employees think the same way, organizational performance and profit suffer severely.

Profit-sharing payments are usually made in the form of incentive bonuses, but sometimes they are paid into pension plans or stock purchase benefit plans. In the latter situation, there is no direct payment to the employees; the payments are invested for the good of the employees' future (and the organization's future as well). Although the real effectiveness of profit-sharing is not clearly known, many organizations believe in the positive symbolic effects it has on the organizational culture and employee commitment. Moreover, the risk of adopting such a plan is not too high, as organizations need not pay out if they are not making good profits.

## Employee Stock Plans

Employee stock plans are plans that either provide employees with the company's shares at no cost or allow employees to purchase the company's shares at a price lower than the market price. As this type of rewards is tied to the value of the company's shares, which depends on the organization's performance, it is considered an organization-based incentive. Such rewards may be given to all employees in the organization or certain employee groups. Through the ownership of shares, employee stock plans have the general advantage of enhancing employees' organizational commitment and prompting them to be more concerned about the organization's performance. There are different types of employee stock plans.

Stocks can be paid as simple bonuses, in which case the shares are provided at no cost to the employees. Stock option plans are those that provide employees with the option to buy some company stocks at a specific price after a vesting period. They are often offered to senior management members as a form of executive compensation and are expected to provide some longer term incentive for the executive to drive up the organization's performance. Employees need not exercise the option to buy if the market price plummets, but when both the organization and the stock market is performing well, stock options are a very attractive reward for executives. Sometimes, rather than providing actual stocks to employees (so that the market shares are not "diluted"), organizations provide cash rewards that are based on the appreciation of market price of the company stocks. This has the benefit of motivating employees to improve the organization's performance without the trouble of going through brokers or securities commissions.

As individual-, group-, and organization-based incentives all have their advantages and disadvantages, organizations may choose a combination of incentive plans to elicit the best performance from individuals without creating unfavourable competition that will drive sub-optimal group or organizational performance. The weight attached to the different incentive components depends on a number of factors, including the organizational goals, the overall management philosophy (particularly the rewards philosophy), and the organizational culture.

## INTERNAL AND EXTERNAL EQUITY

*Job evaluation* helps organizations determine the relative worth of jobs within the organization and, by benchmarking pay to comparable organizations in the external market, can also supposedly achieve external equity. However, there are situations when internal and external equities are not totally compatible. For example, job A has a lower job value than job B within the organization but because job A is in demand in the market, the market pay for job A is higher than for job B. What can the organization do? The organization does not want to upset the internal equity situation but it does need to hire the necessary people to do job A. One alternative is to make an additional payment for job A in terms of a market premium. That way, it signifies that it is an anomaly due to the market situation. As the premium is not built into the job base pay, there is more flexibility relating to it. For example, benefits related to base salary (such as pension or overtime) need not increase with the market premium, subsequent salary increases need not apply to the premium amount, and the premium can also be subject to periodic review. Of course, care must be taken in communicating the terms of such employment to potential hires. If the terms are clear, there is less chance of resentment or even lawsuits for constructive dismissal, which may arise from a unilateral change in a fundamental term of employment.

In the global economy, many organizations have offices and plants worldwide and employees are deployed overseas on various projects. Internal equity then becomes a much more challenging area. Due to the differences in the cost of living, should similar jobs in different locations be paid the same? Most organizations realize the need to compete for labour and talent in the local market and thus have little choice but to pay the local market rate. However, what should the compensation be for expatriates coming from another country or who return to the parent country after a job assignment period? Some organizations choose to pay either the home-based pay or host-based pay, whichever is higher, to ensure the expatriate employee does not lose out. Based on a similar principle, organizations may pay equalization benefits as needed to ensure that the expatriate employee is not losing out due to exchange rate fluctuations, higher income tax rate at the host country, or higher cost of living at the host location.

Compensation is only one of the many areas of concern in expatriate assignments. As discussed in Chapter 6, unsuccessful overseas deployments are often due to adjustment problems of the employees or their families. Hence, strategic human resource flow in an international setting requires detailed consideration of many integrated areas of human resource management, including proper design of rewards, provision of cross cultural training and other support, and careful selection of expatriate staff.

## PAY-RELATED LEGISLATION

In designing any pay system, it is crucial to understand the laws applicable to the organization. Many statutory laws are in place to limit what an organization can or cannot do in its payment to employees. For example, in Canada, the Canada Labour Code (for organizations under federal jurisdiction) or the provincial employment standards legislation have explicit requirements for minimum wage, overtime pay, and wages in lieu of notice in dismissal situations (other than when it is for just cause). The legislation also stipulates when a person is entitled to certain types of payment (such as basic wages). Moreover, tax laws require specific employer and employee payments for the Canada Pension Plan and Employment Insurance. The employee portion of the payments, including the income tax payments, is to be deducted up front from the employee's pay cheque.

Human rights legislation at both the federal and provincial levels forbids employment and pay discrimination based on prohibited grounds (certain personal characteristics unrelated to their job performance or tenure). In particular, some jurisdictions in Canada, including the federal jurisdiction, have explicit pay equity legislation that specifically targets gender inequity in wages paid to employees. Pay equity is premised on the concept of equal pay for work of equal or comparable value (or job worth as determined by job evaluation). While such legislation may apply only to public service organizations in certain provinces (such as Manitoba, Nova Scotia, New Brunswick, and Prince Edward Island), the legislation is applicable to all employers in Ontario and Quebec with ten or more employees (Human Resources and Social Development Canada, 2006). By requiring the comparison based on job value or job worth, it is possible to compare between jobs of totally different nature, such as between an accountant and a plant foreman. This is much broader in applicability than some forms of equal pay provisions, such as in Alberta where the same wages need only be paid to both genders if they are performing the "same or substantially similar work".

In accordance with the pay equity legislation, employers are required to identify job classes as male- or female-dominated, depending on factors such as the percentage of job holders in the class being of one gender or how the job class has been traditionally viewed (Long, 2002). If a gender-neutral job evaluation process indicates a difference in the pay between a female job class and a male job class of equal job worth, then adjustments must be made for the incumbents of the lower paid gender job class, which can be done over a period of time and may vary across jurisdictions.

The cost and administration related to the pay equity issue can be quite substantial. In the event of major disputes and complaints, it can take years of litigation to achieve a decision. For example, in the case of *Public Service Alliance of Canada vs. Treasury Board of Canada* (judgment dated October 1999), the litigation process lasted almost 15 years and involved a potential payout of 3.6 billion dollars for over 200,000 employees and ex-employees (Sulzner, 2000, p. 89). This probably represents the longest-lasting complaint and largest payout in Canadian history on pay equity.

A less well-known legislative constraint on pay relates to the prohibition of adjusting salaries during a union organizing drive (other than if the adjustment is made in the normal course of business, e.g., increments have always been given annually) as is explicitly stipulated in some Canadian labour relations legislation. This is to prevent employers from interfering with the union organizing efforts by promoting pro-management sentiments and discouraging pro-union votes during the critical period. Therefore, it is important for employers to provide pay increases fairly at all times and to be particularly cautious during a union organizing period in order to avoid being charged with unfair labour practice.

## BENEFITS

Benefits are a major expense for organizations, representing possibly as much as forty percent of the payroll cost (Eligh, 2012, slide 4). Benefits include a wide range of components. In Canada the mandatory benefits are Canada Pension Plan premiums, Employment Insurance premiums, Workers' Compensation premiums, statutory holidays, and certain leave periods such as maternity.

Company-initiated benefits include but are certainly not limited to the following:

- health care and wellness benefits
- life, disability, and accident insurances
- company pension plans or contributions to registered retirement saving plans
- employee share purchase plans
- educational allowances
- lodging allowances
- executive perks (such as car allowance, stock option plans)
- group purchase discounts
- services, such as child care facilities, counselling (psychological or financial) services, outplacement services
- holidays and paid leave periods in excess of the statutory requirements, such as extra vacation days, sick leaves, bereavement leaves, parental leaves, educational leaves.

Why do employers provide such benefits, especially when a high cost is involved? First, a good employer is believed to be one who takes care of its employees. Health and insurance benefits help employees in times of need and the pension plan helps with their financial future. Second, the benefits help to improve productivity. Healthy individuals and a better educated workforce are associated with higher productivity and performance. Employees with share ownership are likely more interested in helping the organization succeed. Third, some benefits serve to attract, retain, and motivate employees. For example, executive perks can be quite substantial in amount to attract the top managers, lodging allowances may be necessary to get people to move to a location where accommodation is much more expensive, pension plans tend to encourage employees to stay, while child care facilities can ensure employees have peace of mind at work knowing their children are nearby in good quality care. Fourth, some of the benefits have a tax advantage or are cheaper to provide on a group basis than on an individual basis. For example, in Canada health care benefits are generally not taxable, and group premiums may be less expensive than the sum of the premiums paid by individual employees themselves. Therefore, an employer is better off paying the group premium than paying individual premiums in the form of salary that is taxed in the employees' hands. Fifth, leave periods serve a number of useful purposes. (Leaves are seen as benefits even though the monetary element attached to them is not as apparent as with cash payouts.) Leave periods help employees recharge and become more productive upon return. They allow employees to take leave for critical events in their lives, such as loss of a family member, so that employees do not have to worry about taking illegitimate leaves or about wage loss.

Since benefits are costly but serve many different purposes, it is an important consideration in rewards management. The benefits composition sends a strong signal to employees of the values of the organization and can be used effectively to support the organization's strategic human resource management and organizational culture. For example, an organization that embraces diversity and wants to attract more qualified female employees is more likely to provide child care services. An organization that values stability and long service will focus on the pension plan area.

## Cafeteria Type of Benefits Plans

Employees obviously do not value all benefits the same way. The older employees may be more interested in the pension plan and health-related benefits while the younger ones may find educational benefits, benefits involving more immediate monetary gains, and leave periods more appealing. Employees with a spouse and children are more likely to view favourably benefits such as child care services and benefits with dependent coverage. On the other hand, an employee whose spouse already has all the necessary health-related family coverage through the spouse's employer is unlikely to feel a need for such plans. Therefore, it is certainly a challenge to find the right balance for all employees. As a result, some organizations are adopting flexible benefits plans where employees choose from a range of benefits, subject to the total not exceeding a certain amount. Of course, not all benefits can be given an absolute dollar term. Moreover, employees do not always choose benefits that are the most appropriate for them (for example, people tend not to think about health benefits until they get sick). So instead of giving total flexibility in substituting one benefit for another, employers may require certain minimal levels of compulsory benefits (e.g., health-related ones) or allow a choice between a few well-balanced benefits packages. Organizations may also

177

allow employees to make changes to their choices only periodically to reduce the administrative burden.

While the concept of providing employees with their choice of what they value most in terms of benefits seems a good one, there are a few disadvantage associated with it. First, as mentioned above, employees do not always make the choice that is necessarily best for them or the organization. Second, the administration of such plans can be costly and time-consuming. Last but not least, it is sometimes questionable if employees can switch from health care or insurance plans to other benefits without increasing the cost to the company. Understandably, those switching are likely to be the ones who least need the plan and thus are partially responsible for keeping the group premium rates low in the first place. If these employees opt out of the plans, it does not necessarily mean that the overall premiums paid by the group will decrease proportionally. Indeed, since insurance companies consider the total previous payouts to set the group premiums, it is not surprising that the total group premiums stay more or less the same, even after some employees leave the plan. If the employees get other benefits in exchange for leaving the plans, the company may end up having to pay more, and benefits (or benefit levels), just like other entitlements, can be very difficult to remove once given.

### Some Future Challenges to Benefits Plans

There are certainly challenges in the provision of various benefits plans. Health care costs continuously increase. In particular, American employers often face a much higher care cost than their Canadian counterparts. How should employers deal with such increasing cost? Should the employer cut the coverage and if so, how can it be done with least employee resentment? Should the deductible be increased, should the employees' co-payment percentage be increased, or should fewer services be covered?

Another major liability arising out of benefits plans is in the pension area. Pensions provide a steady stream of income after retirement for the remaining lifetime of the retirees. There are two major types of pension plans: employee contribution plans and defined benefits plans. In employee contribution plans, employees and employers both contribute certain amounts on a regular basis (usually certain percentages of an employee's salary with each pay). The contributions are then invested, and the pension at the time of payout is calculated based on the contribution amounts plus their investment returns (less administrative costs). There is no guarantee what the accrued benefits amount will actually be when an employee reaches retirement. On the other hand, defined benefits plans provide a formula that specifies the payment amount under various conditions, such as on regular retirement or on early retirement. The formula usually involves multiplying three elements: (1) the number of years in the pension plan; (2) the annual earnings, which can be the latest earnings, the average earnings in the last few years, or the highest annual earnings in the last few years in case a person retires in phases; and (3) a certain factor that represents a percentage or proportion to be applied to the annual earnings. With this type of plans, the future payment is committed, irrespective of the return from investing the funds. Hence, liability may arise for the employer if the investment is not doing as well as expected, such as in a financial market downturn. Shortfall in funds can also arise if unexpected high inflation pushes up salaries, especially if it happens to occur in some years when many employees retire, making the pension payment much higher than anticipated. Longer life expectancies of the retirees also add to the increase in pension payout. As government legislation requires that shortfalls be made up primarily by the employer, such liabilities can be very substantial in cost and not always predictable. Therefore, there seems to be a move away from defined benefits plans in recent years (Long, 2002). Designing and implementing benefits plans, especially ones that have long-term implications, must be done very carefully, with due consideration given to the plans' objectives, potential impact, feasibility, and long-term sustainability.

# HRM in Action
## Benefits Plans at Bank of Montreal (BMO) Financial Group

BMO, in operation since 1817, has been a leading financial institution in North America, with over 29,000 full-time employees just in Canada in 2012. It has consistently been regarded as an employer with not only a strong commitment to employee development, but also good financial rewards and benefits plans. BMO ensures its salary is competitive through taking part in market surveys and reviewing individual salaries yearly. Bonuses, share-purchase plans, defined benefits pension plans, and discounted financial products are some examples of the financial benefits provided. Its flexible health plan applies to a range of benefits for the employees and their family, some automatically covered while some dependent on employee choice with adjustable premiums to suit individual needs. No waiting period is required. Benefits available include life, accident, and disability insurance, employee assistance plans, and coverage for prescription drugs, dental, eyecare, medical supplies, and alternative medicine. Flexible plans are particularly important in the United States where health costs are high and employees can choose their preferred provider, plan package, and dependent coverage. Employees can also contribute to a health spending account to pay for extra health-related expenses at the pre-tax rate. Specially worth mentioning is that health plan coverage extends to retirees too. For employees keen in lifelong learning, the continuous education assistance plan offers financial support for business-related learning. At times of financial hardship, employees and retirees may obtain help from a specially set up benevolent fund.

BMO also has generous leave policies, such as parental leave, compassionate care leave (for caring for ill family members), people care days (for any personal matters), and extended leaves of absence as needed. As well, the company offers flexible work arrangements like flextime, flexplace (work from home), compressed work week, reduced summer hours, and job sharing to allow for a good work and life balance. Phased-in retirement is another work option available to the older workers. To help employees with young children, the bank partners up with a national day care provider to offer quality emergency day care services (up to 10 days paid for by the employer). These initiatives are considered helpful to attract and retain talent.

BMO was selected as "one of Canada's Top 100 Employers, Top Employers for Canadians over 40, Financial Post's Ten Best Companies to Work For, and Greater Toronto's Top Employers for 2012" (Yerema & Leung, 2011).

Sources:
BMO. (n. d.). *Work and life effectiveness.* Retrieved June 25, 2012 from www.bmo.com/home/about/banking/corporate-responsibility/employees/work-life-effectiveness
BMO. (n. d.). *BMO responding to working parents' need for more flexible day care options.* Retrieved June 25, 2012 from newsroom.bmo.com/press-releases/bmo-responding-to-working-parents-need-for-more-f-tsx-bmo-201202100765316001
Yerema, R., & Leung, K. (2011, October 6). *Chosen as one of Canada's top 100 employers, top employers for Canadians over 40, Financial Post's ten best companies to work for and Greater Toronto's top employers for 2012.* Retrieved June 25, 2012 from www.eluta.ca/top-employer-bank-of-montreal

# HRM in Action
## Value-Based Health Benefits at Procter & Gamble (P&G)

Prior to 2004, P&G had been paying a flat percentage co-insurance for prescription drug coverage for employees. Due to rising cost upon the arrival of many specialty drugs, the company strategically implemented a value-based health benefits plan with the following goals: to recognize the importance of employee health to company performance, to contain cost, and to change employee behaviour to foster a healthy workforce. The plan involved two tiers of drug coverage. The first tier covered drugs that were required for preserving the major bodily functions. The company paid 70% of the drug costs for this tier to ensure that needed drugs were affordable to employees to maintain fundamental health. The second tier covered drugs that were not essential but nice to have, such as acne treatments, contraceptives, and hormonal therapies, for which the company paid 50% co-insurance, down from the previous coverage. Other medications that were simply to enhance one's lifestyle, such as sexual enhancing drugs and appetite-suppressants, were not covered. However, together with this change was the emphasis on maintaining a healthy living through preventive incentives, such as payment for employees to complete online health risk assessments, weight-loss programs, smoking cessation programs, and personalized condition management programs for certain health conditions (e.g., diabetes, heart disease, depression, etc.). The change resulted in substantially reduced numbers of prescription use in the tier two drugs and overall decrease in medical costs especially in areas of hospital and emergency room costs, while many employees took advantage of the preventive incentives. Overall, employees seemed to be taking their medications and managing their well-being more responsibly than before. Hence, the value-based redesigned plan was able to positively change employee behaviour in their health management.

Source:
Ceplenski, C. (September 19, 2007). Value-based health benefits pay off for P&G. *BLR HR and Employment Law News*. Retrieved January 26, 2012 from http://hr.blr.com/HR-news/Benefits-Leave/Healthcare-Benefits/Value-Based-Health-Benefits-Pay-Off-for-PG/

## References

Adams, J. S. (1965). Inequity in social exchange. In L. Berkowitz (Ed.), *Advances in experimental social psychology* (Vol. 2, pp. 267–299). New York: Academic Press.

Belcher, J. G. (1996). *How to design and implement a results-oriented variable pay system.* New York: American Management Association.

Belcourt, M., & McBey, K. (2000). *Strategic human resources planning* (2nd ed.). Toronto, ON: Nelson Thomson.

Chen, H., & Chen, C. (2004). Direct financial payments within an organization: A competitive advantage perspective. *International Journal of Management, 21*(2), 202-210.

Eligh, L. (2012). Chapter 12: Managing employee benefits [Powerpoint presentation]. In *Human resource management* (Canadian second edition, 2011). Retrieved February 26, 2012 http://www.pptsearch365.com/Human-Resource-Management-11e.html

Herzberg, F. (1968, January/February). One more time: How do you motivate employees? *Harvard Business Review, 46,* 53-62.

Human Resources and Social Development Canada. (2006). *Pay equity legislation in Canada by jurisdiction.* Retrieved November 12, 2006 from HRSDC, Labour Law, Employment Standards Legislation in Canada website: http://www.sdc.gc.ca/en/lp/spila/clli/eslc/table_pay_equity.pdf

Long, R. J. (2002). *Strategic compensation in Canada* (2nd ed.). Scarborough, ON: Nelson Thomson.

Maslow, A. (1954). *Motivation and personality.* New York: Harper.

Skenes, C., & Kleiner, B. H. (2003). The HAY system of compensation. *Management Research News, 26*(2-4), 109-115.

Sulzner, G. T. (2000). A pay equity saga: The Public Service Alliance of Canada vs. The Treasury Board of Canada.... *Journal of Collective Negotiations in the Public Sector, 29*(2), 89-122.

Vroom, V. H. (1964). *Work and motivation.* New York: Wiley.

Zingheim, P. K., Ledford, G. E., Jr., & Schuster, J. R. (1996, Spring). Competencies and competency models: Does one size fit all? *ACA (American Compensation Association) Journal, 5*(1), 56-65.

 **Chapter 9**

# Performance Appraisal and Performance Management

## Introduction

To most managers and employees, *performance appraisal* (PA) is a familiar annual or periodic exercise in which one's past work performance is assessed. It is also a process that many seem to dread and is reportedly one of the most disliked management tasks, right next to firing employees (Heathfield, 2007). Employees being appraised may be wary of scrutiny or criticism, while appraisers may be concerned about offending the appraised employee and the tremendous amount of time demanded of the process. Many simply do not have the confidence and the skills required to do a PA properly. Yet, it has been a process firmly in place in many organizations for decades.

In more recent years, some organizations have begun to see the need to look beyond PA into what is called *performance management* (PM) in order to become a high performance work organization. PM aims at recognizing good performance and continuously improving the performance of the employees and the organization by fostering a culture of cooperation and partnership between management and employees. This means having employees participate in the performance review and development process, integrating their efforts in alignment with the organizational vision and strategies, and putting in place HR and work systems that support the management philosophy. Whereas PA is backward-looking, PM is more concerned with going forward. Mutually agreed goals and measures are commonly set, and ongoing feedback and development are emphasized. PA is still a very important component of PM, but PM takes a holistic approach in managing performance. It is not just an assessment tool.

PM can serve a number of purposes for an organization. Some of the general ones are

- to show employees that the organization cares about their performance;

- to formally communicate the organizational and departmental goals and strategies and how the individual performance goals tie in with them;

- to provide feedback for past performance with a view to removing performance obstacles and providing performance enablers to help improve individual and thus organizational performance;

- to set future challenging performance goals and plans jointly between the supervisor and employee so that the employee is motivated to achieve them;

- to jointly set developmental goals and plans to improve employee knowledge and skills; and

- to provide the records for human resource decisions, such as promotion, pay increase, and terminations.

To achieve effective PM, there must be commitment and support at all levels of the organization. The process must be seen as fair and able to attain its objectives, while the PA tools are reliable and valid.

Since PM has two major components, assessment and development, how should the two parts be conducted and integrated? Generally, separating the assessment part from the development part in the PM design is desirable because their different emphases require different corresponding tools and methods. For example, whereas quantitative measures are more helpful with assessment and human resource decision-making, qualitative feedback provides more information for development purposes (Toegel & Conger, 2003). It is also a good idea to separate the two processes, such as separate appraisal and development interviews. In the next section, the conflicting roles of the appraiser in being a judge (critical in assessment) and a coach (helpful in development) are discussed. Basically, switching between incompatible roles in the same process compromises the effectiveness of the appraiser in both roles.

This chapter starts with a look at some PA problems and suggestions to address them. The commonly available PA methods are introduced along with their strengths and weaknesses. Next is how a method should be chosen with regard to the organizational goals, the organizational culture, and the PM objectives. A specific section is devoted to multiple rater and 360-degree feedback, which are being increasingly used in organizations. The chapter closes with some suggestions for providing productive feedback.

## PROBLEMS WITH PERFORMANCE APPRAISAL

When properly managed, PA is an effective tool to enhance individual and organizational performance. However, the process is also associated with a number of potential problems. A few of the major issues are summarized here.

### Assessment versus Development

The appraising supervisor is often placed in the conflicting roles of judge and coach, making it difficult for the supervisor to do a good job (McGregor, 1957). On the one hand, the appraiser is the boss who makes a performance judgment of the subordinate. On the other hand, she or he is a colleague, mentor, and coach, someone who is supposed to provide support and help for the appraised. Imagine a situation where the appraiser has to mention all the unfavourable incidents that justify a low rating and the consequences of such performance (e.g., demotion, no salary increase) but then switch his or her role immediately to show a positive attitude and support in trying to develop the employee. It is very common that once the assessment part is discussed, employee defensiveness gets in the way with a shift of focus to the employment and financial implications, making it almost impossible to direct the conversation to the coaching and development part. In other words, the judge role has the potential to create defensive responses from subordinates and dissatisfaction for both parties, thereby jeopardizing the effectiveness of both the appraisal and developmental aspects. Therefore, if two separate processes and forms are used, so that the assessment and development discussions are done at different times, the supervisor may be able to have the proper focus for each meeting and the employee may be more receptive to developmental suggestions.

### Appraisal Biases

Appraisals inevitably involve judgment, which in turn is associated with subjectivity and biases. Biases are intentional or unintentional. Listed in Table 9-1 is a summary of common biases related to appraisals.

Most biases can be reduced by proper training and appraisal design. Often, raters are unaware of their unintentional biases. Raising self-awareness of the raters and teaching them techniques for self-reflection and checking may lower incidences of such biases. For intentional biases, raters should be educated on the adverse implications of the bias, and hopefully, in combination with proper built-in safeguards in the system, such occurrences will be reduced. To ensure the appraisals are done appropriately, performance management skills should be an appraisal dimension for the raters themselves. This holds them accountable for the process so that PA gets the serious attention it deserves.

185

**Table 9-1  Appraisal Biases**

| | |
|---|---|
| **Halo** | Having one facet of performance influence the assessment of other (probably unrelated) facets.<br>For example, if a person is known to be good with presentation skills, he or she is rated as good with analytical skills too without objective consideration of the evidence for the latter. |
| **Central tendency** | Rating everyone just around the central point.<br>This is a safe approach for appraisers because fewer supportive comments are usually needed to substantiate a middle rating. |
| **Leniency** | Rating everyone higher than they deserve.<br>Some raters do this intentionally to get their subordinates a higher pay increase or to avoid potential conflicts or confrontations. |
| **Harshness** | Rating everyone lower than they deserve.<br>Some raters do this to reduce the necessary pay increase for the department in order to fit the budget. A rater who him- or herself got a low rating may also be reluctant to rate his or her subordinates any higher. |
| **Recency** | Allowing recent performance to mask over the performance demonstrated earlier in the appraisal period.<br>Raters who do not document performance behaviours and who are forgetful are prone to have this bias. |
| **Primacy** | Allowing the earlier performance to mask over the performance in a later period (i.e., first impression counts too much.) |
| **Spillover** | Allowing past evaluations to influence the current appraisal period evaluation. Hence, it is sometimes suggested that past appraisal forms should not be available for review for the new appraisal period, other than perhaps the part of the development plans which require follow-up actions in the current period. |
| **Contrast** | Allowing the performance of others to influence the evaluation of a particular individual.<br>For example, an average performer may be rated excellent when appraised together with a large proportion of poor performers due to the favourable comparison. |
| **Similarity** | Rating someone higher just because the person is similar to the rater him- or herself. |

## *Time and Commitment*

The appraisal process is very time-consuming. Preparing the documentation and conducting interviews takes a lot of the supervisor's time, especially if he or she has a large span of control. In situations where there is a lack of top management commitment to the process and the human resource department is left only with the role of collecting the PA forms, PA is often ignored by line managers. Moreover, the real purpose of the appraisal process is sometimes not clear to the managers and employees. With rapidly changing environments, the annual or semi-annual appraisal process is at times considered not very useful. People are not inclined to spend much effort and time on it if they feel that the forms are just filed on record. On the other hand, if it is done more frequently, supervisors and subordinates can be overwhelmed. Therefore, a balanced approach is necessary to allow for sufficient flexibility without creating an undue amount of work. As well, both top management and HR must play a major role to generate the necessary commitment and support for PA from line management.

## Budget Constraints

When the appraisal process is too closely tied in with the budget and the merit pay increase, the PA ratings may be manipulated: upwards to provide more rewards for the appraised employees if the budget is not tight or downwards to fit within a tight budget. Departments with more top performers than others may also find themselves in need of downward adjustments in order to keep within a budget set independent of departmental performance levels and committed to prior to the appraisal period, thereby making it grossly unfair to the high performing employees. Hence, it is important that the PA process is fair and employees are given an assessment based on their performance as compared with established performance criteria, not the budget amount. (Note that top performers can still get a low salary increase if there is a budget constraint, but in no way should their performance ratings be lowered to justify a low salary increase.)

## Lack of Skills

The appraiser may not really know how to conduct a proper appraisal due to a lack of training. Many forms used for PA are not well-designed, with the scales meaning different things to different people. With proper education and training and well-designed processes and forms, such a problem is alleviated. These areas are covered further in the following sections.

## PERFORMANCE MANAGEMENT DESIGN ISSUES

In designing a PM process, it is important that the purpose of the PM be identified and agreed upon by the main stakeholders. A number of questions then need to be asked, including but not limited to the following:

- How can organizational goals be translated to the group and individual goals?
- Should performance assessment be group-based or individual-based or a combination of both?
- Should the appraisal be tied in with the budget or merit pay and, if so, how tight should the link be?

- Who should do the appraisal: a supervisor, coworkers, customers, or the employee him- or herself?
- Who should coordinate the process, especially if multiple-raters are used?
- Who has ownership or are accountable for the appraisal process?
- How should the measurement standards and criteria be set?
- What appraisal method is appropriate and who is best to design the appraisal form and associated processes?
- How often should appraisals be done?
- How often should follow-up actions take place for the developmental plans?
- To what extent should the appraisee be involved in the process?
- What is the appeal process in case of disagreements with the appraisal?

## COMMON APPRAISAL METHODS

### Ranking

Ranking is easier to use in small departments with few assessment criteria. In multi-dimensional criteria situations, it can be very tedious and difficult to determine the rank order of every individual, especially the ones in the middle, some of whom perform better only in some areas than others. Ranking also has the tendency to make at least half of the individuals unhappy if they know that they are below the middle rank. Comparing employees with each other pits them against one another, especially when pay is tied tightly to their rank; colleagues may become less cooperative and even fight for the top ranks and the associated rewards. In some organizations, a forced ranking approach is adopted in which employee performances are grouped into different rank categories and only a certain percentage of employees are allowed for each performance category. For example, the top performer category is limited to five percent of employees. While this approach overcomes the situation where there are rating inconsistencies across areas, it does not allow for proper recognition of excellent performance in units where there are a number of very capable employees. It also unnecessarily over-recognizes some average or poor performers in units where there are fewer top performers.

### Rating

There are various forms of rating scales. In some organizations, certain common dimensions are set and are expected to apply to all positions. In other organizations, more specific dimensions are identified for each departmental or occupational group. Common dimensions used are along the lines of quality and quantity of work, work knowledge and skills, initiative, and relationships with others. A rating scale of 3 to 10 points may be used. Sometimes, the scale only has the two ends defined, for example, as "high" and "low" or "strongly agree" and "strongly disagree." Sometimes each point involves a brief description of what it means. This is what is used in the popular *graphic ratings scale* (GRS). Figure 9-1 is a partial illustration of a graphic ratings scale.

**Figure 9-1  Graphic Ratings Scale Example**

|  | 1<br>Outstanding | 2<br>Very Good | 3<br>Average | 4<br>Fair | 5<br>Poor |
|---|---|---|---|---|---|
| Job Knowledge |  |  |  |  |  |
| Initiative |  |  |  |  |  |
| Cooperation |  |  |  |  |  |

The advantage of GRS is that it is simple to use. Its main disadvantages are the vague dimension and scale point descriptions give rise to inconsistency in interpretation and that simply selecting a point for each dimension does not provide detailed information for feedback. Therefore some organizations require supplemental descriptive information to support the point assigned.

Another very similar scale that some organizations use is the *behaviour observation scale* (BOS). It specifically measures the extent or frequency desirable behaviours for the job are demonstrated. Figure 9-2 is a partial illustration of a behaviour observation scale for a project team member.

**Figure 9-2  Behaviour Observation Scale Example**

|  | 1<br>Almost Never | 2<br>Seldom | 3<br>Sometimes | 4<br>Regularly | 5<br>Almost Always |
|---|---|---|---|---|---|
| Completion of task on time |  |  |  |  |  |
| Proper consultation with stakeholders |  |  |  |  |  |
| Providing clear documentation |  |  |  |  |  |

Like GRS, this scale is simple to use. Moreover, performance assessments based on actual behaviours are generally viewed as more objective. Hence, appraised employees are more receptive to the feedback provided through such scales. However, it is not always easy to determine the most appropriate set of desirable behaviours. Different sets of behaviour descriptions may be needed for different types of position. The vague BOS rating scale definitions leave plenty of room for inconsistent interpretation as well. This last drawback is addressed by the use of a more complex behaviour-based scale called the *behaviourally anchored ratings scale* (BARS). Under BARS, each scale point has a behavioural description attached to it. Such descriptions are quite specific to the job or job category so the development of such scales requires someone with good knowledge of the job involved. The development process can be quite time-consuming and labour-intensive. Figure 9-3 is an illustration of a behaviourally anchored ratings scale for an instructor in relation to just two job dimensions.

**Figure 9-3  Behaviourally Anchored Rating Scale Example**

| Behaviour Descriptions | Ratings (Select the most appropriate rating for each category) |
|---|---|
| Instructor's promptness in answering student questions:<br><br>1.  My instructor generally answers my questions in a few hours. | ☐ |
| 2.  My instructor generally answers my questions in a day. | ☐ |
| 3.  My instructor generally answers my questions in two to three days. | ☐ |
| 4.  My instructor generally answers my questions in a week. | ☐ |
| 5.  My instructor generally does not answer my questions or takes more than a week to answer them. | ☐ |
| Instructor's effectiveness in helping students apply course concepts:<br><br>1.  My instructor proactively provides examples to link theory with practice and offers constructive feedback on the application of course concepts. | ☐ |
| 2.  My instructor provides occasional examples to link theory with practice and offers feedback only as necessary on the application of course concepts. | ☐ |
| 3.  My instructor lets students come up with examples of applications of course concepts and provides feedback on them. | ☐ |
| 4.  My instructor lets students come up with examples of applications of course concepts and offers suggestions only if they are inappropriate. | ☐ |
| 5.  My instructor neither provides examples to link theory with practice nor offers feedback when students apply the course concepts to practice. | ☐ |

## Checklist

A number of behavioural statements reflective of job performance (both positive and negative) are prepared. Each of the statements carries a positive or negative weight, the value of which depends on its relevance and importance to the job performance. Appraisers are to check off the statements where they apply, and the weighted score is compiled to reflect an overall score. In its simplest form, all statements carry the same weight and the overall score is calculated just by counting the checked statements. While this method seems simple to use, it does have its drawbacks. Since the statements need to be specific to the job behaviour, a different list may be needed for each job group. The choice of checking or not checking sometimes does not provide the necessary information for good feedback. Moreover, there is uncertainty as to when a check mark should be given: to what extent does the behaviour need to be exhibited? With only two extreme choices (checking and not checking), the chance of bias, especially the leniency bias, is increased.

## Narrative Form

The narrative form provides good information for feedback and discussion and stays away from trying to compare employees with one another in any quantitative terms. The appraisal can take longer to complete than the simple rating or checklist methods. The quality and dimensions of focus can be quite different for different appraisers and such lack of consistency is a drawback for the organization. The narrative form is usually used in combination with other methods, such as the ratings scale, so that the PA has both qualitative and quantitative components.

## Critical Incident

The appraiser (often the supervisor) documents all the major incidents where the appraisee performs very well or very poorly. The cumulated information over a period indicates the effectiveness of the appraisee on the job. With proper documentation, specific examples can be cited to support the evaluation. This method provides more objectivity in the assessment and reduces some of the bias due to the recency effect. However, subjectivity is still involved in converting the incident information into an overall assessment over a number of dimensions. The major problem with this approach is that most supervisors do not have the time to document every critical incident. Many just rely on what they can recall at the time of the appraisal, which basically defeats the purpose of the approach.

## *Goal Setting*

Under the goal setting method, goals and targets are set in advance of the appraisal period. One popular goal setting approach is *management by objectives* (MBO) in which goals are jointly developed by the employee and his or her supervisor. As discussed in Chapter 3 under "Goal Setting Theory", goal setting is a motivational as well as an appraisal tool. The goals set should be aligned with the organizational and departmental objectives. The goals should also be specific (S), measurable (M), attainable or achievable (A), relevant (R), and timely or time-bound (T), or in short, SMART. Proper goal-setting can motivate performance because employees know where they should direct their efforts and what to aim for. By focusing on actual results, this is a more objective approach than many others. Moreover, the joint goal setting process, if used, has the added advantage of getting better employee buy-in.

However, as with any other methods, there are a few drawbacks to this approach. The setting of individual goals and target measures for individual employees is a time-consuming process. With a rapidly changing environment, the goals and measures set may not be applicable if circumstances change during the appraisal period. If goals are not periodically adjusted, they become meaningless at the end of the appraisal period. If they are changed constantly, there is no point in setting the goals before the appraisal period as the basis for comparison of performance. Moreover, constantly updating the goal-setting document can be exceedingly time-consuming, and few supervisors can afford the time. A well-balance approach is needed to allow the goals and measures to be adjusted as appropriate in warranted circumstances so that the appraisal review properly considers unanticipated changes.

Another major criticism of this approach is that the focus on the outcomes leads to a few problems. First, many factors contribute to the outcomes and some of them are not at all within the employee's control. Should the employee be penalized for something outside his or her control? Second, what gets measured tends to get done. Since only a limited number of goals can be listed in the appraisal form, areas not covered but still important for the job may be neglected. Third, in this approach, the process of achieving the goal may be ignored. Does the end justify any means? For example, how acceptable is it to have team cooperation sacrificed for someone to reach an individual sales target? A suggestion to overcome this issue is to set some team-related goals as individual goals so contribution to team performance is assessed for the individuals as well. Although having specific goals set tends to enhance objectivity in the appraisal, bias can still occur if some supervisors set more lenient goals than others.

## Link between Organizational and Individual Goals

When it comes to performance measurement and goal-setting, many people think of the balanced scorecard approach, which has gained much popularity since its introduction in 1992 by Robert Kaplan and David Norton. The balanced scorecard approach was not developed for individual employee performance assessment. Rather, it is aimed at the organizational or departmental level performance. Basically, as mentioned in Chapter 1, the approach recommends that organizations not just focus on the financial outcomes, but also consider other dimensions. The four dimensions of performance measures Kaplan and Norton (1992) propose are: financial perspective, customer perspective, innovation and learning perspective, and internal business perspective. The last three operational measures are important complements to the financial aspect as they are believed to be "the drivers of future financial performance" (p. 71). It recognizes the importance of customers who provide the revenue, internal processes that affect productivity and customer satisfaction, and innovation and learning that help to improve business processes and meet customer needs. All these, in turn, have an effect on the shareholder value.

Although it is intended for measuring performance at the organizational or departmental levels, the balanced scorecard can have an impact on individual appraisal situations. As introduced in Chapter 1 and emphasized throughout the text, individual goals should be integrated and aligned with the organizational and departmental goals. Therefore, if an organization adopts the balanced scorecard approach, outcomes other than the financial perspective should also be considered in setting individual goals. For example, what are some of the individual performance goals in relation to provision of customer service, to contributions to internal processes, and to improving knowledge and learning practices? In any case, the goals set indicate explicitly to the employees what criteria are used for the performance evaluation and what is valued by the organization.

## Choice of Method

There is no single appraisal method that is right or wrong. The choice really depends on the objectives of the PM system, the culture of the organization (e.g., joint goal-setting does not go well in a highly authoritative culture), and the resources that can be provided for the system. If PM is to serve a few objectives, especially when it relates to both pay and development, a combination of approaches is appropriate. Managers should be aware that the choice of the appraisal method, what is emphasized, and the way it is implemented all send messages to employees about the management philosophy. For example, what does the organization care about? How employees are valued? Is the organization fair to employees in terms of both distributive and procedural justices?

Greer (2001) suggests that while selecting an appropriate measurement approach is important, it is crucial to obtain employee buy-in because a performance management system can only function effectively if its purpose is understood and well supported by not just the appraisers, but also the appraisees. Hence, organizations should ensure that employees

- understand the dimensions of performance on which they are evaluated,
- know that they are being evaluated on relevant aspects of their jobs,
- view the evaluation process as valid,
- believe the evaluations are fair, and
- see reward contingencies.

## MULTIPLE RATERS AND 360-DEGREE FEEDBACK

In traditional organizations, the supervisor is usually the one doing the PA. The supervisor is assumed to be in the best position to know what the subordinate is doing. With organizations becoming flatter and employees being required to multi-task, an employee's work has many facets and it is doubtful the supervisor is able to sufficiently observe all these dimensions to provide a valid evaluation. For example, in a matrix organization where functional roles intersect with cross-functional responsibilities (like in a project team), a functional supervisor may never actually have the opportunity to observe an employee in action in a cross-functional team and may have to rely on feedback from others to render the judgment. In such a case, the team leader is an appropriate appraiser, as are some of the other team members. To overcome the inadequacy and inaccuracy of single-rater appraisals, *multi-rater assessment* has become quite common in recent decades, especially for supervisory and management positions. Due to the demand on time and resources, multi-rater assessment is less common for junior positions with more standardized work performance criteria.

In any position, an employee is likely to be working with and for a number of people. Who is an appropriate rater in the multi-rater process? The supervisor usually still plays a critical role. Peers of the employee can provide essential feedback on areas such as contribution to teamwork and helpfulness to coworkers. Subordinates of the employee may have valid comments on areas such as leadership ability and administrative skills. Customers, clients, suppliers, or any other contacts, both within the organization and outside, may be able to provide essential information on areas such as service quality and efficiency. In the situation where the appraisers can be anyone working above, below, or at the same level in the organization as the appraisee, the multi-rater process is also called a *360-degree appraisal* or *feedback*.

Last but not least, many PAs involve the element of *self-assessment* as well. Self-assessment is often considered appropriate as the individual should know best about his or her own work performance. It gives employee the opportunity to actively participate in the process and to seriously reflect upon his or her work. It also prepares the employee for discussing the past performance and future plans with the supervisor. However, research provides a few interesting insights into and cautionary suggestions on the self-rating situation. Some of the concerns with self-assessment, as well as with the overall 360-degree feedback process specifically, are discussed below.

## Problems with Self-Assessment

Eichinger and Lombardo (2003), in their review of PA literature and their empirical study, report that self-ratings are generally significantly different from ratings by others and that they often bear little or no relation to performance, actual promotion, or promotion potential. Moreover, people tend to overestimate their strengths, especially in the case of the poorest performers. More bragging is also associated with a higher level of difficulty in checking the validity of the claim. Under-raters, on the other hand, are likely to be high performers with high expectations.

Employees are also concerned about self-assessment for fear of being seen as over-rating themselves (the supervisor may feel they are not trustworthy by inflating the ratings) or under-rating themselves (as it may actually contribute to the lowering of their final evaluation). Hence, self-appraisal may add not just work but also stress for the employee. While self-rating may not be a good tool for performance assessment and employment-related decisions, it is helpful for raising self-awareness (Toegel & Conger, 2003). For example, a comparison of self-rating and ratings by others helps the individual see his or her blind spots and provides the individual and his or her supervisors with a better understanding of how the employee sees him- or herself.

## Rater Selection Issues

How should one select from the pool of available appraiser candidates? For example, an employee may have twenty peers working with him or her. Obviously, not all of them can be or need to be involved. Should the choice be made by the employee, the supervisor, or by some random selection? Nomination by the employee gives the employee more satisfaction in knowing that his or her view counts, but there is the possibility of collusion and upward bias. Hence, while the employee may be consulted on the candidate pool, the selection is best determined by someone with a good knowledge of the employee's work contacts and who may be able to provide an objective assessment of the raters' knowledge and assessment abilities. Alternatively, the selection can involve a balanced number of appraisers nominated by both the employee and management.

### Lack of Skills

As mentioned earlier, appraisers may not possess the skills necessary to do a proper appraisal. This is so even in traditional settings where mainly managers and supervisors are the appraisers. With 360-degree feedback, a number of additional appraisers are involved, with many of them in lower level positions who may not have done any appraisals before. In such a situation, proper training is particularly critical to ensure understanding of the system, how an appraisal should be conducted, and how development plans should work. Fostering a culture of openness, empowerment, and participation also helps employees feel at ease with such a feedback process.

### Undermining of Supervisor Authority

The supervisor may feel that his or her authority is undermined by sharing the appraiser role with others, especially with subordinates. Hence, 360-degree evaluation should not be implemented as a standalone system misaligned with the organizational culture. It works best only in a culture where employee participation and empowerment are valued and embraced by both management and employees.

### Rater Biases and Inconsistent Ratings

Supervisors, peers, and subordinates alike may fear retribution in a 360-degree evaluation environment if the person being appraised does not get a good evaluation. Hence, they are less likely to be honest or candid in their assessment and may provide higher ratings than justified (Chappelow, 2003). In particular, research shows that subordinates tend to provide higher ratings as compared with raters who are supervisors or peers. The difference was found to be as high as a full standard deviation on average (Eichinger & Lombardo, 2003, p. 36).

Peers may also provide a somewhat biased evaluation, either being too generous because they want to do their colleague a favour or have an implicit reciprocal arrangement or being too strict because they are competing for limited resource rewards. With multiple raters assessing on different dimensions, it is also very likely that some areas of evaluation are not compatible.

### Suggestions for 360-Degree Feedback

As discussed earlier, helpful measures to counter rating biases and inconsistencies include educating the raters and providing safeguards in the system, such as checking for inter-rater reliability, removing outliers (extreme ratings) or ratings not properly substantiated, and having a coordinator or facilitator review the inconsistencies, make sense of the interpretation, and consolidate the assessment as needed.

Keeping the appraisal process anonymous also helps promote honest evaluations as there is less fear of retribution. There is evidence that when the rating is not done anonymously, higher scores and lower variance result (Antonioni, 1994; Eichinger & Lombardo, 2003). Of course, with anonymity, there are the odd situations where the raters act irresponsibly in providing ratings because they are not accountable. That is why rater training and proper rater selection are essential.

Should 360-degree evaluation be used for assessment or development or both? Due to the various problems with rater bias and inconsistency in the multiple rater evaluation situation, it is very difficult, if not impossible, to consolidate the various results into an overall assessment, especially one that leads directly to human resource decisions. How are the various rater inputs to be weighed? Hence, 360-degree evaluation is best used for developmental purposes, where raters feel free to provide honest comments, knowing that the appraisal is not going to jeopardize someone's job or income (DeNisi & Kluger, 2000).

## PROVIDING PRODUCTIVE FEEDBACK

The way feedback is provided largely determines its effectiveness. DeNisi and Kluger (2000) suggest a few tips for feedback interventions:

- Focus on the task and task performance, not the person. Once the feedback gets personal and threatens the person's self-image, defensive behaviour and subjective arguments may ensue.
- Provide helpful information on how the performance can be improved.
- Develop a goal-setting plan (for both performance and personal goals) for the next period.

Ongoing feedback is also more useful than annual feedback as performance improvement can be made in a timely manner, especially when incidences of substandard performance are fresh in the memory. Feedback should be provided in a constructive manner, with encouragement and support to the employee. Sensitivity and active listening skills are also crucial for providing effective feedback. By putting him- or herself in the feedback recipient's shoes, an appraiser can have a better understanding and appreciation of the views and perspectives of the other side. Paraphrasing is a good tool to ensure the other person is not misunderstood. Asking for input and suggestions is a good way of getting the other person on board and signals the commitment to a partnership rather than a unilateral arrangement. When setting feedback meetings, it is also important to minimize distractions, such as unexpected visitors, phone calls, or pagers.

## Conclusion

In sum, PM is an ongoing commitment, even if formal PA is only done periodically. It requires a supportive and participative culture, good training and resource support, and alignment of other HR and work systems. For example, if performance improvement is to be driven by intrinsic motivation, then the work system must allow for growth and enrichment. If better skills and competencies are believed to lead to better performance, then skill-based pay should be considered over other systems such as seniority-based pay. Last but not least, PM involves two-way interaction. Management and employees are partners, working together for both the good of the organization and themselves.

---

# HRM in Action

## Performance Management Program (PMP) for Executives in the Federal Government (Canada)

The main objectives of the PMP for executives in government departments include motivating employees to excel in performance through goal-setting and rigourous evaluation, ensuring consistency and equity in performance management, and providing the basis for recognition and rewards (performance pay).

The program starts with establishing performance agreements between the executives and their supervisors, comprising 5 or 6 specific results-oriented commitments related to program and policy arising out of the department's business plans, management of organization's priorities and resources, and demonstration of leadership competencies (values and ethics; strategic thinking; engagement of people and organizations; and management excellence including people and financial management). Clear, observable, and/or measurable performance indicators for each commitment must be documented. At the beginning of the performance cycle, executives are made aware of the assessment criteria and how rewards are tied to the achievement of the results of demonstration of competencies. Changes to the agreement can be made in the period if agreed to by the parties. Formal performance evaluations are conducted once in the mid-point of the performance cycle and once at the end, with additional assessment done as circumstances warrant or at the request of the executive or the supervisor. Departments are expected to have a process to ensure a review of the executives' performance collectively for equity and consistency purposes. Where appropriate, feedback from the appraised executive, his or her peers, subordinates, as well as other relevant sources may be considered.

In determining the executive's performance ratings, the performance as shown by demonstrable behaviours and accomplishments, as well as the scope and the level of difficulty of the commitments are taken into account. Not only are results considered, but also the means of achieving so. The performance ratings categories include: did not meet expectations; succeeded - (either did not fully succeed or the expectations set were less challenging than those of others); succeeded (fully meet expectations); succeeded + (exceeded expectations or fully succeeded in a highly challenging type of commitment); surpassed (way above expectations); and unable to access. As endorsed in 2004 by the Advisory Committee on Senior Level Retention and Compensation, the "best practice" distribution of the ratings for an effective PMP should have not more than 65% in the "succeeded" and "succeeded +" categories, not more than 20% in the "surpassed" category, not less than 10% in the "succeeded -" category and not less than 5% in the "did not meet" category.

Guidelines on the PMP are provided by the Secretariat (the administrative arm) of the Treasury Board of Canada. The Treasury Board is responsible for "accountability and ethics, financial, personnel and administrative management, comptrollership, approving regulations and most Orders-in-Council" in the federal government.

---

Sources:
Treasury Board of Canada. (2007). *About the Treasury Board.* Retrieved March 17, 2012 from http://www.tbs-sct.gc.ca/tbs-sct/abu-ans/tb-ct/abu-ans-eng.asp
Treasury Board of Canada. (2007). *Guidelines on the performance management program for executives 2009-2010.* Retrieved March 17, 2012 from http://www.tbs-sct.gc.ca/hrh/gorgl01-eng.asp

## References

Antonioni, D. (1994, June). The effects of feedback accountability on upward appraisal ratings. *Personnel Psychology, 47*(2), 349-356.

Chappelow, C. T. (2003). 360-degree feedback. In C. D. McCauley & E. Van Velsor (Eds.), *The Center for Creative Leadership handbook of leadership development* (pp. 58-84, 2nd ed.). San Francisco: Jossey-Bass.

DeNisi, A. S., & Kluger, A. N. (2000). Feedback effectiveness: Can 360-degree appraisals be improved? *Academy of Management Executive, 14*(1), 129-139.

Eichinger, R. W., & Lombardo, M. M. (2003). Knowledge summary series: 360-degree assessment. *Human Resource Planning, 26*(4), 34-44.

Greer, C. R. (2001). *Strategic human resource management: A general managerial approach* (2nd ed.). Upper Saddle River, NJ: Prentice Hall.

Heathfield, S. (2007). Performance appraisals don't work – What does? *Journal for Quality & Participation, 30*(1), 6-9.

Kaplan, R. S., & Norton, D. P. (1992). The balanced scorecard – Measures that drive performance. *Harvard Business Review, 70*(1), 71-79.

McGregor, D. (1957). An uneasy look at performance appraisal. *Harvard Business Review, 35*(3), 89-94.

Toegel, G., & Conger, J. A. (2003). 360-degree assessment: Time for reinvention. *Academy of Management Learning and Education, 2*(3), 297-311.

Vonk, R. (1999). Impression formation and impression management: Motives, traits, and likeability inferred from self-promoting and self-deprecating behavior. *Social Cognition, 17*(4), 390-412.

# Diversity Management and Inclusiveness

## Introduction

*Diversity management* in an organization is about the recognition of individual differences, valuing the diverse perspectives, and integrating them with the view of bringing out the best contributions of people to achieve a competitive advantage for the organization. Successful diversity management often involves a culture of inclusiveness in which all employees, irrespective of their demographic characteristics or individual differences, feel respected and valued.

Individual differences are related to demographic characteristics, such as race, ethnicity, gender, sexual orientation, age, disability, marital status, family status, and religion. They are also related to differences in personality, life experiences, value systems, and views and approaches to work. The demographics list is similar to the list of prohibited grounds of discrimination under most human rights legislation in developed nations. Generally, under such laws, organizations must not engage in activities that provide different treatment to individuals based purely on the prohibited list of characteristics that do not have a direct bearing to the job requirements or performance. An interesting question that ensues is whether organizations should treat all employees the same way or differently (within the legal bounds). Some managers think that being non-discriminatory means treating everyone the same way, but how can organizations reconcile this need to treat people the same way and yet cater to individual differences? The essential point is that people should be treated fairly and that any differential employment treatment is based on valid grounds such as differences in needs (as in the case of training), tenure, ability or performance (as in the case of promotion), and job requirements (as in the case of salary level). Decisions should not be made on the basis of the demographic group to which an employee happens to belong. For example, English language training should not be offered only to a specific racial or ethnic group, but rather to anyone who has English as a second language or who, as shown through some form of valid assessment, has not yet mastered the language skills. Similarly, managers should not base decisions on unfounded impressions of work ethic just because a person is in a certain age group or comes from a certain background.

In this chapter, workplace discrimination in general is discussed, followed by more specific discussions on diversity related to gender, culture, age, and disability. General approaches are suggested for managing diversity and how a culture of inclusiveness can be built to create a competitive advantage for the organization. The controversy of reverse discrimination and the role of unions in diversity management are also covered.

## DISCRIMINATION

Why would employers discriminate in the first place? Discrimination can be due to stereotyping or other forms of personal bias and prejudice. Stereotyping refers to characterizing someone according to the group(s) to which he or she belongs. For example, if an employer perceives that members of a certain ethnic origin are generally less trustworthy than others, then job applicants from that ethnic origin may not be hired irrespective of their individual characteristics. Stereotyping tends to make complex decisions simpler for employers. Indeed, employers may intentionally practice statistical discrimination because trying to get to know each individual is time-consuming and often impractical. Making decisions based on the statistics of the group to which a person belongs greatly cuts down on the time and cost involved in making the decision, even though the outcome of an improper decision can be costly. An example of such discrimination is not hiring anyone with a criminal past because of the statistics on re-offending, regardless of what changes the individual might have gone through or how many years have elapsed since the offence.

Discrimination also occurs for other reasons. People tend to form impressions of others, like or dislike, within a very short time of their first meeting, before they get to know the individual. For example, an employer may dislike people with a certain facial feature. This is a purely subjective feeling, yet if not kept in check, can give rise to overt or subtle discrimination in the workplace.

Many people easily recognize overt forms of discrimination. Nowadays, with various legal protections against outright discrimination, many discrimination cases take more subtle forms. For example, female executives may complain that at times decisions are made outside the boardroom in informal "old boys' clubs" which tend to exclude female participation. Longstanding policies and practices, which were not established with the intention to discriminate, actually end up discriminating against certain classes or groups of workers. Such forms of discrimination are called systemic discrimination. It is important to note that while disparate treatment (intention to discriminate) is clearly discriminatory, discrimination can also be established based on the disparate impact (adverse outcomes) caused by certain actions, albeit unintentional. Systemic discrimination is not always apparent because people generally take established policies and practices for granted. In particular, if something is written into policy there is an aura of legitimacy attached to it, and people often accept it without question. In some instances, managers themselves may even be unaware that their actions in accordance with company policies or practices are discriminatory. Below are some examples of potential systemic discrimination:

- Using a written test in English to screen out applicants for positions that do not require English skills (it can discriminate against racial groups with English as a second language).

- Requiring certain characteristics or qualifications that are not bona fide occupational requirements (e.g., unnecessarily imposing weight or height requirements that discriminate against a gender or unnecessarily requiring Canadian experience that excludes recent immigrants).

- Not providing adequate washroom facilities for women in a male-dominated job environment.

- Relying on employee referral or the word of mouth for recruitment when the existing workforce is obviously underrepresented in the minority groups.

- Setting up decision-making committees based purely on tenure (rather than merits or contributions) which may have the effect of excluding minority members who tend to have been in the workforce for a shorter duration of time.

To reiterate, treating people differently based on any demographic or personal differences not related to the job requirements or performance standards is discriminatory and often unethical and illegal. Some of the common areas involving inequities are discussed below.

## GENDER INEQUITY

While women are no longer underrepresented in the overall workforce participation in many developed nations, gender inequity still seems to exist in many other ways. For example, even though more women are entering the professional and managerial ranks, the gender gap is still very apparent in the upper echelons of organizations. Women also tend to be overrepresented in part-time work, either by choice or otherwise.

According to Hausmann, Tyson, and Zahidi's (2011) study on the global gender gap, commissioned by the World Economic Forum, there has been much improvement in gender equity over the past years, but the reality is that the gender gap still exists in all of the 135 countries studied (representing more than 90% of the world's population). The gap was narrowest among the Nordic countries, while Canada and the United States were ranked eighteenth and seventeenth respectively. The study looks at four critical areas of equality: economic participation and opportunity, political empowerment, education attainment, and health and survival. In particular, the economic participation and opportunity variable captures the "participation gap, the remuneration gap and the advancement gap" in the workforce (p. 4). The following quotations reflect some of its findings, especially related to the first three areas.

> [T]he gap between women and men on economic participation and political empowerment remains wide: only 59% of the economic outcomes gap and only 19% of the political outcomes gap has been closed. (p. 16-17)

> [In terms of regions], North America holds the top spot, followed closely by Europe and Central Asia. (p. 17)

> The United States places 6th in the world in terms of economic participation and opportunity, the results of high rates of women's labour force participation and prominent numbers of women in legislative, senior official and managerial positions as well as professional and technical worker positions. However, the perceived wage inequality for similar work remains high, placing United States 68th in the world on this variable. (p. 23)

> [The Nordic] economies have made it possible for parents to combine work and family, resulting in high female participation rates, more shared participation in childcare, more equitable distribution of labour at home, better work-life balance for both women and men and in some cases a boost to declining fertility rates. Policies applied in these countries include mandatory paternal leave in combination with maternity leave, generous federally mandated parental leave benefits provided by a combination of social insurance funds and employers, tax incentives and post-maternity re-entry programmes. (p. 22)

In recent years, at least in North America, women have certainly been increasingly occupying important organizational positions. Fairfax (2005) indicates boardroom representation by women has increased by almost tenfold in the past thirty years, citing Korn/Ferry International's 2004 finding that "82% of Fortune 1000 companies had at least one woman on the board" (p. 1107). Still, by 2011, women only held 16% of available board seats at Fortune 500 companies" (Knowledge@ Wharton, 2011). Another study by the World Economic Forum specifically on corporate gender gap provides further evidence on the aspect of women's economic opportunity (Zahidi and Ibarra, 2010). Of the 20 major economies studied, including Canada and the United States, "[f]emale employees tend to be concentrated in entry or middle level positions" and "the average number of women holding the CEO-level position was a little less than 5%" (p. 5). It seems there is far more to do to address the gender gap, especially for senior management positions. Norway was a clear exception in this area. This may be due to a law effective January 2008 requiring all public companies to have women comprise 40 percent of their board members ("Business in Norway," 2008). It remains to be seen whether other countries will follow suit to establish some forms of mandatory representation requirements. The corporate gender gap report also found that the United States (together with India and Mexico) had the least generous statutory maternity leave provisions, while some employers in countries with more generous statutory requirements did not even provide the legal minimum in relation to maternity leave and benefits. In terms of advancement to leadership positions, the biggest barriers identified in the report are "general norms and cultural practices in your country", "masculine/patriarchal corporate culture" and "lack of role models" (p. 11).

A few interesting metaphors related to glass are used to describe the gender inequity situation. Other than the commonly known *glass ceiling* phenomenon, which refers to the lack of advancement opportunities for women, women executives are also said to face a "glass cliff," a situation in which women are given leadership positions with a greater chance of failure. Ryan and Haslam (2007) find in experimental studies across various settings a tendency to place women in precarious leadership positions. The reasons suggested for such appointments include the belief that women can handle socio-emotional challenges during crises; purposely setting them up for failure as a scapegoat; male candidates declining these positions in favour of better opportunities that come their way; and a signal for change as the previous traditional leadership has not worked. As this is a relatively new metaphor, further research to study the phenomenon is certainly needed. Another metaphor used in describing the gender inequity situation is the "glass escalator" (Williams, 1992). This term describes the phenomenon where men rise through the career ladder more rapidly than women, particularly in female-dominated areas.

There is a lot of controversy on whether the gender gap is real because there can be many reasons for women's lack of career advancement, including in part, their own choice and effort; differences in educational background, qualifications, and experiences; lack of mentors or female role models; and interrupted career path due to child-bearing, child-care, and elder care. However, the gender gap is still found to exist in rigorous studies that have controlled for confounding effects. For example, Brett and Stroh (1999), studying 1,000 managers in twenty Fortune 500 organizations, find a significant gap in the wage increase between males and females over a 5-year period, with the male managers' increase at 65% and the female managers' increase at only 54%, despite their apparent indistinguishable experience and background. The study also finds different experiences in the external labour market situation in that the gains from changing employers are minimal for female managers but greatly beneficial for the male managers. A more recently published longitudinal research that included thousands of MBA graduates from top U.S. schools as study subjects still shows that woman MBA graduates lagged behind in level and pay after controlling for "work experience, industry, region, and other factors" and it also provides support that the lag was not due to lesser ambitions by women as the women group studied included many who had no children and had explicitly stated their ambition for very senior ranks (Silva & Carter, 2011).

Even when women do get into management ranks, they seem to face more challenges than their male counterparts. For example, an organization may promote female employees just to make the organization look good from the diversity point of view. Due to such concepts, male colleagues may think that women get promotions not because of their ability, but because of their gender, even if it is not the case. Women tend to have a different style of management and communication. The softer approach of being more willing to listen and share power is sometimes seen by others as indecisive or less competent. On the other hand, if a female manager acts more like a male manager in terms of clothing choice and communication style, she may be seen as too aggressive (while men of similar qualities are seen as appropriately assertive). Hence, there seems to be no easy win-win situation for female managers (Oakley, 2000). Female managers in a male-dominated environment are often the tokens who are critically scrutinized and distrusted by the other organization members (Kanter, 1995). As a result, they may have to work a lot harder than their male counterparts to gain the level of respect they deserve. This difficulty faced by women may account for the lack of advancement into more senior leadership positions.

## CULTURAL DIVERSITY

Organizations today are operating in an increasingly pluralistic and ethnically diverse environment as more and more people move across nations. In Canada, immigrants form an important source of labour. Canada's 2011 Census shows that total visible minorities comprise over six million (19.1 percent) of the population, with South Asians, Chinese, and Blacks being the three largest minority categories, respectively representing 25 percent, 21 percent, and 15 percent of the visible minority population (Statistics Canada, 2013). The same census indicates that 20.6 percent of the population is foreign-born (Statistics Canada, 2013). Similarly, in the U.S., visible minorities represent a significant portion of the population. For example, Hispanics represented about 16 percent of the population in 2010, followed by Blacks at 13 percent, and Asians at 5 percent (U.S. Department of Commerce, 2011). In a Census Bureau study commissioned by the U.S. Department of Commerce, minority population is projected to contribute to 90 percent of the population growth in the period 1995 to 2050 (He & Hobbs, 1999, p. 1). This phenomenon of increased cultural diversity is also happening in the South Pacific region where Australia and New Zealand have seen substantial increase in the Asian population since the 1970s.

Despite the significant proportion and growth in visible minority population, their representation in senior management ranks lags substantially behind. According to a Conference Board of Canada 2004 report, of those which responded out of 300 organizations surveyed, only 3 percent have a chief executive officer who is a visible minority and only 3 percent of their senior executives are visible minorities (MacBride-King & Benimadhu, 2004). The 2006 Census shows that immigrants earned much less than their Canadian-born counterparts with the same amount of education and work experience. One explanation for the difference is in the level of skills between the two groups. Immigrants were found to score lower overall in prose literacy and problem-solving skills, despite the fact that a higher proportion of immigrants than Canadian-born had university-level education. The human capital accumulated from foreign work experience may also be limited in transferability, and hence, only yields very low returns (Statistics Canada, 2009).

The diversity is already a reality in the current workforce. The rapid pace of globalization involving overseas establishments or partnerships further necessitates the interaction and deployment of employees across national borders. Technological advancement has also made cross-border virtual teams a common occurrence. All these changes mean the need for effective cultural diversity management and cultural inclusiveness is imminently important. Integrating the diverse workforce and rectifying the under-representation situation are not just a human rights issue, but an issue that can have direct effect on the organizational performance. Empirically, firms embracing cultural diversity such as those on Fortune's 1999 list of "America's 50 Best Companies for Asians, Blacks and Hispanics," performed better than firms in the S&P 500 index (Colvin, 1999).

In Chapter 6, the cultural dimensions identified by Hofstede are discussed. They include power distance, individualism versus collectivism, uncertainty avoidance, masculinity versus femininity, long-term versus short-term orientation, and indulgence versus restraint. Understanding these dimensions not only helps in dealing with employees, customers, and other stakeholders in countries elsewhere, but also in managing employees in the parent company who come from different national cultures. Often in a pluralistic and multicultural environment there is no one best way to manage the workforce. Many North American managers naturally assume that applying the same parent company rules and expectations to other overseas locations is fair. However, what is right or ethical usually depends on the cultural context. Buying gifts for employees of an organization for which one intends to secure a contract is seen as a source of conflict of interest or even outright bribery in North America. However, in some cultures it is seen as a usual or expected way of doing business and not following the norm is seen as being disrespectful. North American culture also tends to stress equality which is a reflection of low power distance. Students call professors by name and the young are supposed to freely speak their minds. That is not the expected situation in cultures with high power distance, where the elderly or people in senior positions are to be heard and respected more than others. In countries like Japan, even salary is expected to relate to age and seniority. This is in sharp contrast to North America where employment-related decisions based purely on age are forbidden (but allowed for seniority). Countries that place a higher value on relationships and connections are said to be taking a *particularistic approach*, and from that perspective it is appropriate not to treat everyone the same way. In such a culture, family members and friends should receive higher priorities. Cultures that are sensitive to the nonverbal and situational cues are also said to be *high-context cultures*. They tend to place a high priority on social relations and groups (similar to the dimension of collectivism in Hofstede's classification). High-context cultures include Asian, Hispanic, American Indian, African American, and Arabic, while *low-context cultures* include Northern European, Germanic, and Scandinavian (Allard, 2002). Therefore, organizations cannot simply import any one set of human resource policies and practices suitable for one country into another without thoroughly understanding the type of culture into which they are getting and making modifications and adjustments as needed.

Cultural diversity is usually seen as related to racial or ethnic backgrounds. However, it can broadly be seen as involving differences in individuals' beliefs, values, and characteristics that do not necessarily vary only across national borders or across racial or ethnic lines. People brought up with different family backgrounds, with different exposures to educational systems, or who had worked for different organizations with different organizational norms and values all bring different cultural perspectives into an organization. In many situations, cultural diversity is a source of competitive advantage, as is explained later in this chapter.

## AGE DIVERSITY

With the arrival of the millennials into the workforce, workplaces may now have four different generations of workers. These are the veterans (~1925-1945), baby boomers (~1946-1964), generation X (~1965-1980), and generation Y (~1981-2000) (Jenkins, 2008).[1] Across the generations, there are general differences in personal characteristics, work styles, expectations and views on ethics or social responsibility. Some of these differences are captured in the following descriptions.

### The Veterans

Also sometimes called the Traditionalists, Silents, or Pre-Baby Boomers (Stevens, 2010), this generation of workers are at or around the retiring phase. Some may choose to stay on in the workforce for various reasons (e.g., they enjoy their work or they need the income) and even want to continue working for as long as they are capable of doing so. The veterans have gone through the tough economic times of the Great Depression and World War II, and these might have contributed to their conservative, disciplined, logical, and hard-working nature (Bartley, Ladd, & Morris, 2007). The Veterans are also described as "loyal, consistent and conforming," which favours a top-down management approach involving following the book (Stevens, 2010, p. 79). To the younger generations, they may be seen as rigid or harsh.

### The Baby Boomers

Born after World War II, this generation of workers are much better educated than the previous generation and were raised in a period of economic growth and stability. They are optimistic and eager to better the world, ambitious and determined to succeed, but they are also collaborative, relationship-building, and have a strong work ethics (Bartley et al., 2007; Dwyer, 2009; Stevens, 2010). While they have respect for power, they

---

1 Note that there has been no total consensus on the defining years of each generation and so, they may vary to some extent across research studies.

are less likely than the Veterans to unconditionally conform to rules and authority (Poindexter, 2008; Stevens, 2010).

**Generation X**

This generation has observed the ups and downs in the economy and some organizational downsizing periods. Hence, they do not believe in permanence of jobs and their commitment is not to the organization but to their own work, team, or a respected boss (Bartley, et al., 2007). They prefer ongoing feedback on their work, value autonomy, skill development, and advancement opportunities, and tend to fare well in an environment where the supervisor acts as a mentor, coach, or facilitator (Bartley, et al., 2007; Stevens, 2010). Their independence and preference for work/life balance may at times lead some of the older generation workers to mistakenly believe they are selfish and not caring.

**Generation Y**

This generation of workers are also called the millennials. Generally, this group is technologically savvy, good at multi-tasking and team work, values innovative ideas and ingenuity (rather than authority), prefers leisure time and travelling, appreciative of diversity and social responsibility, works hard for what they believe in, and will change jobs or careers for better challenges, development, or advancement (Bartley, et al., 2007; Dwyer, 2009; Jenkins, 2008; Poindexter, 2008; Stevens, 2010; Yeaton, 2008). Often born to protective parents who shower them with praises to boost their self-esteem, this generation may be less accustomed to receiving harsh criticisms. The high parental expectations may also add pressure for this group to excel (Bartley, et al., 2007).

As the baby boomers age, the age profile of the organization will shift. The retirement of the older workers, which currently form a large portion of the workforce, will lead to labour shortage situations, especially in terms of the more skilled and experienced workers. Organizations must be able to plan the staffing needs well in advance to prepare for such situations. Young workers are often said to hold a different work value, and most people are starting to understand that the current situation is unlike in the past when people tended to have only one career path and to work for one company lifelong. Mobility across jobs is a fact of life and organizations must be prepared to retain their talent by being an employer of choice. Bridging the gap between the old and the young is important in integrating employees with different assets. Properly designed teamwork and mentoring programs allow for better social networking among organization members and help in the transfer of knowledge. Older workers may benefit from the computer skills of the younger generation, while the latter can gain valuable insights from the older workers' practical work experience. Moreover, organizations may need to consider ways of retaining some older workers beyond their "retirement" in response to the labour needs.

Dwyer (2009) outlines some more issues that multigenerational workplaces face. For example, the generation Y workers may be supervising the baby boomers. In such cases, the young managers would need to develop their own competencies in managing others, prove themselves, and have open and honest ongoing communication with the subordinates. If the situation is not properly managed, the older workers may feel alienated. As well, the generation Y workers tend to embrace changes, while boomers are more resistant to changes and uncertainties. This type of value differences can create conflict within the organization. Therefore, organizations may benefit if their employees can learn some conflict management techniques. Furthermore, motivating different generations of workers can present organizations with unprecedented challenges. Different generations of workers have different preferences and needs. For example, older workers are likely to be more concerned about retirement and health benefits. Some may prefer to ease into their retirement by cutting back the hours and striking a better work-life balance. On the other hand, the young workers may prefer higher direct wages, training and advancement opportunities, leave time for travelling, and flexible schedules. Hence, it is not easy to determine a wage and benefits policy that fits and motivates all. There needs to be consistency for fairness and yet flexibility to meet diverse needs.

The recent legislative developments on the removal of mandatory retirement in some Canadian provinces (as described in Chapter 6) can be an indication of the changing attitude towards older workers and the recognition that they have a lot to contribute due to their wealth of experience. Of course, it can also be a reflection of the concern over a potential labour shortage. In any case, organizations are losing out if they are unable to retain and make good use of this important resource.

## PEOPLE WITH DISABILITIES

People with disabilities represent another minority group whose talents are relatively untapped. People often think of disability only in terms of the physical aspect. However, people with disabilities include not only the physically handicapped, but also those temporarily incapacitated due to physical or mental illness, those with chronic diseases, and those with mental impairments. Basically, people who have a condition that adversely affects their ability to carry out normal daily life functions are considered to have a disability. Naturally, employers are concerned about the cost of absenteeism related to short-term or long-term incapacities and the uncertainties in employee attendance or performance due to chronic disease or mental illness. Some employers may just shy away from hiring people from these groups without trying to carefully understand their disability situation, employability, and potential contributions. This often results in lost opportunities for both the employer and people with disabilities.

Here are some facts related to the disabled population in Canada as of 2006:

- 14.3% of Canadians reported having a disability (Statistics Canada, 2008a)
- Only about half of the disabled people were employed; the others were either unemployed or not in the workforce for various reasons (Statistics Canada, 2008b)
- The unemployment rate for the disabled group aged 15 to 64 (i.e., those actively seeking for jobs) was at 10.4%, which was higher than that of 6.8% for the non-disabled group in the same age category (Statistics Canada, 2008b).

In other countries, people with disabilities also constitute a significant proportion of the population, reportedly as high as 20% of the population both in the U.S. and in New Zealand (Coelho, 2000, p. 10; Statistics New Zealand, 2003). The unemployment rate of this group has always been substantially higher than that of the general population. The underrepresentation of this group in the workforce can be largely due to stigmatism and misunderstanding from potential employers: that people with disabilities are not as capable in performing work tasks and that the cost to accommodate them is high. This, however, may not be the case. Since roughly 60 percent of the people with disabilities are limited only in motion, that is, in speed and quality of movement (Wright 2001, p. 47), these workers should not be any less productive than others in many types of white collar jobs that require desk work. In terms of accommodation, the Canadian Abilities Foundation's 2003 survey found that most disabled respondents felt the annual costs to their employer for accommodating their disability would be less than $500, while the Canadian Council on Rehabilitation and Work indicates that about half of disabled workers require no accommodation and only about 20% of accommodation situations exceed $500 (Prost and Redmond, 2005, p. 11). Moreover, it can be much more cost effective to invest some money to provide support for an employee with special needs than to spend additional money to recruit others.

Wright (2001) proposes that to create an inclusive culture, attitudinal barriers against this minority group must be overcome through education. A supportive infrastructure by providing appropriate job tasks, flexible work arrangements, and accessible working environment is also important to remove unnecessarily physical and logistical barriers.

## APPROACHES TO WORKPLACE DIVERSITY

Diversity management is much more than simply removing discrimination. In general, employers' approaches to workplace diversity can be classified into three main categories: assimilation, differentiation, and integration.

Early views on diversity tended to take the *assimilation approach*. This is also called the "melting pot" approach. Individuals with a different background are expected to conform to the general norm of the majority. Differences or uniqueness of individuals are basically ignored or highly discouraged. Employers usually comply with human rights legislation by trying to treat everyone the same way and do not necessarily provide reasonable accommodation proactively to employees since individual differences and needs are generally not recognized. In Canada, the main statutory laws relating to anti-discrimination and promotion of diversity and equal opportunities include federal and provincial acts or codes in the human rights, employment equity, and pay equity areas, all of which are covered in prior lessons on human resource flow and reward management.

The second approach, *differentiation*, takes a totally different standpoint. Individual differences are valued because they can add constructively to the skill base of the organization. Different perspectives enrich decisions and enhance productivity and performance. As discussed in Chapter 5, diverse or heterogeneous groups are often more creative and productive than homogeneous groups. This logic may apply to the organizational setting as well. A problem with this approach is that by emphasizing the individual differences and acting on the knowledge of such differences, the organization may be providing differential treatment to employees, which can be viewed as discrimination if not handled properly. Moreover, too much diversity can create chaos and potentially dysfunctional conflicts.

The third approach is one of *integration*, whereby the merits of both the other two approaches are incorporated; that is, equal opportunities are promoted, individual differences are respected and valued, and diversity is appreciated and properly managed. In other words, this approach takes a more central position, attempting to strike a balance between the two extremes by recognizing differences and seeking out common bonds, complements, and synergies within the workforce. It goes beyond fair treatment just based on the legally protected characteristics. Indeed, a culture of inclusion is promoted. By effectively managing diversity, organizations benefit in a number of ways, which can give them a competitive advantage over others.

Sometimes, the diversity approach of an organization is found or inferred from the organizations' diversity statements or, more broadly, value statements. If an organization focuses on saying that they are an equal opportunity employer, it may imply that they are more concerned about legal compliance. If there are further statements on valuing employees and the contributions resulting from their diverse background, it may indicate the organization's commitment to a culture of inclusiveness. Of course, making a statement is only a first step in communicating the organization's commitment to employees, potential job candidates, and other stakeholders. Whether organizations follow through on those commitments depends on whether they "walk the talk". Later in the chapter, some common organization practices in managing diversity are examined.

## COMPETITIVE ADVANTAGE OF DIVERSITY

Effective diversity management gives rise to competitive advantages for an organization. Some of these advantages are summarized below (Cox & Blake, 1991):

1. *Cost* – Diversity is almost inevitable in the present day organization. If diversity is not handled properly, it can result in significant cost in terms of money, time, and other resources. For example, discrimination lawsuits can occur. There can be substantial cost differences between organizations that integrate the diverse workforce well and those that do not. Organizations successful in managing diversity are able to reduce turnover, absenteeism, and overtime costs because employees are more satisfied and productive in such environments.

2. *Resource acquisition* – Organizations reputable in managing diversity are naturally more attractive to women and the minority groups. In an age of looming labour shortages, having a competitive edge in attracting and retaining talent is extremely important.

3. *Marketing* – For organizations dealing with international settings and customers, having employees from culturally diverse backgrounds is certainly an advantage. Such employees are able to keep management informed of the cultural expectations of the customers and potential local partnering organizations as well as the latest developments in the local area, including changes in politics, law, competition in the region, and shifts in customer tastes.

4. *Creativity* – A diverse workforce has a lot to offer to the organization such as bringing innovative products to the market well ahead of the competition or coming up with innovative ways of doing things that save a tremendous amount of money. Hence, organizations that embrace diversity

and de-emphasize conformity have a competitive edge as compared with other organizations.

5.  *Problem-solving* – Diversity is also associated with more alternatives being generated and potentially better decisions, whether they are related to strategic level issues or day-to-day routine problems.

6.  *System flexibility* – To better manage diversity, corresponding changes are usually made in the organization systems, making them more flexible or fluid. Such changes help the organization respond or adjust more rapidly and efficiently to environment changes.

## MANAGING DIVERSITY AND BUILDING A CULTURE OF INCLUSIVENESS

According to Parris, Cowan and Huggett's (2006) Conference Board of Canada study on diversity in organizations, while most organizations said they valued diversity and inclusiveness, actual diversity-related performance (such as representation rates, diversity-related investments and initiatives) was mediocre. The report reveals a majority of organizations surveyed (58%) had a diversity strategy, but only one-third of them had a diversity budget (p. 10). There is quite some room for improvement in managing diversity. One should also note that the organizations' perspective on diversity and inclusiveness may not necessarily reflect the employees' or women's perspective.

Pless and Maak (2004, pp. 136-139) provide a framework for building a diverse culture. It involves

- raising awareness, creating understanding, and encouraging reflection;
- developing a vision of inclusiveness;
- rethinking key management concepts and principles; and
- adapting HR systems and processes.

In developing a vision of inclusiveness, a work environment must be fostered that appreciates cultural difference, encourages respect for others, and ensures everyone is heard and has equal rights and opportunities. Trust, integrity, mutual recognition, reciprocal understanding, and integration of intercultural views should be the norm. Open and honest communication, participative management style, and diverse team development are some common features of organizations with a culture of inclusiveness.

Hayne and Dipboye (2004) outline a number of common practices organizations adopt in managing diversity. Some of these practices are discussed below.

## Recruitment

Specific efforts can be made to employ people from a diverse group, such as targeting advertisement and job fairs to schools and minority communities. Internship and scholarship programs can also be focused on the targeted groups.

## Retention

Appropriate employee benefits and a well-balanced work-life program appeal to the diverse workforce. For example, providing good child care and elder care assistance or leave is particularly attractive to the "sandwich generation." Provision of group dependent health benefits also help retain workers concerned with the welfare of their family members. Work-life programs that focus on striking a balance between work and quality of life involve flexible work hours, job-sharing arrangements, personal leave for various legitimate needs, on-site child care facilities, on-site fitness and exercise facilities, fitness club membership, wellness account benefits, and employee assistance programs that provide necessary proactive or reactive consultation and counselling.

## Training and Development

Leadership programs should not just focus on training and development for individual workers in the minority categories to help them climb the career ladder. All leaders should be trained to embrace diversity and to integrate it into their organizational decisions. Leaders need to be sensitive to cultural or other differences of individuals and be able to bring together the positive effects of the differences, while treating everyone fairly. Awareness training is useful for managers and workers to understand themselves and others, and hence learn to appreciate and handle individual differences. Harassment prevention training alerts members to acceptable and unacceptable behaviours within the organization. Mentoring programs are particularly helpful for orientating new employees, especially members of minority groups, to help them get to know others and become familiar with the organization. Such programs also have the potential to improve intergenerational relationships in the workplace. Team-building and group process training are particularly important in today's organizations as they move away from the hierarchical structure. Such training helps members gain the skills of collaborating with others from diverse backgrounds to achieve a common goal.

## Communication

Top management's commitment to diversity and inclusiveness must be properly communicated to staff as well as external stakeholders. Awards that recognize outstanding achievements in the area of diversity management can be provided. Diversity management can be explicitly made a performance goal for staff, whereby their contributions to diversity management are formally recorded and rewarded. Newsletters, bulletins, and staff messages can reiterate management's position on diversity, which helps develop a culture of inclusiveness.

## Staffing and Infrastructure

Specialized staff can be recruited or assigned to foster an environment of inclusiveness. Formal committees can also be formed to spearhead diversity management initiatives. Such staff or committees may be able to answer any diversity-related questions. Proper committees can also be established to investigate complaints of discriminatory treatments or cases of harassment. Grievance procedures and due processes are useful in addressing situations where employees feel they have been treated unfairly.

As with any management initiatives or programs, successful implementation of diversity programs depends on top management commitment, middle-management support, and buy-in from all staff. It requires devotion of resources for training and development purposes. Research is also needed to identify employee attitudes related to diversity and gaps in diversity management so that proper measures are taken to address them. It is also critical that programs are evaluated to determine the extent the diversity goals have been accomplished. A monitoring process with good feedback sheds light on what is needed to be done in the future. Some ways to conduct an audit of effectiveness of the diversity management initiative include

- identifying representation of minority groups in various units or occupational groups within the organization and comparing this to the labour market composition;

- evaluating recruitment and promotion data to ensure that employment decisions are not prejudiced;

- reviewing grievances or complaints on discrimination to ensure that due processes are in place and appropriate follow up actions are taken to eliminate potential root causes of discrimination;

- comparing minority turnover data with the overall turnover rate to ensure that minorities members do not feel more dissatisfied than the others because of any treatment they receive; and

- analyzing employee survey data or exit interview information to highlight potential issues with discrimination.

## Reverse Discrimination

In attempting to address the issue of minority representation, it is important that the needs of the majority are not overlooked. Sometimes, employees complain that they did not get a job because of reverse discrimination. They claim that since the organization needs to fill certain quotas for minority groups, they are bypassed in promotion or training opportunities. Some people also say that by specifically targeting women or certain minority groups for recruitment, the organization is practicing reverse discrimination against the majority members, which is comprised mainly of the white male population. Organizations that adopt reverse discrimination are certainly not doing anyone a favour. Hiring or recruiting a minority member not suitable for the job is unlikely to work in the long run. The employee will not be happy due to his or her incompetence on the job, the organization will suffer, and the majority members in the organization will resent such decisions. Therefore, hiring or promoting someone just to fill a quota defeats the underlying purpose of equity and diversity. That purpose is to level the playing fields between the minority groups and the majority group (not to create an unfair advantage for the minority groups) by rectifying past practices that created unjustified employment barriers for the minority members and promoting and advancing the employment opportunities for members of these underrepresented groups. Appropriate diversity management should focus on ensuring that the right person gets the job due to individual merit. It is inappropriate to hire a minority member just because of his or her minority status. Communication of organization policies and procedures and transparency in the selection criteria help employees understand the fairness in management decisions and prevent resentment in perceived reverse discrimination.

## Unions' Role in Diversity Management

In a unionized setting, unions have a major influence on the terms and conditions of employment through collective bargaining. Do unions allay or accentuate employer discrimination? There are two opposing views on the union position: the inclusionary view that unions are open to any groups of workers as members and the exclusionary view that unions want to exclude certain groups of workers from their membership.

Arguments for the inclusionary view are as follows:

- Unions have a social democratic mission, one that "promotes reforms within both the economy and society, in general, such as an improved workers compensation system, reduced wage inequality within and across firms, and support for human rights concerns" (Godard, 2000, p. 523). As such, one of unions' missions is the reduction of economic and social inequality.

- Unions are facing declining membership and they need to organize non-traditional members, most of who come from the minority groups.

- If unions organize all groups of workers, employers will have a more difficult time finding cheaper non-union labour sources. This helps the unions' power leverage against the employer. Moreover, the more the members, the greater the union voice.

Arguments for the exclusionary view are as follows:

- Unions can press for higher wages by limiting the membership. This is in line with the monopoly argument and the craft union philosophy. According to this view, having a diverse membership dilutes the skills and lowers the productivity of the union workforce, leading to more difficulty in securing high pay increases for the members. Limiting the available labour naturally leads to better pay and conditions for members, especially if the union can negotiate a closed shop or union shop agreement with the employer (the former means that the employer can only hire union members as workers in the bargaining unit while the latter means that anyone hired must join the union within a certain period after employment).

- Many senior union executives are white males who have risen through the union ranks and it is possible that they are not very receptive to workers who are different from them.

- According to the median voter theory (Downs, 1957), union executives are not able to please all factions within the membership and most likely will favour actions that please the majority of the members or the median voters rather than the marginal ones. Since many workforces are still dominated by traditional workers (e.g., full-time Caucasian members), there may be limited incentive for union executives to focus on the needs of the minority members.

- Union executives may believe that a more diverse membership reduces union solidarity.

The recent developments suggest a shift away from the traditional work setting and craft unionism to a work setting and union philosophy more conducive to adopting an inclusionary practice. Yet, the controversy is far from over and further empirical work is certainly needed to indicate the union influence. It is also quite likely that union attitudes towards women and minority workers are different across work settings as some of these groups are larger and potentially more influential in certain settings than others. Nonetheless, if unions take an overall inclusionary view, they can affect the employers' decisions because the employers have to abide by the collective agreement provisions negotiated with them. Hence, unions that adopt an inclusionary philosophy help reduce discriminatory practices in organizations and enhance equity among the majority and minority workers. It should be noted that unions, like other organizations, need to comply with provincial and federal laws such as those on human rights and labour relations. Indeed, fair representation of all employees in the bargaining unit is expected of all Canadian certified bargaining units.

## CONCLUSION

Recognizing the value of diversity is only the first step towards effective diversity management. Concerted efforts from various stakeholders are needed to help organizations embark on a journey of change to foster a culture of inclusiveness. Government legislation sets the minimum standards to combat outright discrimination. More subtle forms of discrimination must be overcome through objective reviews of policies and processes within the organization and education of both managers and workers to enhance understanding of the importance of diversity and fairness. Most important of all, visionary leaders can be the main drivers of change in diversity management. The will and commitment expressed from the top levels sets the direction and priorities for the organization.

# HRM in Action
## Diversity and Inclusion at Xerox

Xerox operates in 160 countries and hires employees from all over the world. Diversity and inclusion was much valued in the organization. Specifically, at Xerox Canada, its President and CEO Mandy Shapansky says,

> Diversity is a constant we can be proud of at Xerox. We live and work in a diverse world and having a diverse workforce is a competitive advantage and makes good business sense. When we foster an inclusive culture it allows us to leverage our differences, reach our full potential, and ultimately be an employer and supplier of choice (www.xeroxcareers.ca/working-at-xerox/diversity-inclusivesness).

To ensure that the company devotes the necessary attention and resources to this valued objective, a Diversity and Inclusion Manager was specifically appointed. A diversity and inclusion website was also created to educate employees on various diversity topics like employment equity, issues in multi-generational workforce, gender, culture, and Aboriginal relations. Employment equity targets are reviewed quarterly and in 2011, the company conducted a global diversity survey to obtain views and feedback from employees on diversity and inclusion.

Some of Xerox Canada's diversity and inclusion initiatives include diversity-related training workshops for managers and employees, flexible work arrangements, employee assistance programs, virtual work, sabbatical programs, and programs on respect. The company also support various employee resource groups organized along gender, ethnic, or sexual orientation commonalities and interests.

In 2012, Xerox Canada was chosen by Mediacorp Canada Ltd. as one of the top 50 Canada's Best Diversity Employers. (It was also an award recipient for 2011.) At the time of the award application, Xerox had 136,000 employees worldwide. They have over 3,600 employees in Canada, 37% of them were women and 15% were visible minorities. As for the U.S. employee composition, according to their website information as of February 2012, minorities comprised almost 30% of the U.S. workforce. For the Vice President and above levels, females represented 19.2%, minority females 7.8%, and minority males 15.1%.

Xerox's diversity initiatives do not just end at the employee level, but also extend to their suppliers. It has formed partnerships with many diverse companies and "found that Minority- and Women-owned Business Entreprises (MWBEs) meet and surpass corporate supply standards" (www.xerox.careers.ca/working-at-xerox/diversity-inclusivesness).

---

Sources:
Xerox Canada. (2012). *Working at Xerox: Diversity and inclusiveness*. Retrieved March 5, 2012 from http://www.xeroxcareers.ca/working-at-xerox/diversity-inclusivesness
Mediacorp Canada. (2013). *Canada's best diversity employers*. Retrieved from www.canadastop100.com/diversity
Mediacorp Canada. (2013). *Xerox Canada Inc.* Retrieved from www.eluta.ca/diversity-at-xerox-canada

## References

Allard, M. J. (2002). Theoretical underpinnings of diversity. In C. P. Harvey and M. J. Allard (eds.), *Understanding and managing diversity: Readings cases and exercises* (pp. 3-27, Rev. ed.). Upper Saddle River, NJ: Prentice-Hall.

Bartley, S. J., Ladd, P. G., & Morris, L. (2007). Managing the multigenerational workplace: Answers for managers and trainers. *CUPA-HR Journal, 58*(1), 28-34

Brett, J. M., & Stroh, L. K. (1999). Women in management: How far have we come and what needs to be done as we approach 2000? *Journal of Management Inquiry, 8*(4), 392-97.

Business in Norway: Girl power. (2008, January 3). *The Economist* [Business section], pp. 54-55.

CBS Broadcasting Inc. (2003, January 21). Hispanics now largest U.S. minority. *CBS News.* Retrieved April 19, 2004, from http://www.cbsnews.com/stories/2003/01/21/national/main537369.shtml

Coelho, T. (2000). Cultural diversity and people with disabilities. *Diversity Factor, 8*(2), 10-13.

Colvin, G. (1999, July 19). The 50 best companies for Asians, Blacks, & Hispanics: Companies that pursue diversity outperform the S&P 500. *Fortune, 140*(2), 52-59

Cox, T. H., Jr., & Blake, S. (1991). Managing cultural diversity: Implications for organizational competitiveness. *Academy of Management Executive, 5*(3), 45-56.

Downs, A. (1957). *An Economic Theory of Democracy.* New York: Harper and Row.

Dwyer, R. (2009). Prepared for the impact of the multi-generational workforce! *Transforming Government: People, Process and Policy, 3*(2), 101-110.

Fairfax, L. M. (2005). Some reflections on the diversity of corporate boards: Women, people of color, and the unique issues associated with women of color. *St. Johns' Law Review, 79*(4), 1105-1120.

Godard, J. (2000). *Industrial relations, the economy, and society* (2nd ed.). North York, ON: Captus Press.

Jayne, M. E. A., & Dipboye, R. L. (2004). Leveraging diversity to improve business performance: Research findings and recommendations for organizations. *Human Resource Management, 43* (4), 409-424.

Hausmann, R., Tyson, L. D., & Zahidi, S. (2011). *The global gender gap report 2011.* World Research Forum. Retrieved February 28, 2012 from http://www3.weforum.org/docs/WEF_GenderGap_Report_2011.pdf

He, W., & Hobbs, F. (1999, September). *Minority population growth: 1995 to 2050* (U.S. Department of Commerce, Minority Business Development Agency report). Retrieved September 25, 2006, from http://www.mbda.gov/documents/mbdacolor.pdf

Jenkins, J. (2008). Strategies for managing talent in a multigenerational workforce. *Employment Relations Today, 34*(4), 19-26.

Kanter, R. M. (1995). The job makes the person. In C. Harvey & M. J. Allard (Eds.), *Understanding and managing diversity: Readings, cases, and exercises* (pp. 111-117). New York: HarperCollins.

Knowledge@Wharton. (2011). *Limited seating: Mixed results on efforts to include more women at the corporate board table.* Retrieved March 3, 2012 from http://knowledge.wharton. upenn.edu/article.cfm?articleid=2861

MacBride-King, J. L., & Benimadhu, P. (2004). *Toward maximizing talents of visible minorities: Potential, performance and organizational practices* (Conference Board of Canada Leaders' Summit on Visible Minorities Report, Publication #608-04). Retrieved September 15, 2006, from http://www.conferenceboard.ca/MTVM/608-04MaxTalentsBooklet.pdf

Oakley, J. G. (2000). Gender-based barriers to senior management positions: Understanding the scarcity of female CEOs. *Journal of Business Ethics, 27*(4), 321-334.

Parris, S., Cowan, A. P. , & Huggett, N. (2006). *Report on diversity: Priorities, practices and performance in Canadian organizations.* Retrieved March 3, 2012 from http://www. conferenceboard.ca/temp/746a400c-5553-446a-b25c-a8db4884a315/067-07-Diversity%20 Outlook%202006-web.pdf

Pless, N. M., & Maak, T. (2004). Building an inclusive diversity culture: Principles, processes and practice. *Journal of Business Ethics, 54*(2), 129-147.

Poindexter, K. (2008). Passing the torch but not just yet. *The Public Manager, 37*(2), 11-14.

Prost, A., & Redmond, D. (2005). Integrating people with disabilities. *Canadian HR Reporter, 18*(22), 7, 11.

Ryan, M. K., & Haslam, S. A. (2007). The glass cliff: Exploring the dynamics surrounding the appointment of women to precarious leadership positions. *Academy of Management Review, 32*(2), 549-572.

Silva, C., & Carter N. (October 6, 2011). *New research busts myths about the gender gap.* Harvard Business Review Blog. Retrieved March 3, 2012 from http://blogs.hbr.org/cs/2011/10/new_ research_busts_myths_about.html

Statistics Canada. (2008a). *Growth in disability rates from 2001 to 2006.* Retrieved February 28, 2012 from  http://www.statcan.gc.ca/pub/89-628-x/2007002/4125018-eng.htm

Statistics Canada. (2008b). *Participation and activity limitation survey of 2006: Labour force experience of people with disabilities in Canada.* Retrieved February 28, 2012 from http:// www.statcan.gc.ca/pub/89-628-x/89-628-x2008007-eng.htm

Statistics Canada. (May 1, 2009). *Earnings differences between immigrants and the Canadian-born – The role of literacy skills.* Retrieved February 28, 2012 from http://www.statcan.gc.ca/ pub/81-004-x/2008005/article/10798-eng.htm

Statistics Canada (2013). *Immigration and ethnocultural diversity in Canada.* Retrieved May 10, 2013, from www12.statcan.ca/nhs-enm/2011/as-sa/99-010-x/99-010-x2011001-eng.cfm

Stevens, R. H. (2010). Managing human capital: How to use knowledge management to transfer knowledge in today's multi-generational workforce. *International Business Research, 3*(3), 77-83.

U.S. Department of Commerce. (March 24, 2011). *2010 Census shows America's diversity.* U.S. Census Bureau News. Retrieved February 28, 2012 from http://2010.census.gov/news/ releases/operations/cb11-cn125.html

Williams, C. L. (1992). The glass escalator: Hidden advantages for men in the "female" professions. *Social Problems, 39*(3), 253-267.

Wright, R. (2001). *Tapping the talents of people with disabilities: A guide for employers* (Conference Board of Canada Special Report). Retrieved on September 15, 2006, from http://www.conferenceboard.ca/documents.asp?rnext=85

Yeaton, K. (2008). Recruiting and managing the 'Why?' generation: Gen Y. *The CPA Journal, 78*(4), 68-72.

Zahidi, S., & Ibarra, H. (2010). *The corporate gender gap report.* World Research Forum. Retrieved February 28, 2012 from http://www3.weforum.org/docs/WEF_GenderGap_CorporateReport_2010.pdf

# Chapter 11

# UNION-MANAGEMENT RELATIONSHIP

## INTRODUCTION

Throughout the past chapters, various HR considerations in the union setting are discussed in relation to the chapter topic. In this chapter, the roles of unions and the union-management relationship are specifically discussed, including management strategies towards unions, union certification, interest negotiation, and collective agreement administration. While the discussion of these areas mainly focuses on the North American setting, the chapter closes with a brief look at the international context where unionism can vary greatly from country to country.

When people hear about industrial relations, they often think automatically of unions. Actually, industrial relations, in its broadest definition, is the study of the employment relationship in either a union or non-union setting. The three main sets of actors in the industrial relations system are the employer and their associations, employees and their associations (the unions), and the government. The government is a main player because it establishes and enforces legislation that sets the minimum employment terms and conditions (e.g., employment standards, occupational health and safety, human rights legislation) and regulates the labour-management relationship (labour relations legislation). Unions play an important role in providing a collective voice for the employees in collective bargaining and in grievance handling. Collective action counters the imbalance in power between individual employees and the employer. Whereas individual action is easily ignored or even subject to employer reprisal, collective action, especially one that is protected by law, gains much more employer attention and possibly concession. Indeed, in unionized workplaces employers are required by law to bargain in good faith with the unions. Hence, the employee voice channel in a union setting is very different from a non-union one. For the latter, it is totally at the employer's discretion. Some organizations have initiatives like employee sug-

Note: An earlier version of some sections of this chapter written by the author was included in the *Human Resource Management Study Guide* (2007), Centre for Innovative Management, Athabasca University.

gestion programs, quality circles, and autonomous teams, where employees may have various degrees of input and control over decisions, but they are often related to the operational processes, rather than the employment terms. If employees in a non-union setting really do not like their work situation, their voice influence is mostly limited and the usual recourse is exit (Hirschman, 1970).

Studies show that unions have significant impact in a number of areas affecting the employment relationship. They are cited as contributing to the increase in the wage levels of union members, thus creating a wage gap between union and non-union labour; but they also help to reduce the wage differential between minority workers and those in the majority group (e.g., Ashenfelter, 1972; Budd & Na, 2000; Card, 1996; Freeman & Medoff, 1984; Jakubson, 1991; Kornfeld, 1993; Lewis, 1986; Smith, 1992). Unions also enhance fringe benefits for union members (e.g., Clark, 1980; Miller & Mulvey, 1992), ensure better employer legal compliance on health and safety issues (Weil, 1991, 1992), and influence internal career progression, turnover, and termination (e.g., Hartmann, Spalter-Roth, & Collins, 1994; Huselid, 1995; Kaufman & Kaufman, 1987; Lincoln & Kalleberg, 1996; Miller & Mulvey, 1993).

While the union membership rate has significantly declined in the U.S. in the past few decades, the rate has only decreased slightly in Canada where approximately one out of three workers belongs to a union. In the U.S. or Canada, once a union has been certified by the labour relations board (after sufficient support from the employees is established) as the exclusive bargaining agent of a bargaining unit, the employment relationship is no longer just between the employee and the employer. The employment terms are determined by the collective agreement negotiated between the employer and the union. While the collective agreement covers all the employees in that bargaining unit, it may not be necessary that all such employees join the union. This is something the union must negotiate into the agreement. As mentioned in Chapter 6, a union shop agreement is one that includes a provision for all the new hires in the unit to join the union within a certain time period while an open shop does not have such a provision. A closed shop is basically an agreement that requires the employer to hire only members from the union. (Note that the union can be much larger than the bargaining unit because the latter is often a local unit whereas a union can be a national union with many members in different locations, working for different companies.) An agency shop (or Rand formula as it is called in Canada) requires employees in the bargaining unit to pay full or partial union dues but union membership is not compulsory. The union, as the exclusive bargaining agent, must represent all employees in the bargaining unit fairly, irrespective of membership. Such representation includes negotiation with the employer and handling of employee grievances arising out of the collective agreement violations.

In order to effectively work with a union (a major stakeholder in the organization) management must develop a strategy. Traditionally, union-management relationships are adversarial. The parties are seen to have totally different and highly incompatible objectives. More recent developments illustrate a more co-operative approach in some organizations. As organizations struggle to stay competitive, many challenges to employee relations develop. Those organizations that effectively manage their employee relations have a competitive advantage over others. How employee relations are managed effectively, however, is not a simple question to answer. In this chapter, some theories and practices are shared, but it is important to note that there is no single standard best practice.

## MANAGEMENT STRATEGIES ON UNION RELATIONSHIP

Anderson (1989) outlines three main management strategies towards unions.

### *Union Replacement or Suppression*

One assumption under this strategy is that the union already exists within the organization. Management tries by all means to minimize the union influence, if not totally drive out the union. Management may involve itself in hard bargaining and make it very difficult for the union to gain any ground. The ultimate hope is that the union will be decertified. *Decertification* is possible if there are many disgruntled union members in support of such a move. Decertification also occurs in situations where the parties fail to negotiate a first contract, but in Canada most jurisdictions (other than Alberta, New Brunswick, and Nova Scotia) have provisions that require a first contract arbitration in the case of such an impasse (Taras, 2006).

Relocating the plant, establishing new firms, or selling part of the business from one subsidiary to another in order to take advantage of greenfield sites where the union is unlikely to successfully organize are other common ways to move unionized work to non-unionized places. However, organizations wishing to engage in such activities may be constrained by various labour relations code provisions aimed at preventing the intentional circumvention of unions. These provisions involve situations of spin-offs and successor rights.

Another common method organizations use to decrease the union influence is to reduce the union workforce through automating or contracting out work. Labour relations legislation generally applies to employees but not independent contractors. Hence, it is not uncommon to find contracting out a main area of contention in negotiations between management and the union as it not only impacts workers' job security, but also adversely affects the level of union membership.

At times, some employers even resort to unlawful practices to try to work against the union. Firing union officials and activists and bypassing or undermining the union to negotiate directly with the employees are just some of such unfair labour practices prohibited by legislation.

## Union Avoidance or Substitution

Under this strategy, the organization uses proactive and progressive HRM policies and utilizes employee participation so that employees do not feel the need to have a union. Management tries to resist union organization. It is not uncommon for management to challenge the scope of the bargaining unit and who should or should not be in the unit. In some situations, including or excluding a few workers who are particularly supportive of one side results in totally different certification outcomes. However, it is important that employers do not cross the line, because legal restrictions exist as to what are and are not acceptable actions during an organization campaign. For example, hiring contracts that require employees not to join a union ("yellow dog contracts") are void; any actions that intimidate, threaten, or discriminate against an employee and that cause him or her to refrain from becoming a union member or representative are prohibited. In general, employers are not to interfere with the formation and administration of the union. That, however, does not mean that the employer cannot communicate with employees or provide them with company information during the union organization campaign, but any such communication must be done cautiously and should not be anti-union. In serious cases of unfair labour practices by the employer, some provinces allow their labour relations board to automatically certify the union if the board believes that, had the employer not interfered, the union would have gotten sufficient support from the bargaining unit employees.

## Union Acceptance

Under union acceptance, the employer recognizes the legitimacy of the union and understands the need to work with it rather than against it. At one end, employers just accept the union the way it is required by law. At the other extreme, employers embrace the union and work together as partners in a cooperative manner. Although there seems to be a move towards the cooperative model, the traditional approach (i.e., the adversarial model) is still very much the norm. Apparently, employers are usually not thrilled to have unions in their organizations. When unionization is inevitable, the question remains: what is the best way of handling the relationship?

While unions are sometimes seen as being an obstacle to the efficient running of a business, some researchers (e.g., J. Pfeffer, P. Kumar) suggest that unions can play important roles in organizations (other than just improving the employees' welfare). For example, if a union is involved in strategic changes in the workplace, management can have a much easier time in garnering employee support. Unions also help to strike a balance between long-term and short-term goals and to counteract some of the forces that shareholders exert for short-term profits.

The relationship between a union and management depends on a number of factors. The leaders certainly have a major influence in the organization's philosophy. Union solidarity, union density, the parties' resources, and their expertise (in communication, negotiation, and decision-making) all have significant effects on relative bargaining power and how the parties treat each other.

## Union Organizing and Certification

Union membership decline in many developed nations is a concern for union supporters and workers interested in collective forms of representation. For example, in the U.S., private sector union density fell from a peak of 35.7 percent in 1953 to merely 6.9 percent in 2011, leading some to conclude that the early twenty-first century signifies the "twilight of the old unionism" (Troy, 2004, p. 4, Bureau of Labor Statistics, 2012). Even in Canada, where union protection legislation is generally more favourable, total union membership declined from 38% in 1981 to just below 30% in 2010, when the private sector rate stood only at 16% (Statistics Canada, 2005; Uppal, 2012). Similarly, in the U.K., union density dropped from 32% in 1995 to around 27% at the end of 2010, when the private sector rate stood at 14% (National Statistics, 2010). The decline is due to a number of reasons, including structural changes in the economy; white collar workers, service industry workers, and part-timers being less attracted to union representation; the arguably inadequate level of protection offered by labour relations laws to workers and unions with regards to workplace organizing (especially in the U.S. setting); and the degree of management anti-union sentiments and actions, all of which are likely to be responsible for the level of union support and certification outcomes. In view of the declining trend, unions have to develop strategies to attract more non-traditional workers such as those in the minority groups.

Certification of a union to be the exclusive bargaining agent of a unit is often based on the community of interest of the members of the unit. Therefore, a bargaining unit normally includes workers of similar occupations or at a similar location. Often, managers, supervisors, and employees handling confidential labour relations matters are excluded from the unit (or are required to have a separate unit) due to possible conflicts of interest. Where there is a question on the bargaining unit coverage, the labour relations board in the respective jurisdiction is the decision authority.

During an organization drive, the employer must be very cognizant of the rights of the organizing union and the workers. Employer unfair labour practices generally include firing or adversely affecting the employment terms of the union organizers or main union supporters (other than for valid reasons unrelated to the organizing), threatening employees about supporting the union, granting incentives to workers with a view to enticing them to vote against the union, or intervening in the union's lawful attempts at communicating with employees.

Union certification is normally granted upon showing of adequate union support, either by voting or by a card check system (acceptable in some Canadian provinces). The former is probably less favourable to the union because of the extra time and opportunities for the employer to initiate counter-union actions.

Once a union is certified, the employer can no longer directly negotiate terms and conditions of employment with individual workers in the bargaining unit. The employer is bound to engage in good faith bargaining with the certified union.

## COLLECTIVE BARGAINING

After certification, the union must negotiate the first contract with the employer. This is often a critical transition because it sets the stage for the future relations between the parties. At times unions find it difficult to negotiate a contract with an anti-union employer and have to resort to taking legal actions to force the employer to negotiate in good faith in accordance with the labour relations legislation. In view of this difficulty, some jurisdictions have established provisions specifically assisting in the formation and finalization of the first contract (e.g., by arbitration as discussed below).

In the collective agreement negotiation, the union and the employer each present their demands to the other side. It is particularly important for unions to negotiate explicit terms into the contract as management is generally assumed to retain the right to determine employment terms unless otherwise specified in the collective agreement. After a tentative collective agreement is negotiated, the union must present it to the membership for ratification.

Even if both the parties, employer and union, are willing to negotiate, there is no guarantee that they will achieve an agreement since they have different interests. Approaches to negotiation are broadly classified as win-win (integrative) or win-lose (distributive) bargaining. The former is a collaborative approach where each party is willing to understand the perspectives of the other party to try to find common interests and be involved in creative solutions to "enlarge the pie" so that the needs, concerns, and interests of both sides can be addressed. The win-lose approach, on the other hand, is competitive and assumes that it is a zero-sum game: that is, if one party gets more, the other party must lose correspondingly. The win-lose approach is particularly prone to cause an impasse in negotiations. At an impasse, either party may invoke an economic sanction or an alternative dispute resolution mechanism.

*Economic sanctions* generally refer to a strike by the union employees or a *lock-out* by the employer. A union needs to have the support of the members in a strike vote and give advance notice to the employer before a strike action can take place. Advanced notice to the union is also required of an employer lockout. The loss of productivity by striking workers as well as the impact on the employer's business by the picket lines may drive the employer to give further concession to the union demands, especially in situations where replacement workers are not allowed by legislation and product inventory is low. Striking workers lose their regular pay but may be eligible for strike pay from the union (the amount varies depending on the financial strength of the union).

As the strike or lockout approach seems to be a lose-lose situation, at least in the short run, some union-management parties agree to use an alternative form of dispute resolution: mediation or interest arbitration. *Mediation* involves a neutral third party who assists the parties to reach an agreement by facilitating the process, by providing industry and labour relations information, or even by making non-binding recommendations which the parties can take or ignore. In certain jurisdictions this is a mandatory process before a strike or lockout can occur. Contrary to mediation, *interest arbitration* involves a third party making a binding decision for the parties. The arbitrator(s) selected by the parties or appointed by the labour relations authority, as is allowed or required in the jurisdiction, hears the presentations of both sides and decides on the contract terms. Conventional interest arbitration often involves "splitting the difference" so that each party gets part of what is demanded. Given the parties' tendency to make extreme demands to allow the arbitrator room to cut back, another approach called *final offer arbitration* is advocated as a better choice in getting the parties to bargain reasonably. Under this approach, the arbitrator is only allowed to select an offer package from one of the sides, and the side with unrealistic demands usually loses out. In the private sector, arbitration is usually a mechanism voluntarily agreed to by the parties. However, compulsory arbitration can be required by law as in the case of some bargaining units involving public workers or workers providing emergency or essential services because of the undesirable consequences of strikes by these workers on the public.

# Contract Administration

After contract terms have been negotiated and settled and the collective agreement is in place, there are times when interpretation or administrative problems arise. Terms may be ambiguous or, occasionally, may even conflict with each other. There may be areas that have not been addressed. (Usually, when a right is not specified in the agreement, it is seen as under management's prerogative.) For example, a contract term that says promotion is based on both seniority and merit leaves much room for interpretation. Even if these two factors are given the same weight, how are the parties to determine equivalencies between better performance and years of service? Even if the contract states that seniority is the only criteria for promotion, there still can be concerns over how seniority is calculated: is it calculated based on service within a certain job, a certain job grade, a department, or the organization? Moreover, how are part-time employments and leave periods viewed? While it may be good to spell things out clearly in the contract, the more that is stated, the less flexibility there is. This is a trade-off with which both parties must live.

When a dispute arises regarding contract administration, the parties can file a *grievance*. An employee affected by employer's contract violation submits a grievance to the union steward, who then takes it up with the junior levels of management to try to resolve the issue. If unresolved, the grievance is brought to higher levels. In the event that the parties cannot settle, arbitration is the recourse, as required by legislation. The arbitrator (or arbitration board), whether selected and agreed to by the parties or assigned by the labour relations board, hears the presentations of both sides and makes binding decisions. Such arbitrations are called *rights arbitration* because they deal with the issue of rights established in the contract.

Arbitrators will try to right the wrongs and compensate the grievors as necessary. They are allowed to substitute lesser penalties, if deemed appropriate, unless explicitly stated otherwise in the collective agreement. In the case of dismissals that are found to be not justified or against the contract, arbitrators may reinstate the grievors. (This is quite different from common-law wrongful dismissal suits in non-union settings where the outcome is monetary compensation rather than reinstatement.)

# UNION INVOLVEMENT

In unionized organizations, the unions affect almost every aspect of HRM. The collective agreement provisions often involve rewards, HRF, job classifications, and performance appraisals. The presence of unions certainly has an impact on the organization's strategy regarding employee influence. There may not be any legal requirement for the organization to involve a union (or its members) in the redesign of workplace processes, unless it involves changes to the collective agreement's terms and conditions. However, as workplace changes inevitably lead to changes that affect workers and perhaps ultimately to changes in employment situations, involving the union early in the process is a good way to solicit input and enhance buy-in. The problem is that many organizations see the union as an obstacle in the change process and prefer to deal with the union only when it becomes inevitable. Unions placed in such situations are often very skeptical of management initiatives and try to resist any workplace changes for fear of job loss, work overload, or pure uncertainty. They may feel that they are only called upon for concessions without any sincerity of really working together. So when workplace changes fail to work effectively, management and unions tend to blame each other; by then, it is often too late to remedy the situation.

Employee relations are not an isolated aspect: they are largely dependent on the management philosophy, organizational culture, and leadership of the parties. There is no off-the-shelf employee relations package that can be plugged into an organization. Many facets have to fit and fostering new relationships takes time. That does not mean it cannot be done. While unions can be a challenge to organizations and organize resistance, such as strikes that cause huge business losses, unions can be cooperative and can even be strategic partners that help organizations gain a competitive advantage. Many examples exist that indicate joint union-management efforts are mutually beneficial. Such efforts occur where both parties have similar interests, such as promoting health and safety. Whether such beneficial partnerships can be achieved depends on many factors, including the willingness of the parties to move in the cooperation direction, the levels of trust, the organization members' stand, and each party's relative bargaining power.

# THE INTERNATIONAL CONTEXT

Freedom to join a union is sometimes taken for granted, as if it is a universal worker right, because this freedom is often protected by constitutional or statutory law in many developed nations. However, in some less developed nations or in countries where fundamental human rights and labour rights are not as

233

well-respected, union representation and collective bargaining are less prevalent or even non-existent.

Even for countries that formally recognize the legitimacy of unions, the unionism system and membership situation varies drastically from country to country or even from state to state. For example, in the U.S., closed shop union security provisions are disallowed and in the right-to-work states, even union shop provisions are prohibited. In Canada, however, either of these types of union security provisions can be negotiated. In both countries, once a union is certified as the exclusive bargaining agent, no other unions can simultaneously represent any other members in the unit. In contrast, New Zealand has embraced voluntary unionism in that multiple unions can represent different workers within a unit and employees are not required to join any union even if a majority of workers choose a specific union, nor are they compelled to pay union dues (Harcourt & Lam, 2006).

In Western Europe, a dual industrial relations system is widespread. Countries such as Sweden and Germany actually have two levels of worker representation, works councils and unions. The *works council model*, also called the codetermination model, is usually supported by either legislation or national agreement (Ramsay, 1997). Under this model, worker-selected representatives serve on the council to decide with management on matters at the strategic level concerning economic, operations, personnel, and social issues. The rights conferred to the councils vary across countries and across issues, involving joint decisions, consultations, right to information, or veto power (Weiss, 2004). In countries with a two-tier management system (involving a board of directors and a supervisory board), the works council can also nominate a certain proportion of representatives to serve on the company's supervisory board, which is generally composed of non-executives to oversee and advise the board of directors on matters of best interest to the company. This codetermination approach allows workers access to important information and input into changes that can adversely affect employees. For example, when innovative productivity-enhancing work practices are introduced, employee representation on the council helps reduce the chances and extent of employer opportunism (Hübler & Jirjahn, 2003). When it comes to the actual negotiations of specific workers' terms and conditions of employment, the responsibility rests with unions.

Unlike in the U.S., where most collective agreements reflect plant level settlements, collective agreements in some European countries like Germany are negotiated mainly at the national union level. Another major difference between the two levels of representation is that unions are allowed to use the economic sanction of legal strikes, while works councils cannot call for such an action. The usual dispute resolution mechanism for council matters is arbitration. As for the relationship between the two levels of employee representation, while works councils and unions are, in principle, independent entities, they do have a close relationship with each other. Works councils are said to be associated in either "complementary or conflictual ways with collective bargaining, and [they] may assume differing roles within management-labour relations" (Ramsay, 1997, p. 315). In some situations, many council representatives are union members and advocates, such as in the case of Germany. German trade unions are also given some specific rights to participate in certain works council functions, including attending council meetings when some conditions are met (Weiss, 2004). The variation in the codetermination model effectiveness and the implications on union-management relationship is attributable to differences in legislation; the social, political, and organizational institutions; and frameworks as well as employee and employer attitudes and approaches in different national contexts (Ramsay, 1997). For example, in Sweden, where codetermination rights are exercised by union-appointed shop stewards, it is not difficult to understand why unions have a strong control over the codetermination outcomes (Muller, 2000; Streeck, 1995).

As seen, unionism and workers rights to representation vary greatly across nations. Managers involved in doing business in other countries must familiarize themselves with the political and legal environments in this regard as well as the general cultural environment relating to management-employee relations.

## THE FUTURE OF EMPLOYEE RELATIONS

Although union density is generally in decline, Freeman and Rogers (2006, p. 175) find 87 percent of employees actually want a strong or somewhat independent organization to represent them regarding their everyday work concerns; however, most (63 percent) do not want a representative organization that is adversarial to the employer, which unfortunately, tends to be quite common in traditional unionized settings (Freeman & Rogers, 2006, p. 85; Taras, 2002). Apparently, if union and management can cooperate with each other, the needs of the employee and likely the employer are better met.

With non-union representation and voice channels like employee involvement programs flourishing in recent years, will they replace formal union representation? How is their effectiveness compared with that of union representation? These topics are controversial and the verdict is still out there. They are beyond the scope of this text. Nonetheless, it is important for organization leaders and managers to understand and respect the role of any employee representation bodies, be it unions or other forms, because they are an important part of the industrial relations system and can have significant impact on an organization's performance. If organizations are able to garner the support and cooperation of such bodies, they have a much better chance of leveraging their employee resources.

# HRM in Action

## Alternate Dispute Resolution (ADR) – National Defence/Canadian Forces (CF) and a Union (UNDE)

Most civilian members of CF (e.g., general labour, trades, and clerical members) are represented by the Union of National Defence Employees (UNDE). Although they have access to the grievance process when encountering conflicts relating to their collective agreement, the formal grievance process seems to create a win-lose situation not necessarily conducive to a long term relationship. In August 2001, with the support of UNDE, the department launched a pilot project on Conflict Management Program, a form of ADR, as an additional tool for resolving workplace conflicts and improving the work environment. It was a challenge for a traditional command-and-control type of organization. However, both the organization and the union saw the potential benefits of the system to try it out. As indicated by the union's former Executive Vice President, the grievance system does not work well with interpersonal issues The alternative tool could also help those who would be hesitant to file a formal grievance as well as save valuable time and resources for the union by keeping the number of formal grievances down.

Mediation was introduced as part of the ADR. It has the advantage of keeping discussions confidential and having the parties retain full control in terms of accepting or rejecting the agreement, thereby prompting freer expression of ideas and more creative solutions. Under the pilot project, management and union leaders identified the worst grievances and tried them through mediation. When most of them got resolved, the success led to further expansion of the program. Workshops were set up, agreement on the guiding principles for the processes was reached with representation from various stakeholders including other major unions, and more pilot sites were established.

After the pilot results were evaluated, although UNDE had some concerns about their officials not having been adequately consulted, it was confident to support moving the program into full-scale, and ADR was eventually made applicable to both military and civilian members across the department. Demand for ADR has grown since its inception and mediation is offered to all grievors, but acceptance to use it is voluntary. For example, from 2002-2005, over 3300 members used the service and 78% of mediation cases were satisfactorily resolved. Today, ADR includes not just mediation, but also conflict coaching and other intervention services such as consultation, facilitation and group processes.

As for the union role, in the early stages, UNDE was a supporter, but basically left the decision of whether or when to use ADR to local unions, realizing that ADR's growth had to be from the bottom up. By June 2009, when a department internal evaluation on the ADR was done, survey results still suggested that, while there was general support from various national level unions, more efforts would be needed to promote the program at the local level. Ongoing training and promotional activities are being held. Just in the fiscal year 2007-2008, as many as 14,000 personnel were trained on ADR. The department's ultimate goal is to incorporate ADR methods into various policies and processes.

Sources:
Department of National Defence, Chief Review Services. (2009). *Conflict management program (Alternative dispute resolution) follow-up evaluation.* Retrieved April 10, 2012 from http://www.crs-csex.forces.gc.ca/reports-rapports/2009/122P0837-eng.aspx
Department of National Defence, Chief Military Personnel. (2012). *Alternative dispute resolution (ADR).* Retrieved April 10, 2012 from http://www.cmp-cpm.forces.gc.ca/adr-marc/index-eng.asp
Ponak, A., Painter, B., & Shenfield, D. (n. d.). *Beyond collision: High integrity labour relations: National Defence/Canadian Forces – UNDE case study.* Retrieved April 10, 2012 from http://www.moderntimesworkplace.com/DVD_Collection/video_DND_case_study_final_.pdf

## References

Anderson, J. C. (1989). The strategic management of labour relations. In J. C. Anderson, M. Gunderson and A. Ponak (Eds.), *Union-management relations in Canada* (2nd ed., pp. 99-124). Don Mills, ON: Addison-Wesley.

Ashenfelter, O. (1972). Racial discrimination and trade unionism. *Journal of Political Economy, 80*(3), 435-464.

Budd, J. W., & Na, I. (2000). The union membership wage premium for employees covered by collective bargaining agreements. *Journal of Labor Economics, 18*(4), 783-807.

Bureau of Labor Statistics. (2012, January 27). *Union members summary.* Economic News Release. United States Department of Labor. Retrieved March 19, 2012 from http://www.bls.gov/news.release/union2.nro.htm

Card, D. (1996). The effect of unions on the structure of wages: A longitudinal analysis. *Econometrica, 64*(4), 957-979.

Clark, K. B. (1980). The impact of unionization on productivity: A case study. Industrial and *Labor Relations Review, 33*(3), 451-469.

Dunlop, J. T. (1958). *Industrial relations systems.* New York: Holt.

Freeman, R. B., & Medoff, J. L. (1984). *What do unions do?* New York: Basic Books.

Freeman, R. B., & Rogers, J. (2006). *What workers want* (Updated ed.). Ithaca, NY: ILR Press.

Harcourt, M., & Lam, H. (2006). Freedom of association, freedom of contract, and the right-to-work debate. *Employee Responsibilities and Rights Journal, 18*(4), 249-266.

Hartmann, H., Spalter-Roth, R., & Collins, N. (1994). What do unions do for women? *Challenge, 37*(4), 11-18.

Hirschman, A. O. (1970). *Exit, voice, and loyalty: Responses to decline in firms, organizations, and states.* Cambridge, MA: Harvard University Press.

Hübler, O., & Jirjahn, U. (2003). Works councils and collective bargaining in Germany: The impact on productivity and wages. *Scottish Journal of Political Economy, 50*(4), 471-491.

Huselid, M. A. (1995). The impact of human resource management practices on turnover, productivity, and corporate financial performance. *Academy of Management Journal, 38*(3), 635-672.

Jakubson, G. (1991). Estimation and testing of the union wage effect using panel data. *Review of Economic Studies, 58*(5), 971-991.

Kaufman, R. S., & Kaufman, R. T. (1987). Union effects on productivity, personnel practices, and survival in the automotive parts industry. *Journal of Labor Research, 8*(4), 333-350.

Kornfeld, R. (1993). The effects of union membership on wages and employee benefits: The case of Australia. *Industrial and Labor Relations Review, 47*(1), 114 - 128.

Lewis, H. G. (1986). *Union relative wage effects: A survey.* Chicago: University of Chicago Press.

Lincoln, J. R., & Kalleberg, A. L. (1996). Commitment, quits, and work organization in Japanese and U.S. plants. *Industrial and Labor Relations Review, 50*(1), 39-59.

Miller, P., & Mulvey, C. (1992). Trade unions, collective voice and fringe benefits. *Economic Record, 68*(201), 125-141.

Miller, P., & Mulvey, C. (1993). What do Australian unions do? *Economic Record, 69*(206), 315-342.

Muller, M. (2000). Employee representation and pay in Austria, Germany, and Sweden. *International Studies of Management & Organization, 29*(4), 67-83.

National Statistics. (2010). *Trade union membership 2010.* Retrieved March 19, 2012 from www.bis.gov.uk/assets/biscore/employment-matters./docs/t/11-p77-trade-union-membership-2010.pdf

Ramsay, H. (1997). Fool's gold? European works councils and workplace democracy. *Industrial Relations Journal, 28*(4), 314-322.

Smith, T. L. (1992). The impact of university faculty unionization on the male-female wage differential. *Journal of Collective Negotiations in the Public Sector, 21*(2), 101-110.

Statistics Canada. (2006, August). *Perspectives on labour and income: Unionization.* Retrieved February 12, 2008, from http://www.statcan.ca/english/studies/75-001/comm/02.pdf

Streeck, W. (1995). Works council in Western Europe: From consultation to participation. In J. Rogers & W. Streeck (Eds.), *Works councils: Consultation, representation and cooperation in industrial relations* (pp. 313-350). Chicago: University of Chicago Press.

Taras, D. G. (2006). *First contract arbitration: Alberta requires an amendment to the labour code* (Policy Brief No. 06002). Retrieved February 12, 2008, from University of Calgary, Institute for Advanced Policy Research website: http://www.ucalgary.ca/iaprfiles/policybriefs/iapr-pb-06002.pdf

Taras, D. G. (2002). Alternative forms of employee representation and labour policy. *Canadian Public Policy, 28*(1), 105-116.

Troy, L. (2004). *Twilight of the old unionism.* Armonk, NY: M.E. Sharpe.

Uppal, S. (2012, February 14). *Unionization 2011* [Statistics Canada Publication 75-001-X]. Retrieved March 19, 2012 from http://www.statcan.gc.ca/pub/75-001-x/2011004/article/11579-eng.htm

Weil, D. (1991). Enforcing OSHA: The role of labor unions. *Industrial Relations, 30*(1), 20-36.

Weil, D. (1992). Building safety: The role of construction unions in the enforcement of OSHA. *Journal of Labor Research, 13*(1), 121-132.

Weiss, M. (2004). Collective representation in labour law in Germany. *Managerial Law, 46*(4/5), 71-103.

*Chapter 11*

**Chapter 12**

# THE FUTURE OF THE HUMAN RESOURCES ROLE

## INTRODUCTION

Throughout the book, there has been much discussion on the need for HR to be a strategic partner in an organization. The need for this HR role is reflected in a 2010 survey on the Profit 100: Canada's Fastest Growing Companies, which suggests that "putting the human resource function at the head table is a first step toward eliciting the results businesses need" (Zugec, 2010). As for how well HR has been faring in this regard, a recent survey on over 500 HR practitioners shows that about one-third of the respondents consider themselves as business partners, with approximately another 30% indicating that they are probably seen as business partners (Balthazard, 2009). However, only 11% of the respondents indicate that it was "relative easy for them ... to establish themselves as a business partner," while the majority "still need to prove themselves ... to be accepted as a business partner" (Klie, 2009a). This shows that the concept of HR as a strategic business partner has gained increasing support in recent years, but there is still certainly more progress to be made.

In another survey of over 2,200 readers of Canadian HR Reporter and members of the Human Resources Professionals Association, about 70% of the respondents think that professionalization is an important issue for the profession (Klie, 2009b, p. 10). Apparently, other professionals do not necessarily see HR as a true profession. The national HR certification program as well as the raising of the overall education level and business knowledge of HR practitioners has helped the professional profile, but again, there is more work to be done.

So, what is the state of HR at this time and what should HR focus on in the future? A survey conducted by Queen's University Industrial Relations Centre on over 450 HR professionals in Canada attempted to answer these questions (Juniper & Hill, 2011). According to the survey, the areas of HR activities reported to have the most significant growth are ethics, succession planning, change management, organizational culture, and HR governance. The biggest challenges seen are in the areas of talent management, employee engagement, succession planning, change management and organization culture. The survey suggests that the outlook is positive, with HR "increasingly viewed as a value-add to organizations, as senior management relies more heavily on HR to participate in strategic decision making, and realized the linkage between effective people management and corporate performance" (p. 10). The same survey also shows the critical skills area for HR professional, namely, communication, analytical/critical/strategic thinking, interpersonal skills, technical skills, and conflict resolution. Similar results were found by The Society for Human Resource Management (SHRM) in their 2009 poll on over 2,200 HR professionals in the Canada, United States, India, the Middle East and North Africa, which shows effective communication and strategic thinking as the key HR competencies for all the countries' involved (SHRM, 2010). Other top competencies shown by Canadian respondents are persuasiveness, leading change, and credibility, whereas by the U.S. participants are HR knowledge, integrity, and ethical behaviour. The same survey also found that as organizations are becoming more globalized, additional competencies are needed for global HR leaders including global intelligence or mindset and cross-cultural intelligence.

For HR to move forward, HR must overcome a number of challenges and obstacles that stand in the way of effective strategic HRM in both the external and internal organizational environment.

Some of the internal constraints include the following:

- *Management philosophy* – Strategic HRM tends to work in organizations with a management philosophy that values employees and considers them an asset. If management believes that workers are lazy and need to be controlled, they can only drive compliance and not commitment. In such situations, HR is unlikely to be considered as having a strategic role.

- *Leadership* – As covered in Chapter 4, an important role of leadership is to set the vision to guide effective employee performance. Management of meaning is essential in that it signals to employees what is valued and what should be done. Sharing of information and power with employees often creates a more capable and productive workforce. However, many leaders either lack the leadership skills or are unwilling to part with their power. This severely limits the contributions that employees can make to the organization.

- *Unions* – Unions are representatives of employees and provide a good channel of employee voice. As employee influence is a key HR policy area under strategic HRM, in unionized organizations cooperation and support from unions is crucial in getting employees to fully and willingly participate in various organizational initiatives. Unfortunately, despite the general recognition of the importance of the union-management relationship, empirical evidence indicates that HR professionals tend to spend only limited amounts of time in this area (Ramlall, 2006). Moreover, the adversarial union-management relationship is still very common in the North American context. Unions are trying to re-invent themselves, and strategic partnership with them is one of the options that present management with an opportunity to move the relations forward. Nonetheless, since unions' fundamental role is still to protect jobs and membership, while management generally prefers flexibility both in numerical (relating to the number of workers) and functional (relating to the job tasks and worker roles) terms, both management and unions must find ways to address these potentially diverging needs, especially in a competitive global environment.

- *Resource constraint* – If organizations do not place sufficient resources in the HR department, it is not able to effectively perform its important and complex roles. In such situations, the HR professionals likely can only focus on the functional aspects to ensure that day-to-day administrative tasks run smoothly and have no extra capacity to handle the higher level strategic role. More importantly, if there is only limited investment funding for expanding the human capital, the workforce is unlikely to develop into one that can create a competitive advantage for the organization.

External environmental constraints on effective strategic HRM include the following:

- *Labour market* – With the looming retirement of the baby boomer generation and the overall shrinkage of the working population in most developed nations, the supply of labour, in particular experienced workers, is falling short of demand. Organizations will find it difficult to attract or retain a full complement of competent staff.

- *Competition* – With increasing competition worldwide, many organizations are forced to focus on the financial bottom line. Those who have a short-term sight, in particular, are likely to see workers as a tool or simply a factor of production, rather than an asset to be valued or developed. For such organizations, even if they manage to grow and prosper in the short run, their performance is often not sustainable in the long run.

- *Technological advancement* – Technological changes help in organizational performance improvements but also contribute to quite a few problems. Workers' skills, knowledge, and their jobs become obsolete with changes and time. Constantly keeping workers' skills and knowledge up to date can be a challenge in terms of money and time, and not all workers' are willing to be retrained. Job changes may lead to uncertainties or even displacements that can threaten employee commitment and trust. Therefore, while technology creates opportunities for learning and job enrichment, if not properly managed it can have negative repercussions on HRM, and can even invite lawsuits in the areas like wrongful dismissal and invasion of privacy (where employees are monitored improperly or potential job applicants are inappropriately screened via the social media).

- *Knowledge economy* – Our society is in an era totally different from the time decades ago when the focus of production was mass manufacturing for which Taylorism (involving a de-skilling of work) was deemed a suitable approach. With the shift to a knowledge economy, talent acquisition and management has become critical for organizational success, and knowledge workers are key members in organizations. Hence, a shortage of knowledge workers or a failure to retain key members and talent severely hinders the capacity of HR to play a strategic role in organizations.

## HUMAN RESOURCES' ROLE

With all the challenges ahead, HR will continue to play many essential roles in the organization. Jackson and Schuler (2000, pp. 652-655) describe these roles as follows in Table 12-1:

The traditional HR role involves only the enabler and monitoring roles (the administrative side of HR) but, as shown, HR has many other roles to fulfill. Recent surveys indicate that day-to-day service delivery still seems to take most of HR's time and attention (Deloitte, 2003; Ramlall 2006). However, HR must start focussing more on activities that clearly add value to the organization instead of just the transactional activities (Ramlall, 2006; Ulrich, 2007). In the future, the non-traditional roles are likely to become more crucial. As such, the HR department needs to be filled by qualified professionals with the necessary competencies (Deloitte, 2007), many of which have been discussed earlier in the chapter. To have a strategic and macro-organizational perspective, HR professionals should have a broad range of knowledge of other intertwining functional and disciplinary areas (Ulrich & Eichinger, 1998). These include strategy, marketing, economics, finance, operations management, and information technology. In particular, to allow HR to ascend to its strategic and partnership roles, HR must receive the recognition of top management, with the HR department head reporting directly to a very senior level executive (Lawler III, 2005). If HR is subordinated to finance, operational, or other areas, its strategic importance is easily overshadowed by the priorities placed in the primary functions of these areas.

**Table 12-1  HR Roles**

| Role | Description |
|------|-------------|
| Partnership | HR acts as a business partner as it helps address the organization's needs and balance some of the business's competing goals and priorities. As a business partner, HR helps to "identify, steer and measure for example HR related programs that impact the business drivers such as market growth, customer retention, productivity and quality improvement" (Deloitte, 2007, p. 21). |
| Strategic | HR contributes to the business direction and long-term planning. |
| Enabler | HR assists line departments to get the right people for the right jobs and provides line departments with necessary HR related information (e.g., employment laws, HR policies and procedures) to help managers and employees do the job right. HR has an important role to educate managers on how to manage people, but HR should not try to do the job for them. |
| Monitoring | HR ensures the policies and procedures are properly adopted and that the effectiveness of HR programs is monitored and reviewed for further improvements. |
| Change facilitator | HR acts as a change agent in an ever-changing environment by developing leaders' change management skills, acquiring and developing new talents and skills required of new or changed positions, creating flexibility in HR systems to accommodate changes, and doing proper forecasting in HR planning. |
| Innovator | HR helps develop productivity-enhancing programs or quality improvement initiatives that can benefit both the organization and the work life of the employees. HR can redesign their own department processes for greater efficiency and effectiveness as a role model for other departments |

## HUMAN CAPITAL MANAGEMENT

Human capital management (HCM) is a term used to describe the development of "enterprise human capital strategies" through "combining business and workforce intelligence" and ensuring "the human capital portfolio is effectively managed" (Merritt, 2007, p. 14). Whether it is viewed as part of HR or a somewhat separate area, it certainly reflects a newer trend and focus for HR. Merritt (2007) discusses the five strategic HCM domains, as shown in Table 12-2:

Bassi and McMurrer (2007) also identify five similar areas of human capital drivers, namely, leadership practices, employee engagement, knowledge accessibility, workforce optimization, and learning capacity. These categories can, in turn, be measured by a number of HR practices such as communication, executive skills, inclusiveness, job design, work processes, teamwork, recruitment, and training and development.

**Table 12-2  HCM Domains**

| HCM Domains | Description |
|---|---|
| Leadership capital | This involves the leaders' ability to grow the business |
| Structural capital | This centers around areas like the governance structure, management roles, operating processes, and executive compensation |
| Workforce capital | HCM works to determine the optimal workforce composition, such as full-time and part-time mix and the use of contingent workers and partners |
| Culture capital | Much of a company's market value involves intangibles and "[p]erceptions about culture, operational values, ethics, and behaviors of leaders and the workforce influence customer, investor, and employee decisions" (Merritt, 2007, p. 14) |
| Intellectual capital | This is to leverage people and their ideas to achieve the business objectives |

HCM emphasizes not just the employees, but any human capital related to the organization. This includes the human capital of contingent workers or workers in a partner or supplier organization. It takes a more integrated approach on building and utilizing human capital across functions and along the organization's value chain. Certainly, HCM is highly correlated with various HR activities but it also signals the need for HR to further extend their role beyond the current boundaries.

## THE NEED FOR VALUE-ADDED HR MEASURES

Research generally indicates the positive effect HR has on business performance. For instance, HR practices are associated with a 30 percent increase in market value in a 1999 Wyatt survey and accounted for as much as 43 percent of the difference between the market-to-book values among firms in a 2002 Deloitte & Touche survey (as cited in Phillips, 2005, p. 62). However, at the individual organization level, many HR departments are still struggling with establishing their exact contributions. A main reason why HR is encountering difficulty in getting recognition as a strategic business partner may well be the lack of well-developed measures for the HR outcomes. If HR's contribution is not measured or known, then it will not get the attention it deserves. Existing HR measures often relate to deploying resources and cost efficiency (Boudreau & Ramstad, 2006), such as in the areas of absenteeism, accidents, recruitment, training, compensation, and severance.

While cost reduction is a main concern and can help with maximizing profit, HR's real contributions can go far beyond that. For example, by getting and developing the right talent, the organization can develop innovative products and processes that can break into new markets. Innovation is not necessarily a product of the line department or the Research and Development department. Indeed, innovation results from human talent and can be one amongst many measures to reflect HR effectiveness in having the right people. By creating a good knowledge management system, such as coaching and mentoring, HR adds to the human capital value of the organization. By designing employee involvement and participation initiatives, HR adds value to the organization's decision-making process at both the strategic and tactical levels. By having employees with the right attitude and skills to serve customers, HR significantly contributes to the business success. Hence, HR should not be looked as just a cost centre; it adds value to the organization in many respects even if it does not directly generate revenue. Creating measures in HR is not easy, but organizations must start looking at value-added measures for HR in order to fully appreciate the true contributions of HR. Measures need not always be quantitative in nature. Qualitative measures do have a major role in assessing HR effectiveness. Just as in a service department where effectiveness measures normally include not only the number of customers served, but also the quality of the services provided. Indeed, some authors (e.g., Alden, 2006) suggest that even abstract concepts (such as intelligence) can be measured, given time and resources, and more complex factors can be reflected by properly constructed and validated indices (which is a score composed of different measures being summed or average with or without weights attached, as in the case of the well-known consumer price index).

Ulrich (2007) suggests that value must be "defined by the receiver more than the giver" (p. 52). Therefore, communication with the stakeholders must indicate the value HR can provide for these groups: employees, managers, customers, investors, and the communities. Furthermore, an HR value map that links HR activities with the drivers of business values (e.g., revenue growth, operating margins, asset efficiency and market expectations) certainly helps demonstrate the HR contributions (Thom, 2007).

## MAKING HR DECISIONS

Leaders, managers, and HR professionals need to make many HR decisions from time to time. Some are strategic (more at the macro level) while some are functional (more at the micro level). Although there is no absolute prescriptive formula for each and every decision-making, it is useful to remember the following fundamental and timeless *social justice principles* (Deutsch, 1975) to help guide decisions:

- *Equity* – Resources or outcomes are to be distributed in proportion to people's input or contributions (Adams, 1965).

- *Equality* – Resources or outcomes are to be distributed in an egalitarian way without regard to the situation or personal characteristics (i.e., everyone is treated the same way).

- *Need* – Resources or outcomes are to be distributed according to the needs of the individuals, taking into consideration the individuals' characteristics and situations.

As Deutsch (1973, 1985) proposes, the application of different justice principles is associated with different goals: the equity principle with economic productivity, the equality principle with fostering of social relations, and the need principle with the fostering of personal development and welfare. Hence, an organization may find it appropriate to adopt a combination of justice principles with the application of any specific principle depending on the situation. For example, training is given on a need basis because receiving training to do the job properly is a fundamental employee right, involving aspects of personal development. For rewards, equity is the principle of choice if productivity is a main goal and rewards are considered a source of motivation. However, for areas like fundamental employee rights such as being treated with respect and having a workplace free of harassment, the equality principle is appropriate. Moreover, organizations' provision of core benefits such as health and insurance benefits should be based on the equality principle.

Although there is no one right way of making a decision, it is hoped that the above justice principles provide a very basic framework for consideration. HR should always be careful to ensure that the decisions made are ethical, reasonable, and justifiable, and in order to allow HR to effectively do so, the organization needs to afford HR much more autonomy as well as an executive or strategic decision role. Moreover, as emphasized throughout this book, in making important HR decisions due consideration should always be given to the organizational objectives, management philosophy, organizational culture, the employees and other stakeholders involved (e.g., unions), and the relation of the decisions to other HR areas as well as to other organizational areas. Often decisions on HR matters are not necessarily a sole HR department matter but as much a line management responsibility. Hence, both HR and line departments must work closely together. HR needs to find ways to gain the trust and respect of not only top management and employees but also line managers in order to have the necessary influence, especially in a traditional line-dominant organization. Last but not least, it is important to remember that in addition to distributive justice, procedural justice should always be a major consideration in HR decisions.

## References

Adams, J. S. (1965). Inequity in social exchange. In L. Berkowitz (Ed.), *Advances in experimental social psychology* (Vol. 2, pp. 267–299). New York: Academic Press.

Alden, J. (2006). Measuring the "unmeasurable". *Performance Improvement, 45*(5), 7-11.

Bassi, L., & McMurrer, D. (2007). Maximizing your return on people. *Harvard Business Review, 85*(3), 115-123.

Balthazard, C. (2009) Great strides for HR, but still some way to go. *Canadian HR Reporter, 22*(2), 11.

Boudreau, J. W., & Ramstad, P. M. (2006). Talentship and HR measurement and analysis: from ROI to strategic organizational change. *Human Resource Planning, 29*(1), 25-33.

Deloitte. (2003) *2003/2004 state of the human resources function in Canada.* Retrieved July 5, 2007 from http://www.deloitte.com/dtt/cda/doc/content/2003_04_HRSurveyResults.pdf

Deloitte. (2007). *HR transformation survey: Creating customer value.* Retrieved July 5, 2007 from http://www.deloitte.com/dtt/cda/doc/content/cz%28en%29_hr_transformation_110607.pdf

Deutsch, M. (1973). *The resolution of conflict: Constructive and destructive processes.* New Haven, CT: Yale University Press.

Deutsch, M. (1975). Equity, equality, and need: What determines which value will be used as the basis of distributive justice? *Journal of Social Issues, 31*(3), 137-149.

Deutsch, M. (1985). *Distributive justice: a social-psychological perspective.* New Haven, CT: Yale University Press.

Jackson, S. E., & Schuler, R. S. (2000). *Managing human resources: A partnership perspective* (7th ed.). Cincinnati, OH: South-Western College Publishing.

Juniper, P., & Hill, A. (2011). *An inquiry into the state of HR in Canada* (Executive Summary). Industrial Relations Centre, Queen's University. Retrieved March 19, 2012 from http://irc.queensu.ca/gallery/1/executive-summary-an-inquiry-into-the-state-of-hr-in-canada.pdf

Klie, S. (2009a). HR increasingly a business partner: Survey. *Canadian HR Reporter, 22*(2), 10.

Klie, S. (2009b). More needs to be done to raise HR's profile as profession: Survey. *Canadian HR Reporter, 22*(19), 10, 12.

Lawler, E. E., III. (2005). From human resource management to organizational effectiveness. *Human Resource Management, 44*(2), 165-169.

Merritt, L. (2007). Human capital management: More than HR with a new name. *Human Resource Planning, 30*(2), 14-16.

Phillips, J. J. (2005). The value of human capital: Macro-level research. *Chief Learning Officer, 4*(10), 60-62.

Ramlall, S. J. (2006). HR competencies and their relationship to organizational practices. *Performance Improvement, 45*(5), 32-43.

SHRM. (2010). *What senior HR leaders need to know: Perspectives from the United States, Canada, India, the Middle East and North Africa.* Retrieved March 19, 2012 from http://www.shrm.org/Research/SurveyFindings/Documents/10-0097%20HR%20Leadership%20Competencies%20Exec.%20Summary-FNL.pdf

Thom, M. (2007). *How does HR create value in an organization?* Retrieved July 5, 2007 from Deloitte & Touche Canada website: www.deloitte.com/dtt/article/0,1002,sid%253D3630%2526cid%253D115059,00.html (page no longer available)

Ulrich, D. (2007). Has HR finally arrived? *Workforce Management, 86*(12), 51-54.

Ulrich, D., & Eichinger, R. W. (1998). Delivering HR with an attitude. *HRMagazine, 43*(7), 154-159.

Zugec, L. (2010, December 22). *Profit 100 survey reveals 3-step strategy for HR success.* HR Voice Organization. Retrieved March 19, 2012 from http://www.hrvoice.org/profit-100-survey-reveals-3-step-strategy-for-hr-success/

# INDEX